Restoring the Ethics of Creation

Challenging the Ethical Implications of Evolution

Andrew Sibley

Anno Mundi Books

ISBN-13:   978-0-9543922-2-2
ISBN-10:   0-9543922-2-1

Published by:
Anno Mundi Books
PO Box 752
Camberley
GU17 0XJ
England

Table of Contents

Foreword

We all have an innate sense of justice that tells us that stealing and murder are wrong. Coveting is perhaps not so clear-cut in a credit card culture that encourages us to borrow beyond our means. Abortion is seen as a complex problem, with competing claims by mother and child in some cases. Townies are happy to support a ban on fox hunting because it is wrong to take pleasure in cruelty, but we are less judgmental about destroying a foetus, possibly the result of the pleasure of casual sex. With technological advances in genetics and biochemistry, we are faced with ethical decisions about genetically modified plants and animals, and the use of stem cells to rectify inherited diseases.

How do we decide what is ethical and what is not? We have an emotional sympathy for a cuddly fox cub, while an inconvenient embryo is out of sight. We have vague notions about not interfering with nature. Former generations would have had religious grounds for saying what was right or wrong. Today scientists actively avoid any talk of a god. Is our conscience a throw-back to our (supposed) primitive past, before our brains developed properly?

In the year 2000, as far as I am aware, only one country called a conference to celebrate two millennia of Christianity. President Yeltsin invited a number of Westerners to Russia's National Academy of Education for a couple of days to discuss what his country should consider as the foundations for ethics, following the demise of the authoritarian communist system. I was one of several speakers who pointed out that if there is no Creator, ethics is a matter of personal preference. The Russian churches were beginning to find their voice after 70 years of suppression. Even the President of the Academy was a creationist Christian. The conference concluded that the best basis for ethics was the Ten Commandments of Exodus 20, acceptable to Russia's large Muslim population as well as to her Jews and Christians. The philosopher David Hume sought a natural basis for ethics, unrelated to religious thought. Darwinians are still looking for it. Darwin himself was puzzled that altruism and cooperation were as common as predation in the natural world.

Andrew Sibley introduces us to the thoughts of Greeks such as Anaximander, natural theologians such as Aquinas and Paley, Bacon with his twin books of nature and Scripture, Locke, Comte, Copernicus and Spinoza, Adam Smith's laissez-faire capitalism, Galton's eugenics and the fascists, C.S. Lewis and the founder of the Evolution Protest Movement, Attenborough's cruel god and Polkinghorne's non-intrusive god, and a host of other scientists and philosophers.

Sibley points out that the cessationists from the Reformation onwards deny the power of God today while deists deny the power of God in Creation. He discusses the claim that the dominion commission of Genesis 1 has led to the rape of the environment. He notes that the steady progress inherent in evolution theory, an idea dear to the hearts of Victorian Englishmen, was contradicted by the events of the twentieth century.

At a time when we are concerned with human rights, women's rights and animal rights, we need to realise that the evolutionary atheist has no basis for right and wrong. His ethics must then be based on utility and the survival of the fittest. It is time for a paradigm reversal from Darwinism back to the Bible.

Dr. David Rosevear, Chairman of the Creation Science Movement.

Acknowledgements

Thanks to David Rosevear for encouragement in writing this book. It was David's book, *Creation Science*, which first highlighted to me the negative ethical implications of evolution and the effect on society with loss of compassion and purpose. David was also kind in reviewing the material and offering comments and corrections, plus the written Foreword. Thanks also to David and his wife Joan and other council members of the *Creation Science Movement* for giving me opportunities in developing ministry in Creation Science and apologetics. Thanks also to Mike Gascoigne in providing a second review with very helpful comments and for suggesting the need to be more concise in the relationship between Christian faith and the Law of Moses. Mike also offered to publish the book through his own publishing title of *Anno Mundi Books*, and has worked hard in preparing the book for publication. Thanks also to Christopher Southgate for offering helpful advice on the theodicy arguments. Even though Christopher may not agree with everything I have written, he was kind enough to encourage me to expand on some of the points I was seeking to make.

Chapter 1

Building a Foundation

'For since the creation of the world God's invisible qualities
- his eternal power and divine nature -
have been clearly seen, being understood from what has been
made, so that men are without excuse.'
(Romans 1:20)

The understanding that we place on our origins as human beings has a huge impact on the way we view the world, and our place in it. This also has fundamental implications for ethical standards and our concern for the environment and society in general. The underlying philosophical debate over our origins is a compelling argument that none of us can escape from, not only in Christian circles, but also right across the scientific, philosophical and religious spectrum, whether Atheist, Hindu, Buddhist, Muslim, Jew or Christian. In modern times in the Western world, the shift away from the traditional Judeo-Christian perspective, as revealed in the Old and New Testaments, arose primarily through Enlightenment philosophy that developed over several centuries, and particularly as a result of the theory of evolution, which Charles Darwin and more especially Thomas Huxley and friends promoted in the middle and latter part of the nineteenth century. The rise of the theory of evolution in Britain during this period undermined the traditional teaching and authority of the Church, and placed mankind, Darwin believed, firmly among the beasts of the field. Although ironically these beasts of the field continue to push back moral boundaries, and aspire to sit on God's throne with the right to choose who lives and who dies at the margins of society through, for instance, eugenics, abortion, genetic engineering and euthanasia.

The resultant Darwinian paradigm shift occurred nearly 150 years ago, with a profound negative effect on ethical standards in the

Western world, and the impact remains the same today with natural and social ethics reduced to mere human expediency. The French Republic had toyed with atheistic and deistic philosophies, but it was many decades later that these progressive ideas worked their way into the heart of British life. How this came about is an interesting story, as is the rise of the various theories that led to Darwin's publication of his famous book *The Origin of Species*. Today the popular teachings of evolution and gradual geology are little changed from the original versions as laid out by Charles Lyell, Charles Darwin, Thomas Huxley and Herbert Spencer.

While at face value it may appear that evolutionary and gradualistic concepts have no impact on morality, it is necessary to return to the question of the underpinning ethical assumptions that Darwinism presents, and expose them to fresh critical analysis. Closer examination shows that the ideas of the Social Darwinists influenced a number of philosophies, such as 'greed is good' capitalism, a rejection of social provision for the poor, Marxism and the rise of fascism. While some of these creeds may appear diametrically opposed, they all have one thing common. They are all materialistic in nature, and part of a belief in natural science or scientism, sometimes called scientific positivism, which Darwinism underpins. While Darwin and Huxley tried to maintain that evolution should not lead to a degradation of morality, they failed to give a logical or convincing reason why there should be a discontinuity between sociological and biological evolution. Herbert Spencer had the easier task, claiming that there was no evolutionary discontinuity between nature and humanity, and that survival of the fittest should extend to human affairs and society as a whole. This continuity argument of Spencer led to immeasurable suffering in later decades through the materialistic tyranny of fascism, and it also degraded good business conduct.

Today, big business in the form of biotechnology companies, often multinational in scale, have a vested financial interest in pushing back ethical boundaries, and they also have the financial muscle with which to pressure Governments around the world to allow processes that are ethically questionable. Genetic engineering, it is claimed, offers hope to a starving world by developing disease resistant crops, but often it is carried out for commercial reasons alone with the desire to make farmers dependent on one company's seeds and pesticides. In this sense genetic engineering is also anti-competitive. Genetic engineering also raises the fear of unwittingly releasing harmful new viruses or diseases into the environment by taking genes from one species and putting them into another. Such new diseases may have no known control. This also seems to go against the spirit of the Levitical Law, which forbids the mating of different kinds of animals *(Leviticus 19:19)*. Mankind has a long history of ecological disasters because of the abuse of nature, from BSE, to Chernobyl, to mercury poisoning in the seas around Japan, and some have suggested that other new diseases such as HIV/AIDS arose through scientific mistakes. Pressure is also growing for the genetic cloning of animals and humans to be endorsed, with for instance the creation of new embryos for stem cell research so that another person can receive medical treatment. However, this process leads to the destruction of the embryonic entity, who it would appear is denied any sort of rights whatsoever. How can this be justified in terms of human rights, or utilitarian philosophy, and who is to judge what is right and wrong, or whose happiness is more important? Human cloning and genetic engineering have aspects that are similar to the eugenics programme of the early twentieth century.

Money from taxpayers often funds the training of scientists and research programmes, and so all of us contribute to research and development. This provides all the more reason why society at large has the right to ensure that scientific and technological progress is pursued within a moral framework. With the whole scientific and technological enterprise costing so much, it is surely necessary to ensure that public money is spent in areas of research that are ethically sound. It is also the duty of Christians to be salt and light in a world that constantly wants to pursue godless or selfish agendas without consideration for the effects on humanity or nature. Being guardians of the earth as good stewards is part of the original great commission of the Genesis creation account, to 'Be fruitful and increase in number; fill the earth and *subdue it.' (Genesis 1:28)*. The word *subdue* implies the need to bring a sense of order out of a chaotic wilderness. However, it also implies the need to maintain biodiversity with nature, to be protected from destruction. This stewardship ethic forms a major part of mankind's relationship with nature, and also within society.

Scientists too are deeply wedded to their own areas of research, and are constantly seeking funding. Many scientific researchers, such as those investigating the use of stem cells for medical purposes, or for that matter researchers into climate change, may well face the temptation to overstate the case in order to seek funding for their own areas of expertise. This is something that all scientists must be aware of and avoid. The underpinning scientific assumptions with regard to biological research are also derived from godless evolutionary thinking, which gives scientists a materialistically biased worldview, and this taints the pursuit of knowledge, and unwittingly affects the way in which people and nature are treated. An embryo, for instance, becomes just another biological spare part. Capitalists too believe that business should prosper freely as a reward for risk taking, and this is often joined to an over-confident belief in godless technological progress. Technology companies can also achieve high financial multiples upon flotation, making the founders instant millionaires, and are often born out of university research programmes. When excessive capitalist greed is wedded to an over-confident scientific research programme, ethics are the first to suffer. This is especially so when secular governments fail to consider the full outcome of such practices. Pursuing scientific research with little regard for ethics becomes a way of making a lot of money for unscrupulous people. While it must be stressed that a lot of technological progress is often good, and at worst benign, there remains much which is highly questionable, and careful consideration needs to be given to determine what is ethically sound and what is not.

As well as extreme capitalism, Marxist socialism is also a materialistic creed, and has left its ugly mark across much of Eastern Europe and Asia, with for instance the massive ecological damage in the Aral Sea, and the careless Chernobyl incident. The only difference between the two opposing creeds, unrestrained capitalism and Marxism, is over the distribution of material wealth. Marxist and socialist workers' parties believe material wealth should be redistributed to the many and not the few according to a utopian programme, but once again a lot of damage has been caused to the natural environment within socialist states, where nature is exploited for the benefit of state controlled enterprises, and little financial benefit falls to the workers. This focus on materialistic progress has also affected the health of workers, and social cohesion, as well as the subsequent natural ecological disaster. It is perhaps a mistake to think that nature can be fully tamed through human programmes alone.

Contrary to the godless belief in utopian progress, Christianity recognises that God prospers the faithful with material wealth, but that the faithful have a duty to look after other people, society and the natural environment. Individuals have responsibilities to each other, to society, to God and to nature, not to centrally controlled command economies. Material wealth should always be used for the greater good, and not for purely selfish interests. The faithful also have a duty to leave the land to their children in at least as good a condition as they received it from their parents. This divinely inspired environmental and economic principle of fruitful prosperity, of a continual cycle of sowing and reaping, and giving to others, is a spiritual exercise with the focus being away from the material. This may be seen as *soul* prosperity, and it must come before material prosperity, and should lead to environmental well-being and economic prosperity.

Pride comes into play as well. Instead of a search for truth, knowledge has become a sort of vanity, with pride found in intelligence and scientific knowledge. This is especially so where science is turned into a sort of religion with claims that it can solve all life's problems. There is a desire in all of us to be identified for something, or given credit for achievement in a certain field, and scientists naturally want to be given credit for their work, but there is a need for more humility in science and technology. But it is hard for people who have devoted their whole lives to a cause to admit they may be wrong, and this is partly why Darwinists fight so strongly to preserve their theory against the probing questions of scientific Christians. However, if science is to maintain integrity, it must look for answers in an ethical and truthful fashion. Problems with any theory must be faced head on. There is also a need for Christians who are scientists to accurately state exactly what can be proved, and what is simply assumed, in a humble manner. There is no point in winning a scientific argument, only to harden people's hearts against the Christian message of love and forgiveness. However, we should not be worried, or afraid of peer pressure, but instead take a clear stand for truth and integrity within science for the sake of society and nature.

The purpose of this book is to show that the rise of evolution and atheism, with its belief in scientism as a religion, blended with belief in unrestrained technological progress, has had profound negative implications for ethical standards in the Western world. However, it would seem that many Christians, including leading evangelicals, have accepted a version of theistic evolution or progressive creationism, undermining belief in a recent and powerful creation week. Many Christians have simply accepted the prevailing interpretation of the scientific evidence for evolution, cosmology and geology given by godless science, without looking too deeply into the questionable foundations that lie at the root of such concepts. Christians have been too quick to accept the popular scientific interpretation of evidence with little critical thought for the ethical consequences. However, some Christians have made a stand for ethics, and David Rosevear for instance, in Chapter One of his book *Creation Science*,[1] highlights a number of reasons why the creation verses evolution debate is so important to ethical standards today.

Or perhaps there have been missing pieces of evidence that have only recently come to our attention. Is the speed of light for instance constant? Recent research by leading scientists suggests that it may not be, and this may then have huge implications for our understanding of cosmology and the age of the universe, with regard to distant starlight and time. These new pieces of evidence, along with a re-interpretation, or a correct interpretation of existing evidence, may allow a Christian model of origins to be constructed, which brings together science and the Genesis manuscript in a fresh way. Re-establishing a more recent interpretation of the evidence will allow Christians to challenge evolution afresh. The scientific community must encourage and continue this critical analysis of data, or else we simply maintain evolution as an unsubstantiated dogma. How strongly, for instance, are those who oppose this process committed to *a priori* atheistic or humanist dogmas, with a vested interest in undermining the Genesis account, to attack the central Gospel of Jesus Christ Himself?

It is also necessary to show how evolution came to be believed by Western society, and how the arguments in favour of evolution and the geological record are crafted to build an apparently impenetrable wall of 'facts', which the student finds impossible to breach. As an example, one method that scientists and scientific textbooks use time and again is to take a set of data, interpret it according to an evolutionary paradigm, and then turn it around and claim that the data proves evolution. But this is basically circular reasoning and is known as tautology. Tautologies prove nothing, but are simply the restatement of facts - already stated. Most scientists and many Christians are not even aware of this underpinning philosophical process at work, and believe they are actually building on hard facts. But how firm are these foundational assumptions? Can the old data be interpreted in a different way, especially as we now have an accumulation of fresh data, and what does resistance to this process of re-evaluating the scientific evidence say about the quality and ethical basis of science? What implications does it have for our society? It is necessary to take a critical look at the evidence and ask whether it is possible to piece together the building blocks of the geological record, and the theory of evolution in a different way, and so reach a clearer and more coherent understanding of past events.

However, this is a problem that many Christians struggle to find answers to. School textbooks present unreferenced assertions and diagrams, and it is not easy for the layman or school child to check out the basis of facts for him or herself. People want to know the assumptions that lie at the foot of any theory, and question whether they are credible or not, but the underpinning geological and evolutionary evidences are carefully hidden from view until children have been thoroughly indoctrinated into accepting biological evolution and geological gradualism without question. But upon closer examination it is found that the twin theories of uniformitarian geology and neo-Darwinism are hard to tie together with the geological and fossil evidence.

Neo-Darwinism itself emerged in the 1930s and brought together Darwinian natural selection with the emerging field of genetics. The neo-Darwinists believe that macro-evolution progresses through the accumulation of micro-mutations. Mutations occur from time to time in an organism and it is claimed that a changing environment selects favourable mutations that help an organism to survive. It may of course be noted that the vast majority of mutations are harmful to life and random mutations degrade information in the genetic code. One example given of a beneficial mutation by evolutionists is sickle cell anaemia, which gives some protection against malaria. The malaria parasite is only able to infect blood cells in hosts who do not have the sickle cell mutation. When one copy of the mutant gene is present in the DNA, protection is given against malaria and the sickle cell disease is not expressed. When the mutant gene is inherited from both parents, the sufferer usually dies in childhood. The death rate from malaria is slightly higher than the death rate from the anaemia, so the sickle cell trait gives some selective advantage where malaria is endemic. However, both are terrible diseases, and if malaria were eradicated the sickle cell trait would diminish. Random mutations such as the sickle cell trait do in fact obey the law of entropy and do not provide evidence of the grand evolutionary progression of life claimed by neo-Darwinists.

Phillip Johnson in *Darwin on Trial*[2] highlights these dilemmas extremely well, and demonstrates that even some evolutionists see the problems with the fossil evidence. Stephen J. Gould, for instance, recognised that the fossil record shows sudden burial and no change through the record (which incidentally may be accounted for by one flood event), and Gould himself was instrumental in establishing the punctuated equilibrium Darwinian position. Gould and his followers believed that neo-Darwinism progresses through macro-mutations. However, the disagreement between the neo-Darwinists and those supporting punctuated equilibrium remain confused, because the latter is even harder to defend logically, but it follows more closely the geological evidence. The reason for this continuing confusion is that both sides fail to recognise the clear evidence, that most of the layers were laid down during a short period of time with practically all fossils telling a story of rapid burial.

By way of comparison, the physics of general relativity and quantum mechanics as mathematical concepts are complex, because they are beyond our everyday experience, but physical theories are built on basic mathematical principles. However, with macro-evolution and gradual geology, if current theories are true then they should correlate much more closely with the easily observed fossil evidence. They do not, and many people who look at the evidence for the first time find it hard to tie in with uniformitarian teaching. As a result, they either give up entirely, or bow to the apparent surpassing wisdom and knowledge of the geologists and evolutionists. However, there is no difficult maths, or extra dimensions of time and space to work through, but simple logical deduction from fossils buried in sedimentary layers, and the evidence should easily fit with theory. Interestingly, an increasing number of people are beginning to consider another option, and calling the geologists' bluff with the suggestion that the evolutionary emperor has no clothes.

The fossil evidence problems can be stated as no change through the record, that is stasis, and sudden appearance and rapid burial. Fossils appear suddenly having been buried rapidly in sedimentary layers, and remain the same throughout subsequent layers. As noted, this has led to the development of punctuated equilibrium, with evolution supposedly proceeding through macro-mutations, together with the recognition that successive catastrophic events have played a part in shaping the earth that we know. However, the punctuated equilibrium position, in requiring macro-mutations to work, throws up even greater difficulties in terms of probability when it comes to describing how random mutations might logically account for macro-evolution.

The problem of conflict between gradual theory and fossil evidence arises because it is realised that fossils, including many pelagic organisms, were buried suddenly in terrogenous material, not slowly over millions of years. The *sedimentary* rock layers were laid down as *sediment* rapidly, as can be seen by the many belemnite fossils buried through deep layers of the Dorset cliffs. The belemnite fossil is formed from an internal organ of the squid-like cuttlefish.

Indeed, many of the dead animals and plants would decay or be scavenged within a few days if they were not buried quickly. This is the crux of the problem. Macro-evolution by micro-mutation would require very slow and gradual processes to be at all credible, but the geological evidence points to sudden burial and stasis, despite false assertions by gradualists. Darwin presented the following assertion as an example of the gradualistic basis for his theory:

> 'If it could be demonstrated that any complex organ existed, which could not possibly have been formed by numerous, successive, slight modifications, my theory would absolutely break down.' [3]

However, Huxley was concerned that Darwin had expressed his theory in too narrow terms, believing that giant leaps may be necessary for macro-evolution to occur because of the fossil evidence. He commented: 'You have loaded yourself with an unnecessary difficulty in adopting *natura non facit saltum* [nature does not make leaps] so unreservedly.' [4]

So a number of leading evolutionists have developed the concept of punctuated equilibrium as a result of a re-examination of the geological and fossil evidence, and made some very critical comments about neo-Darwinism. While it is true that they do not reject evolution itself, in reality the unresolved conflict exposes the whole Darwinian paradigm to serious doubt. If indeed the resultant gap between theory and observation is so large as to be unbridgeable, then a paradigm shift is necessary instead to a position that is logically credible.

It must be acknowledged that Steven J. Gould has objected to use being made of his comments to attack the theory of evolution itself, but it would be wrong to ignore them. Gould himself was a believer in evolution, but his comments have shown how evolution and gradualism were established, despite clear evidence for catastrophic deposition in the rock layers. Gould did in fact suggest that Lyell and Darwin used bias and rhetoric to impose acceptance of gradualism in society. This was done to make up for lack of direct evidence, and Gould commented that Lyell and Darwin never actually proved gradualism from the rock layers. Gould commented that this had the negative effect of stifling other hypotheses and led to the science of geology becoming closed-minded to empirical evidence. Gould noted that gradualism had become a dogma of geology, and this was a direct result of Lyell's rhetoric.[5]

Gould also paid the catastrophists a discrete compliment, noting that they were more careful observers than the gradualists. The secular geologist Derek Ager, for his part, has also criticised uniformitarian geology for its philosophical basis, and the effective brainwashing of the general public, commenting that:

> '... I have been trying to show how I think geology got into the hands of the theoreticians who were conditioned by the social and political history of their day more than by observation in the field ... In other words, we have allowed ourselves to be brain-washed into avoiding any interpretation of the past that involves extreme and what might be termed 'catastrophic' processes.'[6]

The science of geology recognises that this conflict is real and that it continues to the present day. However, this problem has not been resolved in the minds of the neo-Darwinists, but it is conveniently glossed over and kept away from school textbooks to maintain the overall dogma of evolution. A recent Government declaration in Hansard records that the House of Lords Minister, Lord Geoffrey Filkin, stated that according to the National Curriculum, children in the UK must learn that the fossil record is evidence for evolution, even though, as we have seen, the academic science of geology does not fully support such a position and evolutionists are in dispute about it.[7]

As another example of the geological community's position today, a recent document produced for the nomination of the Dorset and East Devon Coast for inclusion in the World Heritage List, and supported by the British Geological Survey, comments that river valleys in East Devon and West Dorset were central to the nineteenth century debate between diluvial and fluvial interpretations of landforms. This was only part of a wider debate at the time between uniformitarian and catastrophist positions on the history of the earth, and the document notes that this debate continues to the present day and is fundamental to the earth sciences, giving as an example the potential effects of a comet impact upon the earth.[8]

So today, an increasing number of people, Christian and secular alike, consider that the geological record demonstrates that dinosaurs and fossils were buried suddenly in a number of successive catastrophes. However, this then throws open the temporal debate concerning the long-age dating methods of the rock layers, which many Darwinists and neo-Darwinists find extremely uncomfortable. This debate is not really the subject of this book, but it shows how the evidence is wide open for questioning, without losing one's scientific, theological or philosophical integrity. What is more is that, at a foundational level, the way we view the evidence in the rock layers ultimately moulds our belief system and ethical concern. Terry Mortenson for instance records that Charles Lyell, who pioneered gradualism, was guided by his own deistic faith.

> 'Lyell likewise was not a purely objective observer of the geological facts. A number of recent historians of science and geologists have shown that politics, economics and deistic or unitarian theology had a significant bearing on the interpretation of geological formations given by Lyell (and Scrope, upon whom Lyell heavily relied).' [9]

It would appear therefore that gradualism and evolution have been crafted for political, social and even religious reasons, to undermine traditional Christian faith. Erasmus Darwin was a significant player in the 18th century, frequenting with the Unitarian preacher and agitator for revolution, Joseph Priestly. In fact Erasmus Darwin also supported revolution in America, being a friend of Benjamin Franklin, and helped maintain the work of Priestly. Erasmus Darwin was also responsible for setting up the Birmingham Lunar Society, and brought together men like James Watt, and the geologist James Hutton from Edinburgh, to pursue science and technology for various economic and political motives. While some members of this club were deistic and Unitarian, others such as Erasmus Darwin and James Watt were Scottish Rite Freemasons, and some of Quaker origin. Erasmus Darwin was initiated into St. David's Masonic Lodge No. 36 in Edinburgh in 1754, and was also involved in the

Scottish Enlightenment, which included the philosopher and sceptic David Hume. Erasmus Darwin was also a member of Canongate Kilwinning Masonic Lodge No. 2. Erasmus Darwin's later writing appeals to freemason belief with for instance *The Botanic Garden* (1792), beginning with a declaration that its structure was based on the poetic Rosicrucian understanding of spirits in the elements.[10] This is a purely pagan idea, with the sylphs representing air, undines water, salamanders fire and gnomes the earth, and is later echoed in the evolutionary writing of Pierre Teilhard de Chardin. In *Zoonomia*, Erasmus Darwin wrote:

> 'Would it be too bold to imagine that all warm blooded animals have arisen from one living filament, which THE GREAT FIRST CAUSE endowed with animality, with the power of acquiring new parts, attended with new propensities, directed by irritations, sensations, volitions and associations; and thus possessing the faculty of continuing to improve by its own inherent activity, and of delivering down those improvements by generation to its posterity, world without end.' [11]

The influence of deistic and perhaps masonic thought is clearly visible in these ideas, and they play a part in later works of deism and atheism, with a rejection of Christian teaching and authority. Erasmus Darwin's concept of evolution was in fact first proposed in ancient Greece by Anaximander of Miletus around 550BC, who believed life arose through sea slime. Empedocles in 450BC later reworked this materialism with an early form of natural selection, to overcome the appearance of design in nature.[12] The work of members of the Lunar Club later influenced Charles Lyell's uniformitarianism and Charles Darwin's theory of evolution. Charles Darwin borrowed heavily from his grandfather's earlier theory of evolution, and relied on *Zoonomia* and *The Botanic Garden* for his own research.[13] Francis Galton too could boast Erasmus Darwin as his grandfather.

It would seem that William Buckland's interpretation of the rock layers was also moulded by society's belief in the inevitability of social progress in nineteenth century Britain. He came to believe that the rock layers showed a steady improvement through time after successive catastrophes, followed by divinely inspired re-creations, which tied in with broad Enlightenment thinking. However, his Christian views were considered suitably orthodox to be asked to write for the Christian apologetics work *The Bridgewater Treatise*, to defend Christian faith. Nicolaas Rupke comments that the new ideas of geological progress, that were claimed to be evidenced within the rock layers by Lyell, tied in with increasing expectations of social and cultural progress.[14] But as we have seen, Lyell imposed geological progress on the rock layers because of his political and deistic beliefs. Buckland appears to have become increasingly confused as a result of the clever rhetoric and hidden motives of his colleague Lyell, whose interpretation of the evidence did not tie in with his own observations.

Buckland's work also came under a great deal of criticism from scriptural geologists for its confusion and compromise, and it also failed to please secular scientists for the same reason. However, what all of this shows is that Darwinism and gradualism were established for philosophical and deistic reasons, and not out of a purely objective examination of the evidence.

I am well aware that many Christians within scientific disciplines struggle to come to terms with the different paradigms and philosophies concerning origins, and I want to deal with the issues involved in a respectful and sensitive manner. It is, however, the intention to set out the ethical and philosophical arguments plainly, and give the reader the opportunity to understand why many Christians and scientists believe that molecule to man progressive evolution as a cosmic process is morally, scientifically and historically wrong. Having said that, I don't want temporal arguments over the time frame of the creation week to undermine the central message of this book, that the very fabric of society is changed by our belief in our origins. If God is deistic in nature, then how does that affect our conduct? If we perceive God as both very close and powerful, as I believe he is, then does that not change our conduct for better? I would appeal therefore to progressive creationists and theistic evolutionists to understand the broader argument of ethical concern, and consider how our ethical basis might be improved if we really return to belief in God's complete Word as revealed in the Bible.

The purpose of this book is really to invite the reader to question why they believe what they do, and also to question the underlying assumptions. There is a need for Christians to uphold traditional values in politics and society once again, and stand against the notion that science has an answer for all life's issues. Instead, many of life's problems have spiritual solutions. Bearing all of this in mind, it is important for Christians to begin to address the issue of Christian education and consider how these facts may be taught in schools to future generations.

There is a lot of ground to cover, and it is hard to accurately state people's positions on evolution without making generalisations. However, Christians who believe in theistic evolution or progressive creationism may wish to reappraise their beliefs. I want to stress that mention of any persons is done in a respectful manner, but I believe that a frank discussion is called for. It would seem that many modern Christians, who consider themselves to be either theistic evolutionists or progressive creationists, and believe in some sort of gap theory or pre-Adamic races, have little respect for young earth creationists because they are seen as poorly educated fundamentalists, or at best plain naïve. This is far from the truth and is a most disingenuous attitude for Christians to hold. While some progress has been made to end the division between charismatic Christians and more traditional evangelicals, there is further to go between those who are seen as naïve literalists and those who see their faith in more progressive terms.

Roger Forster and Paul Marston in *Reason, Science and Faith*, for instance, have a tendency towards hyperbole when criticising young earth creationists, and fail to really engage in the complexity of some arguments, despite their undoubted ability as theologians and scientists. As an example of this, one area of research on a possible variable speed of light is called 'statistical nonsense', 'moonshine', and 'the worst piece of pseudo-statistics we have ever read'.[15] Whether or not the work in question is statistically significant, Trevor Norman and Barry Setterfield at least start with observational evidence, which is more than can be said for a large part of cosmology. Roger Forster and Paul Marston may also wish to reconsider their view, bearing in mind recent research by leading secular cosmologists on the subject of a possible variable speed of light as well.[16]

The rejection of young earth creationism among modern Christians may be motivated partly by a desire for human respectability. However, Jesus demonstrated that faithfulness towards God is more important than recognition from man. As a result of this approach, many modern Christians avoid the whole issue of Darwinism, and overlook the negative ethical implications of evolution, preferring social action and friendship evangelism to help build the church. This is akin to treating the symptoms of a disease while leaving the causes untouched, and many people reject Christianity directly because they accept godless Darwinism without question. There is a need for modern Christians to look deeper and challenge the philosophical foundations of Darwinism and its ethical implications, and also challenge the increasingly secular education system with its humanistic basis.

It may be noted that much of Forster and Marston's argument appears to be based on the authority of Christian theologians through the centuries. While it is recognised that some theologians may have accepted a form of evolution over the years, and some rejected a literal reading of Genesis 1-3, this is clearly not universal, with both Martin Luther and John Wesley appealing to a literal reading. But what does human authority prove in theological terms when we consider Genesis 1-3? While the authority of Scripture itself is upheld in theological terms, the reasoning of human theologians is fallible. When we look at science, all authority should be rejected in favour of observations. But where are the observations of events that happened long ago? Observations of origins are sketchy at best, and any conclusion we make is through deductive reasoning, which itself is based on underpinning philosophical assumptions.

Darwinism itself seeks to remove God to a distant and powerless sideline, that is if God is considered at all, and the teaching of evolution in schools has been used to undermine Christian faith. Leading conservative theologians came to accept it even though its scientific basis is unproved, and this has made a belief in evolution acceptable to the laity. Leading Christians continue to accept evolution without a full examination and understanding of evidence

20

and philosophy. This has ethical implications. However, in an age when environmental and social ethics are being undermined for the sake of convenience for those who have a voice, or the profit motive, we must again question our society's ethical basis. The twin political systems of fascism and communism, which found their degraded ethical basis in part from Darwinist thinking, have largely passed, but the fruit of evolution continues to inform ethics today. Evolution continues to allow technological progress to be pursued for profit, and individuals demand their rights with little thought for the welfare of others. Rights today are often divided out according to single-issue pressure groups on the basis of personal preference, sometimes with covert backing from big business which desires to protect ethically dubious practices. Those who shout loudest and appeal to sentiment get their rights respected, but are we not called by Christ to protect the rights of the weak and powerless as well?

On the other side, there is a perception in some quarters that young earth creationists have presented their beliefs in a rather fundamentalist and dictatorial fashion, demanding blind allegiance to the cause without really explaining the poor scientific and philosophical basis of macro-evolution and gradual geology. The faith of Christians who disagree with a literal creation is often questioned as well. This is regrettable, and there is not much point winning an argument while hardening hearts and minds against the cause. Scientific creationists can also become so tied up in petty scientific arguments that they forget why the subject is important in terms of truth, faith and ethics.

It is recognised that even young earth creationists acknowledge that micro-evolution, that is change within species or created kinds, may be a reality, and that survival of the fittest is one probable mechanism for this change. However, even though this process may lead to different forms within created kinds, survival of the fittest follows the path of entropy and is at best isentropic, and natural selection cannot account for creation and the complexity seen in nature. It is also interesting to note that Christians are beginning to re-awaken the natural theology argument of Thomas Aquinas and William Paley, through interest in the appearance of design in nature. This has become known as the *Intelligent Design Movement* (or ID for short).

Although this issue of creation versus evolution may be uncomfortable for many, it is an issue that we cannot walk away from because it has such a huge impact on our ethical and social framework. While young earth creationists face disrespect from progressive Christians and secular scientists alike, their scientific ability and use of logic and reasoning is worthy of much greater respect. It needs therefore to be recognised that young earth creationists are often very capable scientists, despite unfounded criticism. There is also a need for greater unity, understanding and respect between Christians of different persuasions.

The biological theory of evolution, as proposed by Charles Darwin, would probably not have got so far if it weren't for its promotion by Thomas Huxley and others. While Darwin was sick with worry over the implications of evolution, Huxley took hold of Darwin's theory and used it to undermine traditional Christian faith, at a time when Christian opposition was weakening. With clever rhetoric he challenged opponents to produce scientific alternatives, and ridiculed appeals to faith with contemptuous arrogance, all the while gaining the support of scientists and many Christians alike. Huxley used this same technique to establish the scientific process as a sort of positivist religion, whereby science was seen as the only source of truth on which to conduct politics and build society, although Huxley claimed to be agnostic himself. Those who promote atheistic humanism in the present day continue Huxley's positivist crusade, and it is this cult of scientific humanism that is as great a threat to ethical standards than the biological theory of evolution itself.

However, it is recognised that many atheists have adopted broadly Christian ethics based on love and respect, and Darwinism could conceivably account for inter-family or even tribal affections, although this is still based on benefit for survival. This loving family response is though part of people's innermost created being, and it is a blind *a priori* assumption to suggest that it evolved that way in a godless system.

This book is therefore about ethics, and seeks to serve a number of purposes. Firstly, it seeks to show that the Darwinian theory of biological evolution and social Darwinism was the underpinning philosophy that inspired later brutal regimes and murderous dictatorships during the twentieth century. These brutal regimes were responsible for more genocide than any other group throughout recorded history. Also it seeks to show that forms of Darwinism continue to inform ethical standards today, through blind allegiance to technological and scientific progress in combination with big business, and it provides no basis for a coherent, strong and loving Christian morality with regard to society and the environment. Any basis for ethics has become selfish and subjective as a result of the Darwinian revolution. Finally, it will be shown that the Judeo-Christian faith, which should lead to respect for the divinely ordered creation, is the best coordinate system on which to build a loving morality and give effective stewardship of the earth, this despite the mistakes of those acting in the name of Christ in the past, and the tacit approval by some Christians who have possibly turned a blind eye to the suffering of people and allowed the exploitation of nature under a misguided notion of domination.

Notes and References

[1] Rosevear, D., *Creation Science*, New Wine Press, Chichester, England, pp. 11-20, 1991.

[2] Johnson, P.E., *Darwin on Trial*, Monarch Books, Lion Hudson Plc., Crowborough, East Sussex, UK, 1994.

[3] Darwin, C., *The Origin of Species*, 6th ed., Collier Books, New York, p. 182, 1872.

[4] Huxley, T.H., Letter to Darwin, 23rd November 1859. In: Huxley, L., (ed.), *The Life and Letters of Thomas Henry Huxley*, vol. 2, p. 176. (*natura non facit saltum*; nature does not make leaps). Macmillan, London, 1900.

[5] Gould, S.J., *Toward the Vindication of Punctuational Change.* In: Berggren, W.A., Van Couvering, J.A., (eds.), *Catastrophes and Earth History: The New Uniformitarianism*, Princeton University Press, Princeton, New Jersey, pp. 14-16, 1984.

[6] Ager, D.V., *The Nature of the Stratigraphical Record*, Macmillan Press Ltd., London, pp. 46-47, 1981. (Reproduced with permission of Palgrave Macmillan).

[7] Hansard, House of Lords, Written Answer 21.2.05. Lord Filkin responds to a question about the teaching of Intelligent Design in schools.

[8] Dorset County Council, Devon County Council, and Dorset Coasts Forum, *Nomination of the Dorset and East Devon Coast for Inclusion in the World Heritage List*, p. 80, 2000. (This nomination and publication was supported by the British Geological Survey).

[9] Mortenson, T., *British Scriptural Geologists in the First Half of the Nineteenth Century - Part 1: Historical Setting*, Answers in Genesis, TJ, 11(2), pp. 221-252, 1997. See also: Mortenson, T., *The Great Turning Point*, Master Books, 2004.

[10] The Eye (pseudonym), *Erasmus Darwin Centre opens in Lichfield*, Freemasonry Today, Issue 9, Summer 1999. <www.freemasonrytoday.net/public/index-09.php>. Accessed March 2006. For Erasmus Darwin's credentials as a Freemason see: <http://freemasonry.bcy.ca/biography/darwin_e/darwin_e.html>, Accessed March 2006, Source: Denslow, W.R., *10,000 Famous Freemasons*, 4 vols., Missouri Lodge of Research, Trenton, Missouri, 1957-61.

[11] Darwin, E., *Zoonomia*, In: Brookes, M., *Extreme Measures: The Dark Visions and Bright Ideas of Francis Galton*, Bloomsbury Publishing Plc., London, p. 11, 2004.

[12] See for instance Denton, M., *Evolution: A Theory in Crisis*, Adler and Adler, Maryland, USA, pp. 37-40, 1986.

[13] See for instance: King-Hele, D., *Erasmus Darwin*, Charles Scribner's Sons, New York, p. 88, p. 94, 1963.

[14] Rupke, N.A., *The Great Chain of History: William Buckland and the English School of Geology 1814-1849*, Clarendon Press, Oxford, p. 255, 1983. In: Mortenson, op. cit., *British Scriptural Geologists...*

[15] Forster, R., Marston, P., *Reason, Science and Faith*, Monarch Books, Lion Hudson Plc, Crowborough, East Sussex, UK, p. 423, 1999. Commenting on: Norman, T.G. and Setterfield, B., *The Atomic Constants, Light and Time*, Invited Research Report of the Stanford Research Institute / Flinders University, 1987. (Unofficial report, see Bibliography).

[16] For instance: Magueijo, J., *Faster than the Speed of Light*, William Heinemann, London, 2003. or; Albrecht, A., Magueijo, J., *A Time Varying Speed of Light as a Solution to Cosmological Puzzles*, Phys. Rev. D 59, 043516, 1999. or; Barrow, J.D., *Cosmologies With Varying Light Speed*, Phys. Rev. D, 59, 043515, 1999. or; Moffat, J.W. *Superluminary Universe: A Possible Solution to the Initial Value Problem in Cosmology*, Int. J. Modern Physics, D, Vol. 2, No. 3, pp. 351-365, 1993. or; Davies, P.C.W., Davis, T.M., Lineweaver, C.H., *Black Holes Constrain Varying Constants*, Nature, 418 (6898), pp. 602-603, 2002.

Chapter 2

Restoring Creation as Science

'He makes the clouds his chariot
and rides on the wings of the wind.
He makes winds his messengers,
flames of fire his servants.'
(Psalm 104:3-4)

Today many evangelical Christian theologians and writers claim that we cannot do science from the Bible, and that those who promote the literal accuracy and authority of the Genesis account are not being true to theology, Christian tradition or scientific methodology. Traditional views have promoted the two-book approach, which considered Scripture and science as separate but complementary to one another. This tradition has been passed down through Thomas Aquinas, Galileo and Francis Bacon, who viewed the Bible as the sacred written Word of God and nature a result of God's spoken Word. The reason for such a position was in fact respect for Scripture, as it was felt that attempts to do science from the Bible might profane the sacred text. In more recent centuries, this position has been reversed, with greater respect given to scientific research than the Biblical text. This change in emphasis has also influenced the response of theologians to Scripture. Forster and Marston, for instance, believe that the creation account should be read more as an allegory, rather than a literal account, and comment that a literal reading of the Genesis account does not form part of Christian tradition.

'... two kinds of new theology should also be resisted. The Bible is neither to be 'spiritualised' out of all reference to the world of space-time, nor to be used as a source-book for scientific theory. Neither liberalism nor young-earth creationism have any claim to represent the historic mainstream of Bible based Christianity.' [1]

Forster and Marston here equate young-earth creationism with attempts to use the Bible as a 'source-book for scientific theory'. This is a subtle point, but it really misrepresents the young-earth creationist position. While it may be agreed that the Bible does not provide a source for scientific theory, it may be shown that an ancient book like the Bible provides a record of events that may then be used to construct scientific theories. I am sure both Forster and Marston believe in the divine inspiration of Scripture, but part of that revelation is in the form of an accurate record of events. The Bible may be considered a record of observations, and from observations comes science. Indeed there is a lot of science that relies on written records in a similar way. In fact Lynn White asserts that the creation account gave the development of science impetus.

> '... modern Western science was cast in a matrix of Christian theology. The dynamism of religious devotion, shaped by the Judeo-Christian dogma of creation, gave it impetus.' [2]

Forster and Marston go on to attempt to show that throughout Church history belief in a recent creation was not widely or strongly held, and point to Philo to back up their progressive creationist or theistic evolutionary view, commenting that: 'Philo does not believe that the inspired author intended us to take the 'days' either literally or chronologically.' [3] However, Forster and Marston also recognise that Philo considered it possible that God created everything at once, and note that: '... although Philo is very clear that Genesis 1-3 was not meant to be taken literally, at times he writes as though it was.' [4] Forster and Marston also note that Philo influenced early Christians such as '... Clement, Origen, Gregory of Nyssa and Ambrose.' [5]

Philo's philosophy of origins appears rather sublime, believing it possible that God could have created everything at once, but that six days were required for the sake of divine order, or possibly even numerology. Philo also recognised that the creation story was not 'mythical fiction', but about 'making ideas visible'.[6] Whichever way we interpret Philo, it seems that he believed in the immediacy of God's power, released in a short period of time over the creation week, and that the creation story had deeper layers of meaning in the form of allegory as well. In no way can Philo, or Christians like Clement, Origen or Ambrose, be used to imply that belief in a recent, short period creation was not part of Orthodox Jewish or early Christian tradition. What is also evident is that those who do believe in a recent, dynamic creation are not closed to the idea that the Genesis account also contains deeper layers of meaning as well.

One leading theologian who did consider the Genesis account to be in part allegory was Augustine of Hippo. In 415AD, Augustine published a third commentary on Genesis entitled *The Literal Meaning of Genesis*, after two previous, but more allegorical studies. Although this was an attempt to give a more literal interpretation of Genesis, he continued to suggest that the first three days, before the creation of Sun, Moon and stars were not literal, but that subsequent 'days' should be considered literal. However, Mortenson goes on to show the degree to which Augustine accepted a literal understanding.

> 'In any case, he considered that the plants and animals were created miraculously and fully formed in an instant on the various days (rather than gradually by present-day processes of nature), and that creation was complete on the seventh day. In rejecting the uniformitarian and catastrophist views of his day, he argued that 6,000 years had not yet passed since the creation of Adam, the first man, and that the antediluvian patriarchs had literally lived some 900 years. He argued at some length that the Noachian Flood was a historical global catastrophe and that all men were descended from Noah, having been dispersed throughout the Earth after the confusion of languages at the Tower of Babel.'[7]

Mortenson also highlights the fact that Martin Luther, John Calvin and John Wesley all considered the creation account to be six literal days in duration, occurring approximately 6000 years ago.[8] Calvin for instance states: 'Let us rather conclude that God himself took the space of six days, for the purpose of accommodating his works to the capacity of men'[9] In fact one recent theologian, Peter Harrison,[10] has suggested that the Protestant Reformation may also have been essential for establishing the conditions that led to the growth of modern Western science. By promoting literalism and rejecting an allegorical or symbolic view of nature, they allowed a new way of classifying creation based on the elevation of the written word. This more literal treatment of Genesis, insisted upon by the reformers who were concerned with the theology of the fall and creation, led in the seventeenth century to developments in experimental science. While Harrison is rather dismissive of young earth creationists, seemingly labelling them as fundamentalists, it is hard to miss similarities between the young earth position and that of the reformers. While it is acknowledged that some Christian theologians, throughout the history of the Church, have considered the Genesis account to be allegory or non-literal, and others have sometimes been rather vague, the assertion by Forster and Marston that belief in a literal young earth creation does not form part of 'the historic mainstream of Bible based Christianity',[11] is really incorrect. Forster and Marston also appeal to Francis Bacon as an authority to deny the validity of young earth creationism, and accordingly it is claimed that Scripture only provides lessons in the divine character, and for understanding morality. As Forster and Marston claim, observations of the natural world lead to science, and studying Scripture leads to theology.[12]

> 'We would, then, defend the classic Baconian approach to science-faith issues, which was rooted in earlier Christians ideas and has shaped the whole of Christian and scientific thinking on relationships of science and theology.'[13]

However, as Mortenson shows, Bacon's actual beliefs appear at variance with such assertions. The writings of Francis Bacon have also been used by secular geologists to deny the validity of the Mosaic accounts themselves, suggesting that only the fossil record has anything to say about scientific theory. However, these assumptions rely on an approach to Bacon's writing that really takes it out of context. Bacon appeared to believe in the two-book approach with Scripture on the one hand providing an understanding of the will and character of God, and natural philosophy or science providing an understanding of God's power and wisdom as seen in nature. Bacon comments in the *Advancement of Learning* (1605).

> 'For our Saviour saith, 'You err, not knowing the Scriptures, nor the power of God'; laying before us two books or volumes to study, if we will be secured from error; first the Scriptures, revealing the will of God, and then the creatures expressing his power; whereof the latter is a key unto the former: not only opening our understanding to conceive the true sense of the Scriptures, by the general notions of reason and rules of speech; but chiefly opening our belief, in drawing us into a due meditation of the omnipotency [*sic*] of God, which is chiefly signed and engraven upon his works.' [14]

However, to use Bacon's writing to denigrate Scripture, when Bacon seemed to have the very highest regard for God's Word, is to use his work outside of his intended purpose. Bacon seemed to elevate Scripture above natural philosophy, considering the latter temporary and passing, and the former divine and eternal. Francis Bacon also considered the Genesis creation account to be literal history of six days duration.

> 'It is so then, that in the work of the creation we see a double emanation of virtue from God; the one referring more properly to power, the other to wisdom; the one expressed in making the subsistence of the matter, and the other in disposing the beauty of the form. This being supposed, it is to be observed that for anything which appeareth in the history of the creation, the confused mass and matter of heaven and Earth was made in a moment; and the order and disposition of that chaos or mass was the work of six days...' [15]

It may be noted as well that Bacon considered the creation events to have been supernatural, and the ongoing laws of nature were said to have 'began to be in force when God first rested from his works, and ceased to create...' [16] In this sense the supernatural events may be considered outside the realm of natural philosophy, and therefore become part of theology. Mortenson too shows how the scriptural geologists considered themselves to be working within Bacon's criteria.

'... one Scriptural geologist, Granville Penn, argued (and some other Scriptural geologists explicitly agreed with him) that Bacon's beliefs, based on Scriptural revelation, about the nature of the original creation and about when the present laws of nature came into operation, were as much a part of Bacon's philosophic principles as his belief that the study of Scripture and the study of the natural world should not be unwisely mixed. In other words, the Scriptural geologists believed that the former principles of Bacon qualified the meaning of his latter principle. Scriptural geologists also contended that it was unBaconian to be dogmatic about an old-Earth general theory of the Earth, when so little of the Earth's surface had been geologically studied in the early nineteenth century. So while the old-Earth geologists claimed to be Baconian in a strict sense, the Scriptural geologists considered that they too were following Bacon in important respects.' [17]

Bacon's reason for writing as he did was to counteract an abuse of Scripture as he saw it, where a group of scholars were suggesting that all science should only be done through Scripture, and were ignoring the observations of natural philosophy. Thomas Aquinas had developed and adapted the idea of natural theology from Aristotle, but one school of thought was trying to build all natural philosophy on a mixture of Aristotle and Scripture. This is clearly out of step with the intention of the Word of God. Bacon comments:

'The school of Paracelsus, and some others ... have pretended to find the truth of all natural philosophy in the Scripture; scandalising and traducing all other philosophy as heathenish and profane. But there is no such enmity between God's word and his works. Neither do they give honour to the Scriptures as they suppose but embase them. For to seek heaven and earth in the word of God, whereof it is said 'Heaven and earth shall pass away but my word shall not pass away' is to seek temporary things amongst eternal; and as to seek divinity in philosophy is to seek the dead amongst the living ... And again, the scope or purpose of the Spirit of God is not to express matters of nature in the Scripture, otherwise than in passage, and for application to man's capacity and to matters moral or divine. And it is a true rule: 'What a man says incidentally about matters not in question has little authority; for it were a strange conclusion, if a man should use a similitude for ornament or illustration sake, borrowed from nature or history according to vulgar conceit, as of a basilisk, an unicorn, a centaur, a

Brierus and Hydra, or the like, that he must needs be thought to affirm the matter thereof positively to be true … In this vanity some of the moderns have with extreme levity indulged so far as to attempt to found a system of natural philosophy on the first chapter of Genesis, on the book of Job, and other parts of sacred writings; and repression of it is the more important, because from this unwholesome mixture of things human and divine there arises not only a fantastic philosophy but also an heretical religion.' [18]

Bacon here notes that the purpose of the inspired Word of God is not to provide a basis for natural philosophy, but to provide an understanding of morals and the divine character. The reason that Bacon wrote accordingly was not to undermine Scripture, but to counteract inappropriate use of Scripture by 'The school of Paracelsus, and some others', who wanted to base all natural philosophy on God's Word. Even young earth creationists would agree that this practice is wrong because it seeks to use the Word of God outside of its proper context. Scripture must always be used in context, and anything else would be an abuse. In fact most creation scientists are themselves trained in, and approve of the disciplines of the scientific methodology.

Whereas Bacon was trying to counteract an abuse of the Word of God, whereby people were attempting to base *all* science on Scripture, his writings have been used subsequently to undermine the integrity of the Bible, suggesting that God's Word has *nothing* to say with regard to natural philosophy. It may however be noted that Bacon mentions that the Scriptures may express matters of nature 'in passage' which may in itself inform our study of nature. Mortenson also comments that Bacon highlights places were Scripture does provide evidence of natural philosophy. Bacon comments:

'So in this and very many other places in that law, [of Moses] there is to be found, besides the theological sense, much aspersion of philosophy. So likewise in that excellent book of Job, if it be revolved with diligence, it will be found pregnant and swelling with natural philosophy; as for example cosmography and the roundness of the earth; *(Job 26:7)…*' [19]

Bacon therefore considers it possible that we may learn some natural philosophy from the Bible, but it may be asked whether Bacon really managed to explain the full complexity of the arguments for proper use of Scripture, despite his insightfulness in so many areas. From the above quotes it would seem that Bacon did in fact allude to a deeper understanding of the place of Scripture in providing lessons in natural philosophy, as well as providing moral lessons for humanity. Perhaps if he could have foreseen what others would have done to his work, in using it to undermine the Genesis narrative, he might have taken more time to qualify his writing more fully.

As far as science is concerned, Bacon suggested that natural philosophy should continue through observations, followed by an inductive methodology to build up an understanding of how the natural world works. For an understanding of how the process of science actually works, it is necessary to make some observations of events. Observations in natural philosophy must be carefully recorded and catalogued for future reference. As an example, a few weather forecasters working in Cardiff observed a water spout in the Bristol Channel on the 11th January 2004, and for the sake of increasing scientific knowledge wrote a short paper on the observed track, size, and the meteorological conditions that prevailed at the time.[20] Through continued observations of this kind, scientific knowledge of waterspouts and tornadoes increases. However, it may be noted that as a result of the passage of time, records become historic, and therefore scientists become reliant on older records of observed events.

In many ways Scripture itself provides a record of past events, and this record of history may be considered more than incidental to the moral message as Bacon proposed. When we read, for instance, that the Patriarchs lived for hundreds of years compared to our short time span, we may ask, how this can be? Whether or not we accept this data as real, or just imaginary or metaphor or allegory, we must surely conclude that it is presented as a factual record, and that it has little if any theological content. It is a simple observation, perhaps only recorded 'in passage', but from such observations comes natural philosophy.

Science in its purest form is concerned with conducting

experiments that are repeatable today. Ideally, science deals with the present and not the past. Finding out what happened in the past falls into the realm of history, although certain disciplines such as archaeology and palaeontology are engaged in forensic, or historical science and seek to draw inferences from collected artefacts or bones, even though such inferences are heavily weighted by foundational assumptions. When it comes to origins, we must stretch our understanding of the definition of science to the limit, and we can really only label it a philosophical or metaphysical search. The Bible is a book of theology, history and philosophy, so it should have something to say about past historic events, and it is legitimate to look for our origins in the Bible.

In a number of places throughout the Genesis record, the text claims to be 'an account' of events pertaining to a particular line of people, for instance: 'This is the account of Noah' in *Genesis 6:9*. This idea uses the concept of the *toledot*[21] and was best described by P.J. Wiseman in 1936 in a book entitled *New Discoveries in Babylonia About Genesis*, and later re-edited and republished by his son Donald Wiseman.[22] We also find recorded in *Exodus 33:11*, for instance, God speaking to Moses face to face as a man talks to a friend, and elsewhere, in *Exodus 17:14*, Moses is required to write down what he is told. Whether we accept the Wiseman view, or believe that God dictated the Genesis accounts directly, we may legitimately accept that the book of Genesis is an accurate record of events.

The Noahic account in fact reads very much like a ship's log of events, and as has been shown, all scientific observations become recorded history, in the same way that Genesis has come down to us. In fact, bearing witness to real historic events was a very important part of Jewish life, faith and culture. Jewish history provides a very clear cultural identity of where they have come from, what they have been through, and what their divine purpose and calling in life is. The historic accounts also provide moral lessons to develop faith, character and theology, as well as providing rich and sometimes mysterious symbolism. The account of Abraham, who was called by God to sacrifice his divinely promised son Isaac on Mount Moriah *(Genesis 22:1-19)*, is a very odd story indeed, but a fuller understanding of its meaning only becomes apparent after the death and suffering of Jesus Christ in the same place around 2000 years later. Here we find a real historic event conveying deeper layers of meaning.

However, in the examples of the age of the Patriarchs and the Noahic flood given above, there is little theology, which suggests little motivation for fabricating a story, although later the Apostle Peter claims that the Noahic account gives a moral lesson as well. A careful study of *Psalm 104* shows that the Hebrews considered the Noahic event to have been an entirely natural occurrence, but one ordained by God, who for instance 'makes the clouds his chariot' *(Psalm 104:3)*.

Now it may be asked, what is the difference between finding and working from observations in an ancient document, and walking along a beach and finding fossils among the rocks or cliff layers? The geologist seeks to discover which rock layers different fossils come from, in order to piece together an understanding of past events. The person working from an ancient document also seeks to understand past events. The problem comes when we try and harmonise one with the other, especially when philosophical assumptions determine our handling of observational data. In both cases, the past event or events that Scripture and the rocks speak of are not repeatable, and so are in fact part of science history. Our interpretation of past events must be based on philosophical assumptions.

As has been suggested already, Peter later takes the Noahic account and suggests that it provides moral lessons for future generations, and in this sense natural philosophy and moral philosophy meet. Peter comments in a very perceptive piece of prophecy that people will one day deny the Noahic flood to put out of their minds the fear of God. In this prophecy, the evidence for a global deluge is deliberately denied and replaced, for philosophical reasons, by a uniformitarian argument to do away with the God of the Bible who brings judgement for sin.

'First of all, you must understand that in the last days scoffers will come, scoffing and following their own evil desires. They will say,

"Where is this 'coming' he promised? Ever since our fathers died, everything goes on as it has since the beginning of creation." But they deliberately forget that long ago by God's word the heavens existed and the earth was formed out of water and by water. By these waters also the world of that time was deluged and destroyed. *(2 Peter 3:3-6)*

Here Peter defends the literal reality of an event to back up its moral message. A Christian as a theologian may therefore use the moral message of a passage to construct theology, and as a scientist use the literal historic record and other evidence to uphold the reality of the event, and therefore seek to defend the theological content of the same message. For the Israelite and Christian, upholding the moral lesson and defending the literal account go hand in hand, and this approach is sympathetic to the Judeo-Christian tradition itself. Young earth literalists are often accused of failing to see allegory behind the Genesis accounts, but here we find the literalist Peter understanding the message at a number of different levels of meaning. In fact it may be argued that the one who denies the literal meaning is the one who fails to see the different layers.

Pascal also suggests that the logical position for those who accept some of the Bible is then to accept all of it. Pascal comments that although God is hidden, visible signs have existed throughout the ages, and those who wish to search may find evidence of these signs. He states that we have the prophecies, whereas other ages had different signs, and all these proofs draw together in a consistent pattern. Therefore if one is true, all others are as well. Every age has signs that are appropriate, and therefore each age may accept signs from other ages. The Patriarchs who were present around the time of the Flood believed in Creation, and also believed in the coming Messiah. The Israelites who were with Moses and lived among the prophets believed in the Flood and the fulfilment of prophecies, and in our present age we have seen many of those prophecies fulfilled, especially as they relate to the Messiah, therefore we should believe in the Flood and Creation as well.[23]

Young earth creation scientists would deny that they are following in the school of Paracelsus, who sought to build the whole of science on the revealed Word of God. Such an approach would effectively take Scripture out of context, and abuse it by trying to take more out of it than was ever put in, in the first place. Instead, as Lynn White has noted, the account of creation, and religious devotion, have empowered science and given it impetus.[24] Quite clearly, the pursuit of scientific knowledge must follow broadly according to Bacon's methodology of observation and inductive reasoning, although deductive logic and philosophy will always impinge on the interpretation of observations as well. For this reason, Karl Popper's insistence that the scientific process must seek to falsify its own work through repeatable experiment is an important tool for the discipline of science. However, it may be noted that both the geological record and the Scriptural record are not repeatable. It is evolutionists who seek to hide their theory of macro-evolution from critical analysis, while defending it as science. Karl Popper, at one time for instance, called evolution a metaphysical research programme.[25] However, as has been shown in the previous chapter, geology is now beginning to come into the light where the dogma of uniformitarianism is found to be a very incomplete explanation of the geological evidence indeed.

Bacon's twin book approach, with the Word of God revealing moral and divine philosophy as theology on the one hand, and observations of the natural world leading to natural philosophy or science on the other, is broadly accepted but not exclusively so. It may be noted that Bacon himself acknowledged that Scripture provides incidental, observational evidence towards science, and that for instance Job and Solomon also provide lessons in natural philosophy. Solomon's writings also appear to form the basis for the natural theology tradition that was later taken up by Aristotle and Thomas Aquinas, the ant for instance providing a sermon for the sluggard.

While broadly accepting Bacon's approach, it must be recognised that Genesis itself, as an ancient document, claims to be an account of real observed events, and as such consideration of the reality of these events is part of natural philosophy and leads to a scientific discipline. Christians and scientists have every right to explore the literal text of Scripture to develop a greater understanding of past events, without falling into the errors of

Paracelsus. In many ways, this approach is very similar to the scientific search for evidence of past events within the sedimentary rock layers. The two methodologies should eventually lead to a harmonisation of the study of the text of Genesis and geology. But it may be noted that attempts at harmonisation have been hindered for several hundred years by the deistic and godless assumptions of uniformitarian geology, which have been deliberately and falsely crafted to move away from the literal catastrophic reading of the Genesis text. Moreland and Craig have also recently argued that *theistic science*, which includes creationism and Flood geology and uses theological presuppositions, has been seen to form part of science for most of the history of science.[26] Moreland and Craig also note that Darwin in *Origins* used metaphysical arguments in seeking to draw inferences about the character of God if he were the designer, by claiming that a perfect God would not have produced the present created order that Darwin believed to be imperfect. Accordingly, use of metaphysical arguments such as this, by methodological naturalists, leads to inconsistency when they then seek to deny Christians the right to bring theology, or theological texts, to bear on science.

Incidentally, it is ironic that the book of Genesis faces two accusations that are mutually exclusive. On the one hand it is claimed to be a simple book, written by simple people, for simple people. The other claim is that it contains profound theology written as metaphor and allegory. The first three chapters of Genesis do indeed contain some profound imagery that helps to explain detailed theology, such as the reason for evil, suffering and death. These themes are returned to throughout the Bible and indicate tremendous depth of thought. Modern man is still trying to come to terms with them, and Theodore Dalrymple for instance states that the doctrine of Original Sin has not been surpassed in giving an explanation for mankind's wickedness.[27] Such subtlety and complexity demonstrates that Genesis cannot be a simple book. As we shall see in later chapters, when theologians try and blend this rich metaphor and allegory with belief in theistic evolution, they run into some serious problems with understanding evil, death and suffering. It is only when we accept Genesis for both its rich imagery and theology, and for its literal account, that we can really understand who we are as human beings, where we have come from and our purpose in life. It is only then that we can begin to understand the issues surrounding ethics, suffering and evil.

Another aspect of creationism that has been challenged is over the intelligent design arguments, especially those developed by William Paley and much loved by creationists and the Intelligent Design movement. Alister McGrath[28] shows how Paley, with *Natural Theology*, developed earlier 17th century and 18th century ideas of scientific natural theology, known as *physical theology*, and applied them to biology. Previously, aspects of design had been seen in the mechanistic Newtonian laws of nature, and the precise regularity of Newtonian mechanics was believed to be evidence of a divine plan and purpose. By comparing God's creation to the contrivance and mechanisms of a watch, and suggesting that God was a watchmaker, Paley extended the views of the physical theologians to organic life. Physical theology was seeking to develop the apologetic side of natural theology, but it was making the mistake of over emphasising the book of nature and reducing Scripture in importance. There were therefore problems with this approach, not least was the fact that in many ways, seeing God as a mechanistic original lawgiver was really a form of deism, and it was also leading to atheism. God was being removed to a distant past, and atheists were able to claim that the precise regularity of natural laws proved that God was not required at all. It was for this reason that many theologians were seeking to move away from physical theology, at the time when Paley was resurrecting it in biological form.

Paley's arguments were also weakened because he failed to deal with some important theological issues, such as the nature of the Edenic Fall and suffering. Paley was seemingly committing the naturalistic fallacy by attributing all observed design to a perfect adaptation, as originally given by God at creation. It was George Moore[29] who developed the idea of the naturalistic fallacy in 1903 because he recognised that simply because something is natural does not necessarily make it good. This is an extension of David Hume's idea that it is not possible to derive the 'ought' of ethics from the 'is' of facts about nature. Anyone who observes nature sees the brutality, death and suffering that is not consistent with a perfect creation. Darwin was troubled by the idea of God creating nature to suffer, and would rather believe in a meaningless existence and godless process of natural selection, than place his faith in such a God who could create such suffering.

Today creationists have developed the watchmaker concept as given by Paley, and through application of Scripture have a better understanding of the complexity and also the limitations of design arguments. It may be observed that natural selection can lead to changes in an animal's form and enable it to become a more efficient hunter. The white polar bear is better adapted to catch seals in snow than a brown bear would be. The striped zebra is more camouflaged on the plains of Africa than a pure brown pony would be, and therefore has an advantage in escaping the claws of a lion. But these are limited changes within a divinely created order. The horse, lion and bear exist as separate created kinds. Modern creationists who use the intelligent design arguments recognise the reality of micro-evolutionary changes such as these examples, but also maintain that the basic form of a bear or horse have not changed since the fall.[30] At the genetic level, there are quantised pools of information that confine the degree of adaptation of created animal kinds, and the gaps that exist between such gene pools are unbridgeable by natural means. What is more, at the microscopic level, the cell reveals a degree of complexity that cannot have come from slight successive modification. Such systems as the bacterial flagellum and ATP synthase show a degree of complexity that is not reducible to simpler systems.

In many ways creation science design arguments, as a development and extension of natural theology, are a middle ground between those theistic evolutionists who say that there are no limitations to Darwinian natural selection, and those like Paley who believe that all observed design is as given at creation. In so doing, Paley failed to deal with the issue of suffering and the scriptural record of the fall from grace. Ironically, those who accept theistic evolution also struggle with the issue of death and suffering that troubled Darwin, believing that God created through the process of natural selection. It is doubtful whether Darwin would have been any more impressed with the way theistic evolution deals with suffering for this very reason. The example of Paley here reveals to us the mistake of believing that the scriptural record has nothing to say with regard to the natural sciences. In order to understand the world correctly, in terms of science, ethics and theology, we must compare observations in nature with the scriptural record, and this is the approach that creation scientists adopt. Theologians who claim that Scripture can say nothing about natural science, as Paley and some theistic evolutionists do, find themselves in danger of falling into the naturalistic fallacy trap.

Notes and References

[1] Forster, R., Marston, P., *Reason, Science and Faith*, Monarch Books, Lion Hudson Plc, Crowborough, East Sussex, UK, p. 400, 1999.

[2] White, L., Jr., *The Historical Roots of our Ecologic Crisis*, Science, Vol. 155, No. 3767, p. 1206, 10 March 1967.

[3] Forster and Marston, op. cit., p. 193.

[4] Ibid., p. 194.

[5] Ibid., pp. 193-194.

[6] Ibid., p. 193.

[7] Mortenson, T., *British Scriptural Geologists in the First Half of the Nineteenth Century - Part 1: Historical setting*, Answers in Genesis, TJ, 11(2), pp. 221-252, 1997.

[8] Ibid.

[9] Calvin, J., *Genesis*, 1554; Banner of Truth, Edinburgh, UK, p. 78, 1984.

[10] Harrison, P., *The Bible and the Emergence of Modern Science*, Christians in Science, Public Lecture, Cambridge University, 24th May 2005. <www.st-edmunds.cam.ac.uk/cis/harrison/Peter%20Harrison%20-%20index.htm>, Accessed March 2006.

[11] Forster and Marston, op. cit., p. 400.

[12] Ibid., p. 322.

[13] Ibid., p. 400.

[14] Bacon, F., *Advancement of Learning*, Oxford ed., Book I, Part VI.16, p. 46, 1906. (Orig. 1605).

[15] Ibid., pp. 40-41.

[16] Bacon, F., *The Works of Francis Bacon*, London, Vol. II, pp. 482-484, 1819.

[17] Mortenson, op. cit.

[18] Bacon, op. cit., *Advancement of Learning*, Book II, part XXV.16, p. 229.

[19] Ibid., Book I, Part VI.16, pp. 43-44.

[20] Sibley, A., Brown, A., McIlwaine, T., *Bristol Channel Waterspout, 11 January 2004*, Weather, 59(6), Royal Met Soc., pp. 158-161, 2004.

[21] For use of the *toledot* see also: Genesis 2:4, 5:1, 6:9, 10:1, 11:10, 11:27, 25:12, 25:19, 36:1, 37:2.

[22] Wiseman, P.J., (ed. Wiseman, D.J.), *Ancient Records and the Structure of Genesis*, Thomas Nelson Publishing, Nashville, 1985.

[23] Pascal, B., (trans. Krailsheimer, A.J.), *Pensees*, Penguin Classics, London, pp. 333-334, 1995.

[24] White, op. cit., p. 1206.

[25] Popper, K., *Unended Quest*, Open Court Pub. Co., La Salle, Illinois, p. 168, 1985.

[26] Moreland, J.P., Craig, W.L., *Philosophical Foundations for a Christian Worldview*, IVP, pp.356-366, 2003.

[27] Dalrymple, T., *The Evil That Men Do*, The Spectator, p. 16, 20th March 2004.

[28] McGrath, A., *Dawkins' God*, Blackwell Publishing, pp. 60-72, 2005.

[29] Moore, G.E., *Principia Ethica*, Cambridge University Press, 1903.

[30] Whether or not genetic changes occurred at the fall is another question. There is insufficient space to give a scientific description of what constitutes a *kind*, but the word *kind* comes from the Greek *genos* from which we also get our English words *kin* and *gene*. The Latin equivalent is

species. *Kind* therefore implies a genetic link of a group of animals or plants that can be traced back through common ancestry even though the outward form of those animals or plants may look different in the present day.

Chapter 3

Christian Concern and the Rise of Evolution

'What inclines me now to think that you may be right in regarding it [evolution] as the central and radical lie in the whole web of falsehood that now governs our lives is not so much your arguments against it as the fanatical and twisted attitudes of its defenders.' [1]
(C.S. Lewis)

In the previous chapter it was shown that through earlier centuries the study of science and theology were treated separately, and this stemmed in part from Bacon's writing. Bacon developed the twin book approach from earlier times, with the Bible seen as giving theology on the one hand, and nature leading to natural philosophy or science on the other. This made the way for later philosophers to reject the Bible entirely, although it was noted that Bacon proclaimed the greatest respect for Scripture. As a result, the Genesis account of creation and the Flood are today considered at best allegorical, partial or local, and at worst disregarded entirely. Scripture is perceived now to have no bearing on the study of science. Scriptural assumptions were replaced by other non-Christian assumptions, these established through weight of peer pressure alone, sometimes by those committed to Unitarian theology and philosophy. In the late nineteenth century, science moved from an ambivalent attitude towards Scripture to one of outright hostility, through the writings of Charles Lyell, Charles Darwin, Thomas Huxley and others. Many churchmen fell into line through later decades, and even leading evangelicals considered belief in the literal interpretation of Genesis to be unnecessary for Christian faith, although some Christians sought to uphold the Genesis account and the authority of the Bible through for instance the establishment of the Victoria Institute in 1865. However, by the 1950s the Victoria Institute too had lost sight of its original purpose. Forster and Marston comment that:

> 'In the Victoria Institute, as in the Cambridge Conservative Evangelical circles ... in the early 1950s young earthism simply did not exist.' [2]

While it may be true that young earth creationism was not notable within the Victoria Institute in the 1950s, as Forster and Marston claim, there remained a number of Christians in the middle and early part of the twentieth century, who were deeply concerned with the ethical implications of evolution and the negative consequences for social affairs that belief in survival of the fittest implied. Rejection of the theory of evolution and belief in some sort of creation had a strong tradition within the Victoria Institute from its foundation in 1865 until well into the 1930s.

The Victoria Institute, or Philosophical Society of Great Britain was founded by a group of scientists and Christians concerned with countering the growing anti-Christian bias and lack of integrity that was developing within science. They believed that pseudo-science was being used to deliberately attack Scripture with untested theories promoted and accepted without the necessary supporting evidence. In *Scientia Scientiarum*, the Honorary Secretary of the Victoria Institute James Reddie refers to a discourse and correspondence between Professor Adam Sedgwick and Dr William Cockburn, Dean of York.[3] In 1844 Cockburn attacked the nebular theory for the origin of the earth put forward by Dean William Buckland in the Bridgewater Treatises. Although some nineteenth century scientists used this nebular theory to undermine the Mosaic account, it was later rejected as wrong when it became clear that volcanic rocks were often laid down in the presence of water. Dean Cockburn argued that no geological facts exist to support the long ages of the world. Reddie used this example to show how scientific theories that are used to dismiss Scripture are later abandoned as new evidence comes to light. Defending Scripture against false science such as this formed the basis for the purpose of the Victoria Institute. The first

Object of the Victoria Institute read; *'To investigate fully and impartially the most important questions of Philosophy and Science, but more especially those that bear upon the great truths revealed in Holy Scripture, with the view of defending these truths against the oppositions of Science, falsely so called.'* [4] It is apparent that the original aims and purposes of the Victoria Institute were very similar to the aims and purposes of modern day creationist groups.

Gary Ferngren and Ronald Numbers comment with regard to leading creationists in the Victoria Institute that:

> 'Dewar invited Acworth to lecture at the Victoria Institute, a religiously conservative organization that had long served as a haven for the dwindling remnant of British creationists. There Acworth met other like-minded men, including the distinguished electrical engineer Sir Ambrose Fleming (1849-1945), then president of the institute.' [5]

These distinguished gentlemen later set up the Evolution Protest Movement to oppose the teaching of evolution as fact, and this organisation is today known as the *Creation Science Movement*. However, like Forster and Marston, the modern Church historian Andrew Walker has also claimed that most evangelical Christians have had to come to terms with evolution, and that many Christians view creationism as 'a basic category mistake'. [6] Walker goes on to express regret that creationists are failing to engage in the real ethical debate that a belief in godless scientific progress presents, but instead are wasting their time on trivial scientific arguments. He suggests that a belief in a recent literal creation is unnecessary for ethical standards and goes on to comment regarding C.S. Lewis, that he:

> '... led the way in the 1940s, by arguing cogently and convincingly that Genesis chapters 1 and 2 were not written as science but as myth (in the high sense - following Coleridge and George MacDonald - that Lewis used).' [7]

The Genesis account is therefore seen by many Christians today as a way of only making ideas visible, and that the actual mechanisms that God used are not considered important, being possibly beyond human knowledge and comprehension. The early considered opinion of C.S. Lewis, that Genesis 1-3 should be viewed as a high form of mythology, seems to have great bearing on British evangelical opinion in the late 20th century, with a sharing of Lewis's apparent early view that evolution is not that important to Christian faith or ethics. This is, I believe, a serious mistake and it does not take into account Lewis's later views. More importantly, it leaves Christianity exposed to those forces that seek to undermine it. Lewis, in private correspondence with Bernard Acworth, co-founder of the Evolution Protest Movement, comments:

> "I believe that Man has fallen from the state of innocence in which he was created: I therefore disbelieve in any theory which contradicts this. It is not yet obvious to me that all theories of evolution do contradict it. When they do not, it is not my business to pronounce on their truth or falsehood. My "message" on any biological theorem which does contradict (or who I, with my imperfect process of reasoning, do not perceive to contradict) the Creed, is not "equivocal" but non-existent: just as my message about the curvature of space is not equivocal but non-existent. Just as my belief in my own immortal & rational soul does not oblige or qualify me to hold a particular theory of the pre-natal history of my embryo, so my belief that Men in general have immortal & rational souls does not oblige or qualify me to hold a theory of their pre-human organic history - if they have one.' [8]

Lewis here appears to suggest that he does not have a view with regard to the importance of biological evolution to Christian faith, because he considers evolution merely a scientific theory. In later correspondence with Bernard Acworth, Lewis elaborates a little further and appears to neither attack nor defend evolution.

> 'I am not either attacking or defending Evolution. I believe that Christianity can still be believed, even if Evolution is true. This is where you and I differ. Thinking as I do, I can't help regarding your advice (that I henceforth include arguments against Evolution in all my Christian apologetics) as a temptation to fight the battle on what is really a false issue: and also on terrain very unsuitable for the only weapon I have. Atheism is as old as Epicurus, and very few polytheists regard their gods as creative.' [9]

It would seem that the main basis for refusal by Lewis to enter into attacks on evolution is that he recognised that he was no scientist, and that his contribution to apologetics would be damaged if he strayed from his own literary expertise. Lewis comments:

> 'No one who is in doubt about your views of Darwin would be impressed by testimony from me, who am known to be no scientist.' [10]

Lewis's early view, which is perhaps shared by many Christians today, is that Genesis 1-3 is mainly concerned with theology and relationships, a sort of high mythology given to express and visualise spiritual truths. Lewis also did not consider the truth or falsehood of evolution to be that important for Christian faith, and that evolution did not have much bearing on ethical standards, and Walker also considers a belief in a literal creation to be unimportant to Christian faith. However, this evidence, and Walker's statement regarding Lewis's view, fails to address later correspondence where Lewis appears to change his mind and views evolution as a central and radical lie. Lewis later comments that:

> 'I have read nearly the whole of Evolution [probably Acworth's unpublished "The Lie of Evolution"] and am glad you sent it. I must confess it has shaken me: not in my belief in evolution, which was of the vaguest and most intermittent kind, but in my belief that the question was wholly unimportant. I wish I were younger. What inclines me now to think that you may be right in regarding it as the central and radical lie in the whole web of falsehood that now governs our lives is not so much your arguments against it as the fanatical and twisted attitudes of its defenders.' [11]

Walker for his part goes on to elaborate his view that a belief in a literal creation is not important to Christianity, although he does recognise the ethical implications of the excesses of Darwinian evolution. Overlooking the fact that Walker appears to confuse neo-Darwinism with the philosophy of social Darwinism, most of his comments on the logical and brutal consequence of Herbert Spencer's sociological survival of the fittest are perfectly valid.

One phrase sticks out:

> '... in its demonic guise a pseudo-Darwinism stalks the halls of
> scientific sorcery, where the gathered covens are hell-bent on putting
> an end to natural selection and replacing it with biotechnological
> cloning and genetically-engineered spare-part replacements for
> malfunctioning humanoids.' [12]

While creationists may broadly agree with this statement, the next
comment makes for some difficult reading, and requires an effective
response.

> 'Instead of joining forces with the broad stream of Christian orthodoxy
> in order to battle with the pressing theological, scientific and ethical
> issues of the day, creationism is squandering its intellectual and
> financial resources up a Texan creek looking for the footprints of a
> latter-day dinosaur running side by side with early man.' [13]

Walker also accuses creationists of being too literal, and many
evangelical Christians also view creationism as a sort of pseudo-
science for lonely, embittered Biblical fundamentalists. This
fundamentalism allegedly does not show the grace and love of God,
or the open mindedness and sophistication that most modern
evangelical Christians expect. In short, young earth creationism is
seen as a bit of an embarrassment to those who desire family
respectability, and a warm, cosy sort of charismatic spirituality. Very
post-modern indeed. However, it may be noted that one of the most
radical of the Pentecostal and Charismatic pioneers, Smith
Wigglesworth, looked forward to a day when Christians would be
united, filled with the Holy Spirit and committed totally to the Word
of God.[14] This he believed was important if the evangelical church
was serious about seeing a revival of Christianity in the Western
world.

Many other Christians see their expression of faith in terms of
direct social evangelism, and believe that debates or arguments over
words are less important. This would appear to be the case with one
leading Christian social activist, Steve Chalke, who plans to set up
Christian schools. He is reported to have said that those who accept a

literal reading of Genesis 1-3 are neither honest nor scholarly, claiming that such a view is bizarre and rubbish.[15]

Often though, the hard work of many Christians in social evangelism is undermined by the constant and relentless teaching of evolution in school and in the media. This all-pervasive humanist agenda undermines Christian faith, and produces a generation living solely for self for the sake of short term pleasure, personal benefit and survival. There is little consideration for the needs of others in the world. The purely selfish world of survival of the fittest is a very sad and cold world indeed, but evolutionary teaching reinforces it as the only option. This is in sharp contrast to the example of faith that Abraham exemplified when he let his nephew Lot take the best pasture land, while Abraham himself prospered with God's blessing, through the raising of sheep in a barren environment. Social action without a real commitment to the Biblical teaching concerning the state of man as God's direct creation, and the consequential responsibility towards God and society that such a state brings, is akin to taking water to the needy with a bucket full of holes.

Andrew Walker also wrongly suggests that it was Benjamin B. Warfield and the Fundamentalists who were responsible for placing the Creation account on a scientific or literal footing, as opposed to the more poetic and literary one preferred by many evangelicals today. Walker writes:

'At Princeton Seminary in America during the early days of the last century, Protestant theologians such as B.B. Warfield and Archibald Hodge recast the Genesis creation story from a literary-historiographical account into a scientific one.

One major consequence of this was that by the time the intellectual foundations of fundamentalism were laid, with the publication of the 12 volumes of The Fundamentals (printed 1910-15), American evangelicalism had identified itself not only with a principled stance against the new "higher criticism" of biblical scholarship, but also with a radical rejection of Darwinism. Both these positions were seen to be logically connected and together they have been imprinted on evangelical memory as a major offensive in the battle for the Bible.' [16]

There are indeed very good and logical reasons to see 'higher Biblical criticism' and Darwinism as being linked because they are part of the same concerted attempt to undermine Christian faith by 'enlightened' forces. Just because various attacks appear separate doesn't mean the enemy is not working to a deliberate strategy behind the scenes. However, Walker here misrepresents Warfield's position, and Warfield is not really the fundamentalist claimed. Although a rejection of Darwinism and acceptance of Biblical literalism are now seen as part of fundamentalism, it may be noted that both Henry Morris, and Forster and Marston assert, contrary to Walker, that Warfield came to accept evolution. Forster and Marston comment that:

> 'Morris is, however, correct in his assessment that major theologians of the period such as B.B. Warfield and A.H. Strong mainly moved to accept evolution. Moore and Livingstone add numerous other leading Evangelicals including A.A. Hodge...' [17]

Morris for his part comments:

> 'Certain very popular religious leaders of the day who were believed to be orthodox Bible-believers, such as Frederick Farrar, James Orr, Charles Kingsley, and Henry Drummond, were tremendously influential in persuading rank-and file Christians to accept theistic evolution. The same was true in the United States, where even such stalwarts as B.B. Warfield and A.H. Strong - known as strong defenders of the faith - capitulated to evolution.' [18]

Most of those who wrote for *The Fundamentals* accepted Darwinism, and only a few objected to the evolution of mankind. Fundamentalism itself was originally an attempt to remain committed to an orthodox Protestant position over the *New Testament* accounts, and most young earth creationists today regard their position as being in line with classic fundamentalism.

Warfield was also a reformed theologian and objected to modern day miracles because he believed they should cease according to Scripture, and because they appear to violate natural laws and Christian experience. This is at odds with charismatic and

Pentecostal theology and experience, and Warfield's view may legitimately be considered a form of Biblical deism. However, the main focus of Warfield and the Fundamentalists was to counter 'higher Biblical criticism' and uphold the traditional Christian teaching of the life, death, resurrection and miraculous work of Jesus Christ. Although Warfield's aim may be considered noble, it will be shown later how this partial form of Biblical deism actually undermined Christian faith throughout the Western world and unwittingly allowed Darwinism to prosper. By seeking to uphold parts of the Judeo-Christian Scriptures, while at the same time denying other miraculous parts at the beginning, and also denying miracles in the present day, Warfield seems rather inconsistent.

Charismatic evangelical Christians, who accept modern day miracles, want to move away from Warfield's view of rigid fundamentalism and return to the concept of a God of love and grace, believing that the Christian life is to be lived out in union with Jesus Christ and the indwelling Holy Spirit. Scientific creationism is wrongly seen as being part of that fundamentalism by charismatics, and a denigration of the true spirit of the Gospel, although it must be stressed that this is not a universal view among all charismatic Christians, especially those of Pentecostal traditions. Instead, evolution itself should be considered seriously flawed, and those Christians who fail to notice and point out its philosophical and scientific cracks may be considered partly responsible for artificially propping up a purely materialistic godless faith system.

When the charismatic Paul preached in Athens *(Acts 17:16-34)* he faced the atheists of his day, the Epicureans, who sneered at him. However, he was not afraid to respond by upholding God's place as Creator before moving on to the resurrection. Paul used classical Greek arguments, as derived from Aristotle, to demonstrate that design evidence in creation required God as designer, and implied that every cause needs an initial prime mover. He also showed that God has a purpose for mankind from creation. Paul also quoted Epimenides and Aratus.[19]

'The God who made the world and everything in it is the Lord of heaven and earth and does not live in temples built by hands. And he is not served by human hands, as if he needed anything, because he himself gives all men life and breath and everything else [God as prime mover]. From one man he made every nation of men, that they should inhabit the whole earth; and he determined the times set for them and the exact places where they should live. God did this so that men would seek him [man has purpose] and perhaps reach out for him and find him, though he is not far from each one of us. 'For in him we live and move and have our being.' As some of your own poets have said, 'We are his offspring.'

'Therefore since we are God's offspring, we should not think that the divine being is like gold or silver or stone — an image made by man's design and skill. In the past God overlooked such ignorance, but now he commands all people everywhere to repent. For he has set a day when he will judge the world with justice by the man he has appointed. He has given proof of this to all men by raising him from the dead.' *(Acts 17:24-31)*

The Epicureans were the atheists of the ancient Greek world and believed that various pleasures were all there was to live for. Atheists today follow the errors of the Epicureans, basing morality on short term pleasure and denying any purpose in life, this following the writings of David Hume and Charles Darwin. Western society therefore loses a solid foundation for ethics and reduces mankind to a hopeless purposeless state where living for hedonistic pleasure is all that matters. There is therefore a real need for Christians to uphold faith in the power and wisdom of God in creation once again, to re-establish morality and to give people meaning in life. However, with the advent of Darwinism, it would seem that many Christian leaders simply caved in and accepted evolution, perhaps not realising the ethical package that comes with it. Evolution is one branch of atheistic philosophy that is based on the ethics of Epicurus. Evolutionary theory itself is derived from Anaximander of Miletus (c.570BC), possibly a pupil of Thales (c.600BC), and Empedocles (450BC),[20] and undermines the natural theology tradition that Paul appealed to.

While Walker wrongly claims that fundamentalists such as Warfield were responsible for re-awakening a belief in a literal scientific Genesis account, Forster and Marston suggest instead that modern young earth creationism stems from the middle of the nineteenth century with the founding of the Seventh Day Adventists in 1845.[21] This group believed that Christians should adopt Saturday as the Sabbath, but otherwise they seemed to be fairly orthodox, taking their heritage from Christian non-conformists such as John Hus, Martin Luther and John Wesley. However, they seem to have become outsiders among the evangelical community, possibly as a result of their opposition to the fundamentalist Christian theologians who were trying to harmonise science with Scripture by accepting theistic evolution. The Adventists saw this as too liberal. Modern young earth creationists may note that their arguments against the Fundamentalists have some validity. Mainstream Evangelicals as well continue to view Adventists with suspicion, and this has been heightened further following the carnage that resulted at Waco, although as an aside the real culpability of the tragedy at Waco is carefully shrouded in political mystery and intrigue.

Seventh Day Adventists began to take greater interest in the Genesis account following advice from eccentric prophetess Ellen Gould White, who claimed to have been given a vision in which God stated that the creation account should be taken literally. While I am sure atheistic scientists will be having a good chuckle at the mention of this, Evangelical Christians should not dismiss it so lightly. After all, the Apostle Paul gave the instruction regarding prophecy, to 'Prove all things; hold fast that which is good.' *(1 Thess. 5:21 KJV)*. Adventists are also consistent with Luther and Wesley in taking Genesis literally, and White encouraged her followers to seek to uphold creation with enthusiasm and look for flaws in evolutionary theory. It was one of White's followers, George McCready Price,[22] who took up the literal research challenge that Ellen Gould White proposed, and produced a book called *The New Geology* in 1923. This book was to lay the foundation for another book, *The Genesis Flood* by John C. Whitcomb and Henry M. Morris, first published in 1961, which has since raised a lot of interest around the world in so called young earth creationism. While this is an interesting link, it needs to be noted as well that Terry Mortenson has shown that many Scriptural geologists opposed gradual evolution during the nineteenth century, appealing to a literal flood and creation account, and some of these men were leading Christians and careful observers of geological formations.[23] As noted previously, many of those who founded the Victoria Institute in 1865 also accepted the reality of the Noahic Flood and supported a recent creation.

As already mentioned, in Britain the first creationist group to be set up was the Evolution Protest Movement (EPM), which was founded in 1932 by leading British scientists Sir John Ambrose Fleming, Douglas Dewar and Captain Bernard Acworth. Fleming and Dewar were notable members of the Victoria Institute, and argued against evolution, but also accepted the prevailing theories of geology. Fleming, it would appear, believed in pre-Adamic races, whereas Dewar believed in the gap theory. This was common among respected Evangelical Christians, and indeed the footnotes in the 1917 Oxford Schofield Reference Bible on the creation account debate the possibility of the day-age scenario, the gap theory, and a previous catastrophe which left the world formless. However, Fleming, Dewar and Acworth all rejected scientific evolution, as they saw it as unproved and morally corrupting. The first public meeting of the EPM was recorded in The Times of 13th February 1935. Fleming is quoted as saying:

'Of late years the Darwinian anthropology had been forced on public attention by numerous books or highly illustrated periodicals in such fashion as to create a belief that it was a certainly settled scientific truth, and any objections to it were treated as the result of ignorance or bigotry. The fact that many eminent naturalists did not agree that Darwin's theory of species production had been sufficiently established as a truth was generally repressed. If there had been no creation, there was no need to assume any Creator, and the chief basis for all religion was taken away and morality reduced to mere human expediency. It had seemed to a large number of thoughtful persons that it was of national importance to try to counteract the effects of the reckless and indiscriminate popularisation of the theory of the wholly animal origin of mankind, especially among children or young and non-scientific people, by the diffusion of a more rational and truly scientific anthropology which did not omit to take into account an adequate cause for all those altruistic, aesthetic, intellectual, spiritual and religious faculties, latent and actual, in man, of which not the very slightest trace was seen in the animal species. They did not desire to neglect or oppose any certainly ascertained knowledge of past human history, but only to antagonize a one-sided materialistic presentation of human origin which rejected altogether any suggestion of creation, directivity, or control by a Supreme Intelligence. They said that the arguments of the Darwinian anthropologists were logically defective and did not give the proof they assumed.' [24]

Dewar did not object to evolution on theological grounds, although he did object to it becoming a creed. He accepted the gap theory to harmonise science and Scripture, although he rejected any attempt to make evolution part of Christian credentials. Interestingly Dewar saw the fundamental difficulties with the theory of evolution to be rational and experimental.[25] The EPM was therefore set up to oppose materialistic evolution and the moral degradation of society, but at the time Dewar and Fleming accepted the prevailing views on geology with various theological devices to harmonise Scripture with science. However, it would seem that Acworth was more determined in his attitude towards evolution. Ferngren and Numbers comment:

'In a book entitled This Progress: The Tragedy of Evolution (1934), he [Acworth] denounced evolution as a child of Satan.' [26]

Acworth saw the goal of evolution to be moral degradation through psycho-analysis, extinction through mass birth control and sterilisation, and revolution through a social, communist creed.[27] At the time of Acworth's writing, fascism was the main threat to Christian values in the West, although as a result of the events of World War II, fascism went into decline, but communism remained a threat for several more decades. Acworth himself appears a rather independent-minded character, being an opponent of Churchill's war effort, although he himself gained a Distinguished Service Order (DSO) in World War I for his service in submarines. He was the son and grandson of clergymen, a pioneer of sonar, and later a newspaper journalist.

Some years later, as a result of the publication of Morris and Whitcomb's book, *The Genesis Flood*, the EPM changed its view and adopted the new flood geology, together with a recent young earth creation. Today the EPM is known as the *Creation Science Movement* (CSM), and other similar creationist groups have been formed around the world as well, including the Institute for Creation Research (ICR) and the Creation Research Society (CRS).

However, at a superficial level it is not apparent why our beliefs about our origins matter at all. Whether we believe in special creation, as laid out in the book of Genesis, or Darwinian evolution, is not central to Christian faith, and the story of creation only plays a small part in the Gospel message regarding the fall of mankind. As we have seen, many Christians might claim to believe in theistic evolution or progressive creation, or perhaps have adopted one of the more popular creation theories, such as the existence of pre-Adamic races, the gap theory, or the day-age scenario. So at face value we might question why we should care what people believe on this matter?

But there is one question that Christians of all persuasions need to ask. How did the theory of evolution, and hence atheistic humanism, rise so rapidly in the last 150 years? Set against that rise we can see the steady fall that has occurred in Church attendance over the years, and the ethical implications for our society. From a peak in the late Victorian period, those who regularly attend Church now represent less than ten percent of the population in Britain, and a similar picture emerges right across Europe. Not only that, but there has been an increase in social breakdown as well. Ironically, the church went through a period of great revival for some 40 years after Darwin's book was published. Perhaps it was not Darwin's theory itself that caused the problems, but the widespread promotion of science as a sort of positivist religion during the late nineteenth and early twentieth centuries by Huxley and others. John Dewey for instance was responsible for establishing a purely humanistic education system, which was advanced to the many who were previously denied access to higher education.[28]

However, the Christian Church overcame many difficulties through the centuries, and thrived in times of persecution. It has dealt with splits, heresies, wars and many other problems, so how is it that so many people reject organised Christianity in the Western world today? One possible answer to this question is that it is the failure of the leadership of the Church to counteract the arguments in favour of macro-evolution, and the subsequent rise of godless ethics that has caused its decline. Christian leaders will have to answer this question for themselves, but many religious leaders readily accepted the evidence that evolutionary scientists presented without critical analysis. Not only the liberals, but today many leading evangelical theologians accept an evolutionary timescale for the creation account, and believe that Genesis 1-3 should be seen as only an allegory. In the recent past, Pope John Paul II has suggested that evolution may be considered more than a hypothesis (although Benedict XVI seems more critical of evolution). While I am sure theologians can believe in the accuracy of the Word of God, while accepting the Genesis account to be only an allegory, lesser mortals find this to be a form of syncretism and are left in doubt and confusion, preferring to call a spade a spade. Atheistic humanists are then able to exploit this fertile soil of doubt, and plant new seeds of godless clarity in what should be the Christian harvest field. '... if the trumpet does not sound a clear call, who will get ready for battle?' *(1 Corinthians. 14:8)*

As we have seen, some claim that the 'days' recorded in the Genesis narrative should be seen as long periods of time, and indeed the Bible does say in other places that to God 'a day is like a thousand years' *(2 Peter 3:8.* See also *Psalm 90:4).* However, as an aside, one tentative possibility is that this is a reference to a seven thousand year time frame of history, which correlates with the seven days of creation, the final millennium mentioned in *Revelation 20:4* matching the seventh day of rest.

The story of creation gives numbers to the days, and not only that, but it emphasises the point, 'And there was evening, and there was morning' *(Genesis 1:8).* I appreciate that there are problems with this picture, such as the sun and moon being created after day and night, but according to the apostles Paul and John, it was Jesus, the light of the world, who was present and active at the very centre of creation. 'Through him all things were made' *(John 1:3).* 'For by him all things were created' *(Colossians 1:16).* So we can see clearly that, according to Scripture, Jesus Christ was right at the heart of

Creation. 'In the beginning God *Elohim* (plural) created the heavens and the earth … and the Spirit of God was hovering over the waters' *(Genesis 1:1-2)*. The Father gave the command to the Son, the Son spoke the Word, and the Holy Spirit, hovering over the face of the water, brought about creation. It is when we see Jesus at work in Creation, the same Jesus who raised the dead and healed the sick, that we begin to understand how much He loved the world that he created. This should inform our attitude to humanity and nature.

But where incidentally is Jesus Christ in Genesis chapter 1? Hidden in the Hebrew text of Genesis, but not pronounced, are the letters *Aleph*, and *Tau*, the Hebrew equivalent of *Alpha*, and *Omega*.[29]

'In the beginning God (*Aleph Tau*) created the heavens and the earth' *(Genesis 1:1)*

Is it any wonder that John could say '*In the beginning* was the Word, and the Word was with God, and the Word was God'? *(John 1:1)* Later in John's book of Revelation, Jesus says, 'I am the *Alpha* and the *Omega*, the First and the Last, the *Beginning* and the End.' *(Revelation 22:13)*. It would seem that Jesus was there right from the beginning.

Now, no serious Evangelical Christian doubts the miracles that Jesus worked during his ministry two thousand years ago, but was it any harder for Jesus to turn water into wine than create the vine in the first place? Or feed five thousand people from a few loaves and fish than create wheat and aquatic life? Or raise Lazarus from the dead, than create Adam from the dust of the ground? It didn't take Jesus more than a few seconds to refresh the wedding party at Cana, or the multitude who were hungry on the banks of Galilee, so why do we need more than six days for creation? Of course the miracles of Jesus had symbolic, spiritual truths behind them as well. Jesus turned water into wine and claimed to be the true vine. He claimed to be the light of the world and healed a man born blind. He claimed to be the resurrection and the life and raised Lazarus from the grave, and He claimed to be the bread of life after feeding five thousand people from a few loaves and fish. But these were also real, creative miracles, which demonstrated Christ's divinity and symbolised his purpose on the Earth.

There is also a very good philosophical reason why special creation had to have happened in a short period of time, and not over millennia, and that is because the whole of nature is interdependent, through often complex relationships. The Earth's ecosystem is reliant on each part functioning together. As an example, Darwin highlighted this interdependence with reference to the bumble-bee (he called them humble-bees) and the pollination of certain plants.

> 'I find from experiments that humble-bees are almost indispensable to the fertilisation of the heartsease (Viola tricolour), for other bees do not visit this flower. I have also found that the visits of bees are necessary for the fertilisation of some kinds of clover; for instance 20 heads of Dutch clover (Trifolium repens) yields 2,290 seeds, but 20 other heads protected from bees produced not one. Again, 100 heads of red clover (T. pratense) produced 2,700 seeds, but the same number of protected heads produced not a single seed. Humbles-bees alone visit red clover, as other bees cannot reach the nectar ... Hence we may infer as highly probable that, if the whole genus of humbles-bees became extinct or very rare in England, the heartsease and red clover would become very rare or wholly disappear.' [30]

Darwin goes on to show how humble-bees are predated by mice, which in turn are eaten by cats and birds etc. There is therefore a complex web of symbiotic relationships throughout the natural world that require the different parts to function properly. Originally this was expressed in terms of good cooperative symbiosis, but after the fall also in terms of a competitive survival type balance of power.

How are we to deduce any sort of morality from these observations? The observed symbiotic relationships that clearly exist in nature may be illustrated by the perfect Garden of Eden creation account in Genesis. The observed faithless competitive pressure for resources, and space for survival and reproduction, that are also evident today, are illustrated by mankind's fall from grace, which still impacts nature to this day.

Progressive old earth creationism or theistic evolution faces a problem with the appearance of symbiosis, and it surely makes no sense for the bumble-bee, for instance, to have had to wait around for millennia before having the chance to gather nectar from a flower, or for that flower to be pollinated by the bee. If we are to reject godless macro-evolution as scientifically and logically flawed, then the most compelling alternative seems to be creation over a short period of time. C.S. Lewis noted this in a reply to Acworth. Commenting on Acworth's unpublished book, 'The Lie of Evolution', Lewis writes:

> 'The section on Anthropology was especially good ... The point that the whole economy of nature demands simultaneity of at least a very great many species is a very sticky one. Thanks: and blessings.' [31]

It seems that many of the struggles that Christianity in the West is going through are due to doubts over the immediacy and strength of God's power to work miracles today. A large number of Christians view God as very distant and very weak. Although many might deny it, this is in effect deistic Christianity. This struggle is not caused by the fact that some atheistic or deistic scientists try and remove God from the universe, but that many Church leaders have simply caved in to swim with the prevailing philosophical tide. How for instance would Elijah have managed if he had doubted God's creative power, when he challenged the prophets of Baal to a heavenly fire dual on Mt. Carmel? Or how would Moses have coped if he doubted God when he challenged Pharaoh to release the Israelites, and then passed through the Red Sea on his escape? Or perhaps we doubt these miracles as well? Is it any wonder that the Church, including the so-called charismatic branch, is so powerless today when we doubt God's power to work miracles in the past? We might say today, where is the God of Elijah? But the question that really needs to be asked is, where are the Elijah's of God?

It must be noted at this point that Christian faith comes by revelation. The Bible teaches that the Holy Spirit is the giver of faith, which means that faith does not come from our own understanding, or from seeing creative miracles, but is a revelatory gift of God. In fact we can find ample evidence from Scripture that faith does not come from proving, or witnessing miracles, or from hearing brilliant, logical arguments. The Jews demanded signs and wonders, but many of them ignored the works that Jesus accomplished, while the Greeks demanded great philosophies, and the Apostle Paul obliged them, but still many Greeks did not find faith. Some may object to the idea that Christian faith is a revelatory gift from God, on the grounds of unfairness, or find the Gospel message foolish, but the words of Jesus are clear. 'Ask and it will be given to you' *(Matt. 7:7)*. It is only our own pride that stops us from asking and receiving.

> For it is written: "I will destroy the wisdom of the wise; the intelligence of the intelligent I will frustrate." Where is the wise man? Where is the scholar? Where is the philosopher of this age? Has not God made foolish the wisdom of the world? For since in the wisdom of God the world through its wisdom did not know him, God was pleased through the foolishness of what was preached to save those who believe. Jews demand miraculous signs and Greeks look for wisdom, but we preach Christ crucified: a stumbling-block to Jews and foolishness to Gentiles, but to those whom God has called, both Jews and Greeks, Christ the power of God and the wisdom of God...
>
> ... God chose the foolish things of the world to shame the wise; God chose the weak things of the world to shame the strong. He chose the lowly things of this world and the despised things — and the things that are not — to nullify the things that are...
>
> ... My message and my preaching were not with wise and persuasive words, but with a demonstration of the Spirit's power, so that your faith might not rest on men's wisdom, but on God's power...
>
> ... as it is written: "No eye has seen, no ear has heard, no mind has conceived what God has prepared for those who love him" — but God has revealed it to us by his Spirit. *(1 Corinthians. 1:19 to 2:10)*

So faith comes by revelation from God. It also needs to be stated that we may not be able to prove that God created the universe and everything in it in six days in purely scientific terms, as special miracles lie outside of science. The whole question of origins must remain an article of faith to some extent, but natural science cannot preclude the supernatural either. Material science itself requires the 'Big Bang' as a starting point, but even here naturalistic science has to move from philosophy to science in its account of origins. This conceptual leap from philosophy to science is often denied, but it is real and is no different to a faith position. Naturalistic science too faces unbridgeable gaps when it tries to account for the immense complexity of life in purely natural terms, using laws of nature that are dominated by probability and entropy.

What I have tried to show in this chapter is that Christians need to move beyond compromise with Darwinism if we are serious about upholding our faith. C.S. Lewis is often held up as an authority to support this compromise position, but even Lewis was troubled by the impact of evolution towards the end of his life, and he claimed to be no scientist. Belief in our origins has an impact on how we treat each other as people, how we care for the environment as a whole, and it provides mankind with a purpose to live. It is this that forms the main arguments in the remaining chapters and I would urge people to carefully weigh up the overall ethical and theological debate without being put off by the author's personal preferences and beliefs.

Notes and References

[1] Ferngren, G.B., Numbers, R.L., *C.S. Lewis on Creation and Evolution: The Acworth Letters, 1944-1960*, Perspective on Science and Christian Faith, 48 (1), March 1996. Personal letter from C.S. Lewis to Bernard Acworth dated 13th September 1951. (Letters by C.S. Lewis copyright © C.S. Lewis Pte. Ltd. Reprinted by permission.)

[2] Forster, R., Marston, P., *Reason, Science and Faith*, Monarch Books, Lion Hudson Plc., Crowborough, East Sussex, UK, p. 238, 1999.

[3] Reddie, J., *Scientia Scientiarum*, Journal of the Transactions of the Victoria Institute, Vol.1, 1867-68. (First published as a circular in May 1865). The discourse between Prof. Sedgwick and Dean Cockburn began in 1844 at the British Association for the Advancement of Science meeting at York, where Dr. Cockburn, Dean of York, attacked the nebular theory which held that granites were evidence that the earth began as a hot molten sphere and gradually cooled over a very long period of time. See also Cockburn, W., *The Bible Defended Against the British Association* (1844), 5th ed., Whittaker, 1845.

[4] Victoria Institute, Council Members, *Objects of the Victoria Institute*, Journal of the Transactions of the Victoria Institute, 1866-67.

[5] Ferngren and Numbers, op. cit.

[6] Walker, A., *Epistles of Straw - The True Tragedy of Creationism*, Ship of Fools website, December 2001, <www.shipoffools.com/Columns/Walker/Walker1201.html>, Accessed March 2006.

[7] Ibid.

[8] Ferngren and Numbers, op. cit., Letter from Lewis to Acworth, 23rd September 1944.

[9] Ibid., Letter from Lewis to Acworth, 9th December 1944.

[10] Ibid., Letter from Lewis to Acworth, 4th October 1951.

[11] Ibid., Letter from Lewis to Acworth, 13th September 1951.

[12] Walker, op. cit.

[13] Ibid.

[14] Wigglesworth, S., Reportedly spoken in 1947, shortly before his death. Researched and paraphrased: Price, C., *Revival Prophesied*, Renewal magazine, 284, p. 50, January 2000. Monarch Magazines Ltd., Lion Hudson Plc, Crowborough, East Sussex, UK.
See also: <www.thewayofthespirit.com/about/wigglesworth.aspx>, Accessed March 2006.

[15] Curtis, P., *Christian Charity to Open London Academy*, Guardian news report, 13th July 2004. Reference to Steve chalk of Oasis Trust. It is debatable whether Steve intended for his remarks, perhaps spoken 'off-the-cuff', to be made public in this way, although it helps to understand what lies behind his book, (Chalke, S., Mann, A., *The Lost Message of Jesus*, Zondervan Publishing, 2004). This is discussed more fully in chapter 11.

[16] Walker, op. cit.

[17] Forster and Marston, op. cit., p. 227.

[18] Morris, H.M., *A History of Modern Creationism*, Master Books, p. 38, 1984.

[19] Epimenides in *Cretica* (about 600BC) 'In him we live and move and have our being'; and Aratus (315-240BC) in *Phaenomena* 'We are his offspring'.

See: Barker, K.L., et. al., (eds.), NIV Study Bible, Text Notes to Acts 17:28, Hodder & Stoughton, p. 1647, 1987.

[20] See for instance Denton, M., *Evolution: A Theory in Crisis*, Adler and Adler, Maryland, USA, pp. 37-40, 1986.

[21] Forster and Marston, op. cit., pp. 230-234.

[22] Price, G.M., *The New Geology*, Pacific Press, California, 1923.

[23] Mortenson, T., *British Scriptural Geologists in the First Half of the Nineteenth Century: Part 11: John Murray*, Answers in Genesis, TJ, 18 (2), pp. 74-82, 2004.

[24] Sir Ambrose Fleming, speech at the first public meeting of the Evolution Protest Movement, London, 12th February 1935. Reported in: The Times, *Teaching of Organic Evolution: A Protest Meeting*, 13th February 1935.

[25] Dewar quotes Dr. W.R. Thompson. In: Forster and Marston, op. cit., p. 238.

[26] Ferngren and Numbers, op. cit.

[27] Ibid.

[28] Whitcomb, J.C., Morris, H.M., *The Genesis Flood*, Baker Book House, pp. 445-446, 1961.

[29] Missler, C., *Cosmic Codes*, pp. 111-113, Koinonia House, 1999, <www.khouse.org>, Accessed March 2006.

[30] Darwin, C., *On the Origin of Species*, Murray Publishing, London, pp. 51-53, 1859.

[31] Ferngren and Numbers, op. cit., Letter from Lewis to Acworth, 13th September 1951.

Chapter 4

Huxley and Comte's Religion of Science

'For as he thinketh in his heart, so is he.'
(Proverbs 23:7 KJV)

The above quote really encapsulates the main reason why this subject is important. What this short proverb shows is that, the things we believe in our hearts and minds determine the people we are and become, both individually and as a society. It brings home to us in a very simple statement the importance of faith. What is at stake is much more than an argument about origins, or minor theologies, it is actually the very fabric and direction of our society and civilisation that is changed if we don't fully comprehend and understand the importance of this subject. Our faith determines our ethical standards. The arguments regarding the origin of life are much more than simple scientific enquiries. They have become tied up with philosophy and religious belief. This is why it is such a controversial subject.

Darwin's book *The Origin of Species* was finally published in 1859, twenty-eight years after the start of the voyage of the Beagle, but Darwin himself seemed to be unsure as to whether his theory of gradual evolutionary change was correct and his book is well qualified with uncertainty. He also seems uncertain in his agnostic faith and was sick with worry before publication. However, many of his followers were more determined in their support for and promotion of evolution.

Thomas Huxley gained the identity of Darwin's Bulldog, and did much to promote the work of his fellow scientist. Huxley was the most prominent promoter of Darwinian evolution and he was determined in his hatred of organised Christianity and rejection of anything that could not be explained with the laws of nature. He was a very powerful speaker and full of self-confidence and bluster, although it may be noted that such attitudes do not make one correct, and even Huxley had doubts over aspects of evolution through his life. He never fully accepted that evolution was proved scientifically, and never fully rejected the possibility that God may exist either.

However, it was Huxley who set up the secretive 'X Club' with eight colleagues in 1864, with the aim of pursuing scientific knowledge without any hindrance from what they saw as 'religious dogma'.[1] The nine were Thomas Huxley, Herbert Spencer, George Busk, Edward Frankland, Thomas Hirst, Joseph Hooker, John Lubbock, William Spottiswoode and John Tyndall. Three of the members were past Presidents of the Royal Society, and six were Presidents of the British Association and between them they were able to control the direction of science and education policy.

They met before meetings of the Royal Society for dinner to discuss a united policy, and also discussed in a systematic manner other business such as the ongoing warfare against religion and the place of science in education.[2] Although some of the members of this club had the appearance of being Christian, others like Huxley were keen to promote a sense of conflict between science and faith, and they worked hard at promoting rational science without recourse to faith at all. They also felt that scientists had a right to speak authoritatively on a wide range of social and moral aspects of life as well. Thomas Huxley played a major role in promoting evolution, undermining Christianity and dividing faith and science.

Huxley was also concerned with the organisation of scientific knowledge, and wrote to Ernst Haeckel that: 'I would Counsel you to stay at home, and as Goethe says, find your America here ... It is the organisation of knowledge rather than its increase which is wanted now.'[3] Geology for instance should be 'the history of the earth, in precisely the same way as biology is the history of living beings', and stratigraphy was insufficient on its own, but it should become a study of the gradual processes of change and their causes.[4] Huxley was passionate about the promotion of naturalistic science and his faith in science was as committed as that of Auguste Comte. Although Huxley was scathing of some of Comte's ideas, particularly Comte's desire to set himself up as some sort of high priest of science under a positivist religion, he in fact accepted the positivist ideals of this 19th century French philosopher.

> 'Great, however, was my perplexity, not to say disappointment, as I followed the progress of this "mighty son of earth" in his work of reconstruction. Undoubtedly "Dieu" disappeared, but the "Nouveau Grand-Être Suprême," a gigantic fetish, turned out brand-new by M. Comte's own hands, reigned in his stead. "Roi" also was not heard of; but, in his place, I found a minutely-defined social organization, which, if it ever came into practice, would exert a despotic authority such as no sultan has rivalled, and no Puritan presbytery, in its palmiest days, could hope to excel. While as for the "culte systématique de l'Humanité," I, in my blindness, could not distinguish it from sheer Popery, with M. Comte in the chair of St. Peter, and the names of most of the saints changed.' [5]

> Nothing can be clearer. Comte's ideal, as stated by himself, is Catholic organization without Catholic doctrine, or, in other words, Catholicism *minus* Christianity.' [6]

> 'Rightly or wrongly, this was the impression which, all those years ago, the study of M. Comte's works left on my mind, combined with the conviction, which I shall always be thankful to him for awakening in me, that the organization of society upon a new and purely scientific basis is not only practicable, but is the only political object much worth fighting for.' [7]

Although Huxley rejected the apparent vanity of Comte's ideas because it looked like 'Catholicism *minus* Christianity' with Comte as Pope, it was as if Huxley wanted science itself, or more accurately what Huxley and the X Club thought was scientific truth, to form the basis for the whole organisation of society and politics. Essentially Huxley's idea was a non-conformist version of Comtism, effectively Comtism *minus* Comte. With Huxley's energy, he himself effectively came to stand in the place that Comte had previously reserved for himself. It is debatable whether this was his intention or whether he was blind to this outcome. In Huxley's mind, his own opinion was to become the very arbiter of scientific truth, with sometimes poorly thought out logic. Consider the erroneous logic in these few paragraphs and the worrying conclusion:

'What I said was this: that the bringing into existence of an animal, at once, is a thing which is, in the nature of the case, capable of neither proof nor disproof, and is, therefore, no subject for science, which concerns herself only with matters capable of proof or disproof. And I went on to say, that if the appearance of the successive populations of the globe had followed laws at all similar to those by which the rest of the universe is governed, I could not conceive but that these successive races *must* have proceeded from one another in the way of progressive modification.

And that is my hypothesis, and I *do* include man in the same category as the rest of the animal world. But you will recollect, that I begged you particularly to understand that I regarded this notion of mine simply as a hypothesis, reasoned out from general principles, and wholly devoid of evidence amounting to proof.

Well, if you see good to reject this hypothesis, if you think that my reasonings from the principles I started with are fallacious, or that those principles themselves are erroneous, reject it by all means; and if you can show me, *on these grounds*, that you are right, I will reject it also as speedily as possible, and thank you for the refutation. Why should I cumber myself with the burden of an untruth?

But you all know right well that such are not the grounds on which hypotheses of this kind are objected to. The real reason is, that such doctrines are supposed to be antagonistic to religion, or rather, to be opposed to certain traditions handed down to us with our religious beliefs, from a venerable and remote antiquity.

Now let me tell you quite frankly, that I almost think it beneath the dignity of my calling, as a man of science, to listen to such objections as these. If it be *really* true that science is opposed to religion, all I can say is, so much the worse for religion. If science is *really* opposed to traditions, the sooner the traditions vanish and are no more seen or heard of, the better. For science, and the methods of science, are the masters of the world.' [8]

What does Huxley appear to be saying here? Huxley sets out an evolutionary hypothesis that he claims cannot be proved or disproved, although the certainty of it appears clear in Huxley's own mind. Huxley states that evolution is not proved science, but any objection to his hypothesis that is not based on science is rejected.

Huxley suggests that if you can disprove his hypothesis along scientific lines alone, then he would reject evolution because he would not want to believe something untrue. In other words, Huxley's hypothesis, it would seem, had already become scientific truth in his own mind despite stating that it could not be proved scientifically.

Huxley here challenges his critics to give him an alternative, but he rejects those arguments motivated by faith, effectively claiming the right to determine which philosophy is considered real science and which is not. Ravi Zacharias reports a similar response in discussion with a scientist, who admitted that godless scientists do like to maintain selective sovereignty over what they allow to be transferred to philosophy and what they do not.[9] Huxley too claimed selective sovereignty for science.

It would seem that those who reject Huxley's hypothesis on religious grounds are ruled out of court without even gaining a hearing. Any argument that is motivated by religion is considered false and ridiculed even if presented and backed up with impeccable science. Huxley too effectively accepted his own opinion as truth even though he admitted he could not prove it scientifically.

It may be noted as well that Huxley has made a philosophical leap in his deductive reasoning, applying the apparent laws of the universe to the laws of the evolution of mankind in a complete cosmic process of evolution. Here again, Huxley's own philosophy is acceptable as science, while religious philosophy is rejected. Huxley again appears to be the high priest of Comte's positivist religion. Even though Huxley seems to admit his hypothesis cannot be proved, objections on religious grounds are denied, which makes his own thoughts true science by default. Huxley appears to fail to see the flaws at work in his thinking, but presents an argument that appeals to late nineteenth century pride. In his own words, '... science, and the methods of science, are the masters of the world.'

In the next couple of paragraphs, Huxley continues to engage in sophistry to attack faith, on the one hand stating that it is wrong to claim that there is antagonism between science and religion, but then carefully defining science as a religion, and stating that religion only has value if it is treated scientifically.

> 'But it is not true. If you have seen occasion to put any faith in what I tell you, believe me now when I say, that of all the miserable superstitions which have ever tended to vex and enslave mankind, this notion of the antagonism of science and religion is the most mischievous.
>
> True science and true religion are twin-sisters, and the separation of either from the other is sure to prove the death of both. Science prospers exactly in proportion as it is religious; and religion flourishes in exact proportion to the scientific depth and firmness of its basis.' [10]

Science therefore takes its place as a religion, and true religion, which by definition should be based on faith, has no value because, according to Huxley, true religion requires a scientific base, not a faith base. It is ironic, but Huxley, having condemned scientific arguments that are motivated by religion, then asserts that science too should be treated as a religious devotion.

This lack of care is all very reminiscent of the discovery of *Bathybius* by Thomas Huxley in 1868. Huxley was re-examining samples of deep sea floor sediment that had been collected by the *Cyclops* in 1857, and preserved in alcohol. To his surprise he discovered that a thin film of jelly-like mucus had collected on the top of the sediment, with what looked like embedded tiny granules. Upon examination under a microscope, these granules appeared to move, and he thought that he had found the original protoplasm of life. Protoplasm was seen as the organic substance that formed the basis of life. His enthusiasm meant that he did not carry out chemical tests.

Huxley named this apparent single celled organism *Bathybius haeckelii* after the German naturalist Ernst Haeckel, who was the foremost promoter of the theory of *abiogenesis*; the idea that life could arise spontaneously from non-life. Haeckel, after examining Bathybius for himself, claimed that it was the original primordial slime (Urschleim in German) from which all other living things have arisen.

Partly for this reason two other vessels were despatched, *HMS Lightning* and *HMS Porcupine*, to look for evidence of early life, but they failed to find samples of Bathybius. However, the *Challenger* expedition, which left Portsmouth in 1872, was more successful and after two years sailing noted that samples of sea floor sediment that had been preserved in alcohol also contained evidence of the illusive Bathybius, although interestingly samples stored in seawater did not. The ship's chemist John Buchanan had the good sense to test the jelly and he found that it was nothing more than hydrated calcium sulphate ($CaSO_4.2H_2O$), caused by a reaction of the alcohol on the mud.

Huxley owned up to his mistake and wrote an open letter to the journal *Nature*, admitting that Bathybius was not organic. However, many scientists refused to believe that Huxley had made a mistake, and even three years later the president of the British Association was promoting Bathybius as the protoplasm of life. One recent historian of science comments that the reason there was so much reluctance to accept that Bathybius did not exist was because it played a key role in supporting the theory of evolution. Scientists wanted to believe in the reality of Bathybius.[11]

Thomas Huxley had made a very basic mistake as a result of his clouded judgement in attempts at finding evidence to prove his godless hypothesis. This is in contrast to Huxley's own statement that; 'The man of science, in fact, simply uses with scrupulous exactness the methods which we all, habitually and at every moment, use carelessly.'[12] However, his careless mistake served a useful purpose in promoting evolution as truth for at least seven years. I am trying to be as kind to Huxley as possible by recognising this as a simple mistake, but such a level of carelessness does not tie in with Huxley's high-ranking position as a scientist.

He also worked hard at undermining and rubbishing the work of Sir Richard Owen, who made some very significant discoveries in anatomy and was arguably a much better scientist than Huxley or Darwin. One reason for this obfuscation may have been because Owen believed in divine creation to account for the natural world, while another running sore with Huxley was the way the clerical establishment had treated him and others in his youth. Huxley may therefore have felt the need to settle a few old scores.

Huxley commented that:

> 'I believe I am right in saying that hardly any of these speculations and determinations have stood the test of investigation, or, indeed, that any of them were ever widely accepted. I am not sure that any one but the historian of anatomical science is ever likely to recur to them; and considering Owen's great capacity, extensive learning, and tireless industry, that seems a singular result of years of strenuous labour.' [13]

However, Huxley was once again wrong, his opinion blinkered by his own biased rhetoric, and Owen's legacy is recognised as being very distinguished indeed, despite Owen's own flawed character traits. Huxley was perhaps the first to overstate the evidence for evolution without proper investigation, but he was by no means the last. Despite Huxley's faith in the integrity and work of other scientists and the high praise he gave to the scientific methodology, evolutionary science has a rather shameful history in mistakes and fraud following the Bathybius affair. For instance a number of commentators have accused Ernst Haeckel of falsifying his drawings to support his now discredited theory of embryonic recapitulation. Dubois hid a couple of skulls under the floorboards for many years to allow acceptance of his Java Man skull as an evolutionary link, and later an important report *Die Pithecanthropus-Schichen auf Java* that contradicted Dubois's findings was subsequently removed from European libraries. Evolution Protest Movement Secretary A.G. Tilney had to search through sixty libraries in Europe to find a copy.[14] A well-worn pig's tooth was heavily promoted as evidence for ape-men ahead of the Scopes Trial by leading palaeontologists in America despite their increasing private doubts, and they did not publicly acknowledge their mistake until the trial was over. The Piltdown fraud was also allowed to capture people's imagination in favour of evolution for forty years. Bowden has accused Pierre Teilard de Chardin of carrying out the Piltdown forgery, although a number of culprits are possible.[15] All of these errors and frauds have been useful for the propagation of the theory of evolution.

Towards the end of his life, and suffering from ill health, Huxley appears to have softened his attacks on the church and recognised the ethical difficulties that belief in evolution presents to society, even writing a paper in 1888 entitled *The Struggle for Existence in Human Society* that in private correspondence he later admitted was a criticism of Herbert Spencer.[16] Huxley also discussed *Evolution and Ethics* in the Romanes Lecture of 1893.

> 'There is another fallacy which appears to me to pervade the so-called 'ethics of evolution.' It is the notion that because, on the whole, animals and plants have advanced in perfection of organization by means of the struggle for existence and the consequent 'survival of the fittest'; therefore men in society, men as ethical beings, must look to the same process to help them towards perfection.' [17]

Although Huxley asserts this as a fallacy he fails to provide logical reasons why it should be so, commenting that it is a fact that the natural cosmic process of evolution is antagonistic to the human process that works against it, although he says that such a proposition is logically absurd, even saying he is sorry for logic.[18]

The promotion of purely materialistic and godless science was continued through the work of others, with the founders of eugenics for instance talking in terms of a religious devotion to the logical outworking of survival of the fittest. The *Humanist Manifesto* was also discussed at first in religious terms similar to those of Comte and Huxley, but later the promoters of humanism found greater benefit in building a gulf between naturalistic science and religious faith by denying humanism ever had any religious attachment. This is the approach taken today by Richard Dawkins and most other popular Darwinists, but it would not be unreasonable to identify Dawkins as following in the positivist, religious path originally set out by Comte.

So, many of those who promoted evolution were not satisfied with scientific theory alone, but pursued a consistent and concerted attempt to undermine Christianity, and overthrow traditional Christian teaching and morality, even lowering to fraud and malpractice in the process. Similar attacks on Christianity continue today through the writing of popular writers. Alister McGrath shows how Richard Dawkins makes a similar erroneous leap in logic to reject Christian faith as Huxley had done in a previous century. Dawkins is shown to move from a statement that something cannot be proved, to claiming that such a statement is false.

In a debate entitled 'Whether Science is Killing the Soul', Dawkins responds to a question from the audience on whether he thought religion had value in comforting the bereaved. Dawkins responds by suggesting that although religion may console, it doesn't make it true, and then turns this lack of proof into a statement that religion is false, questioning whether people wish to be consoled by a falsehood.[19] McGrath criticises Dawkins for use of such rhetoric, calling it ridiculous, and comments that it is the worst kind of flaky logic.[20] Dawkins fails to acknowledge that just because something cannot be proved scientifically does not make it false.

All of this use of flawed logic and godless rhetoric is done within the cloak of science and reason, with an *a priori* assumption that there is no God. Every attempt is made to account for the whole of life in purely naturalistic terms without reference to God at all, from the big bang, to the creation of the earth, to the existence of humanity, and worse, to claim the right to speak with authority on ethical standards. But why should scientists in the present time have claims over ethical standards? Why should the scientist, who has skills in making observations and repeatable experiments be able to decide ethical issues? Theologians surely have the stronger right and duty to speak up for ethics. If we are to truly uphold a loving Christian ethic within society then the theologian should surely have a greater right to speak. Contrary to Huxley's view, the natural sciences are not masters of the world.

Naturalistic science, which includes the theory of evolution, has become a tenet of a new humanist religion based on a non conformist version of Comtism, or as Huxley aptly called such faith, a 'culte systématique de l'Humanité',[21] a systematic cult of humanism. This is the struggle that Christians find themselves up against. C.S. Lewis as a convert to Christianity finds naturalism holding a powerful sway and comments that many of us find naturalism as a sort of hangover or infection that exists in our bones. Accordingly we need to maintain vigilance to keep such assumptions at bay.[22] Naturalism and evolution are promoted so relentlessly by the media that it is not always easy reminding one's self of the very real logical and ethical objections to evolution.

C.S. Lewis, famous author and Christian convert, accepted theistic evolution for many years, but in his latter life he began to change his opinion. Upon closer inspection, natural science seems to lack a coherent ethical basis. Not only does it seek to account for everything without reference to God, it undermines the basis for any sort of morality at all. As has been shown earlier, in a personal letter to Bernard Acworth, one of the founders of the Evolution Protest Movement, C.S. Lewis highlighted this fact with an apparent change of mind, calling evolution a 'central and radical lie...' as a result of 'the fanatical and twisted attitudes of its defenders'.[23]

Today, Christianity continues to find itself under attack, and the source of this battleground can be traced further back in time than Darwin and Huxley to the beginning of the Enlightenment, where philosophy moved increasingly away from belief in a personal and loving God to one who was at best cold and distant. This movement later found extreme expression in Britain in the latter part of the nineteenth century following the work of Charles Darwin and his close supporters. This battlefield for faith and morality that Christians find themselves in is not one of their choosing. However, it is a reality, especially if we are genuinely concerned about the quality of ethical standards in society, both with regard to human social affairs and to the way in which we treat the environment. Christians have been losing this battle for too long, with a corresponding debasement of ethics and the social fabric with loss of respect for other human beings and the natural world. This can be seen for instance with the issue of genetic engineering, where the darker side of science wants to use people and animals as means to an end with loss of their intrinsic value. An embryo for example becomes just a spare part for use by another human being, or a genetically cloned animal a tool for scientific research. The task of rebuilding morality and faith is monumental.

Many of the attacks that Christianity finds itself under are unfounded, but they are widely believed in the humanistic mindset. Darwin, as a graduate of divinity, was well aware that his book *The Origin of Species*, would cause controversy, and to some extent was troubled by this, even appearing sick with worry before publication. However, others were not so reticent. Huxley, Spencer and Haeckel did much to promote Darwin's work, and at the same time deliberately denigrated the traditional Biblical and Christian worldview. Although Huxley and Darwin tried to claim that evolution should not lead to selfishness, greed and loss of compassion, the more logical aspect of survival of the fittest gained the upper hand, and still does so in the minds of many pressure groups. Fascism and Marxism are in decline, but there is still pressure for technological progress to be pursued outside of the compassionate, traditional Christian worldview. Extreme environmentalists also place little regard on the needs and welfare of humanity, wanting for instance to reduce the human population for the sake of some sort of biocentric romanticism, forgetting that biocentrism is itself of human construction and that such views may be considered a form of environmental fascism.

Throughout the latter part of the nineteenth century, and the first years of the twentieth century, the idea became popular in Europe and America that progress would continue through purely human endeavour without reference to the grace of God. The West passed through the Great War of 1914 to 1918, the stock market crash, and then depression followed, but this did not dent the confidence, or optimism of the humanists. It was the horrors of the Second World War that finally brought a little realisation to humanist confidence. However, the main problem for secular scientists in determining a moral basis for society from evolution remains unresolved, but naturalism remains deeply embedded in scientific enquiry with highly questionable moral practices.

As an example of the influence that humanistic philosophy, or naturalistic science, has gained in the pursuit of scientific enquiry, we need only look at some of the presentations that were given at the centennial celebration of the publication of Darwin's book *The Origin of Species*, which was held at the University of Chicago in 1959. Speakers included George Gaylord Simpson and Julian Huxley.

Julian Huxley claimed that this meeting was one of the first public forums in which it was recognised that all aspects of reality are subject to a single process of evolution. He claimed that this evolution passed from atoms and stars, to fish and flowers, and from fish and flowers, to human societies and even to values. This evolutionary process of thought meant that there was no longer need or room for the supernatural with the whole earth having evolved along with the animals and plants. Accordingly, human attributes too evolved including the mind and soul as well as the brain and even religion. Julian Huxley went on to claim that this evolutionary vision would enable mankind to discern the development of a new religion to serve future needs of a brave new world.[24]

These ideas have become entrenched in Western thought, and it is clear that not only is evolution an atheistic scientific theory that denigrates traditional faith, it has also become part of a new religion with the scientist as high priest. Julian Huxley interestingly claims that this was the first time that it was freely admitted that all aspects of reality are subject to evolution, despite Thomas Huxley's claim that evolution was a grand cosmic process in the nineteenth century. In fact most committed evolutionists throughout the last 150 years have freely taught evolution as a 'cosmic process' from Thomas Huxley to Carl Sagan. At this meeting Simpson went on to state that evolution should be seen as a completely naturalistic process, expressing the view that materialism and humanism are all we have, where mankind must rely on himself, rejecting the existence of any divinity.[25]

It can therefore be clearly seen that the science of the evolutionists is strongly materialistic, rejecting traditional Christianity out of hand and ignoring clear evidence that the whole of nature appears designed for life. They do not rely on empirical evidence alone as claimed, whether through inductive or deductive logic, but their confidence in materialism is based on humanist philosophy. However, if the whole point of science is a quest for truth and knowledge, then we cannot get rid of empirical evidence. It is simply not good enough to sweep evidence for or against a theory under the carpet simply because it is convenient to do so. We cannot gain knowledge by assuming certain things are, or are not. We will look in more detail at the ethical consequences of evolution in later chapters.

It is regrettable that there is such controversial disagreement between the scientific community, and faith communities as both are searching for truth. Yes, scientists are restricted to looking at empirical evidence in the natural, material world, whereas those who have faith are looking for spiritual truth. But natural science cannot account for the appearance of design and extreme complexity seen in nature that instead points to the supernatural. But there is no logic in denying the possibility that spiritual entities exist just because we can't see, feel or touch them. A more logical approach for those who don't have faith would be to keep an open mind over things that can't be proved with empirical evidence.

This was largely the argument of the nineteenth century American philosopher Charles Sanders Pierce who believed that the intangible could be just as real as the tangible. Pierce was at the forefront of the Pragmatic Movement of the early twentieth century, and was also an accomplished scientist in many fields. Although he believed that Darwin's theory of evolution was correct, he also considered that metaphysical concepts, such as the existence of God, could be just as real as physical ones. For Pierce intangible scientific laws such as the law of gravity, or mathematical constructions were just as real as any particle even though they were not physical entities. Much of his arguments stem from Greek philosophy where the physical world of empirical science was seen as a small part of a much larger spiritual reality.

This highlights other metaphysical concepts such as wisdom, knowledge and the intellect. The very fact that we are discussing this subject demonstrates that wisdom and knowledge exist, but if the universe were entirely meaningless as atheistic logic implies, then this would not be the case. Albert Einstein said that the most incomprehensible thing about the universe is that it is comprehensible. Is it really possible that intelligent beings have progressively arisen through some sort of blind chance process in an undirected meaningless universe, especially when we consider that those same beings are able to question their own existence and origins? Descartes made this self-awareness the basis for his philosophy with the famous statement 'I think therefore I am', or in Latin '*cognito ergo sum*'.

The roof of the Sistine Chapel, painted by Michelangelo begins to address this point. At its centre lies the creation of man, with God's outstretched hand touching that of Adam and giving him life. This picture implies a life giving omnipotence, and a desire on God's part for communication with mankind. The image is clear, and yet enigmatic, and only recently a deeper meaning has been revealed. An American neurosurgeon, Dr Frank Lynn Meshburg visiting the Chapel noticed something familiar. On closer inspection, it became apparent that God's cloak looked like a human brain. It would seem that in the painting God is imparting far more than life, He is imparting His wisdom and intellect to mankind. Mankind created in God's image.[26]

Some humanists claim that Christianity has value as a system of human ethics, and claim that Jesus was simply a good teacher, but again if there is no spiritual reality behind faith, then there is no point at all to the universe and no basis for morality, it becomes meaningless. If there is no God, then why are we able to read these words, or understand anything at all? Words in reality convey information and meaning. As a result of godlessness many people have adopted a rather fatalistic or nihilistic view to life and ethics, where the only purpose to life is to gather as much wealth and pleasure as possible in their short period of life.

Solomon adopted this view after losing touch with God for a time, before returning to faith. He was also reputed to be a wise man, and it is believed wrote the book of Ecclesiastes after falling from grace. His harem and many wives seem to have corrupted him in his latter life, and he was led astray into idolatry. He seems to find himself verging on madness in his nihilistic frame of mind, but eventually he acknowledges his error, and in his wisdom produced what appears to be a rather morose piece of literature. However, Solomon comes to some very basic conclusions.

> ' "Meaningless! Meaningless!" says the Teacher. "Utterly meaningless! Everything is meaningless."
>
> What does man gain from all his labour at which he toils under the sun? Generations come, and generations go, but the earth remains forever. The sun rises and the sun sets, and hurries back to where it rises. The wind blows to the south and turns to the north; round and

round it goes, ever turning on its course. All streams flow into the sea, yet the sea is never full. To the place the streams come from, there they return again. All things are wearisome, more than one can say. The eye never has enough of seeing, nor the ear its fill of hearing. What has been will be again, what has been done will be done again; there is nothing new under the sun.

Is there anything of which one can say, "Look! This is something new"? It was here already long ago; it was here before our time. There is no remembrance of men of old, and even those who are yet to come will not be remembered by those who follow.

I, the Teacher, was king over Israel in Jerusalem. I devoted myself to study and to explore by wisdom all that is done under heaven. What a heavy burden God has laid on men! I have seen all the things that are done under the sun; all of them are meaningless, a chasing after the wind.

What is twisted cannot be straightened; what is lacking cannot be counted.

I thought to myself, "Look, I have grown and increased in wisdom more than anyone who has ruled over Jerusalem before me; I have experienced much of wisdom and knowledge." Then I applied myself to the understanding of wisdom, and also of madness and folly, but I learned that this, too, is a chasing after the wind.

For with much wisdom comes much sorrow, the more knowledge the more grief.' *(Ecclesiastes 1:2-18)*

Solomon acknowledges that life without reference to God is meaningless, 'a chasing after the wind'. He simply states that if we view the whole of life in purely material terms, as he himself had done, as viewed from 'under the sun', then life becomes meaningless. At the end of the book he reaches some interesting conclusions.

'Remember your Creator in the days of your youth ... before the silver cord is severed, or the golden bowl is broken; before the pitcher is shattered at the spring, or the wheel broken at the well, and the dust returns to the ground it came from, and the spirit returns to God who gave it...'

'... Now all has been heard; here is the conclusion of the matter: Fear God and keep his commandments, for this is the whole duty of man. For God will bring every deed into judgement, including every hidden thing, whether it is good or evil.' *(Ecclesiastes 12:1,6-7,13-14)*

However, many have not heeded wisdom from Solomon through history. Darwin for instance claimed in *The Descent of Man* that mankind descended from primates and sought to remove God from the creative picture. However, he at times appeared worried over the ethical implications of this theory, and tried to claim that natural selection should lead to altruistic values and good morality, through filial and parental affection. Accordingly, this parental sympathy for close friends and family helped for instance with the protection of defenceless young, and he believed that it would then extend to the level of the tribe because it increased benefit for survivability in inter tribal competition and conflict. He also saw the inter relatedness of nature and believed that some ethical consideration, or communality extended between species despite obvious competition. Darwin's attempt at finding a natural basis for ethics, apart from religious duty, is viewed by many as a possible rational explanation for Hume's atheistic ethical principles.[27]

However, it may legitimately be pointed out that Darwinian affections are weak and based purely on selfish survivability, and therefore do not provide a strong basis for a community wide altruistic ethic that should apply to society and the environment. In whatever way we choose to view Darwinian affections, they are in fact weak, shallow and selfish forms of morality, which presumably can be overridden for the sake of survival, and atheism is left floundering for a consistent, and coherent moral basis for society. Darwinism also places the altruistic cart before the evolutionary horse. The logic goes that human altruism exists therefore it must have evolved that way. The observation in no way provides a proof for the evolution of an ethical system and it does not undermine the Biblical claim that mankind has been made in the image of God with a moral conscience.

Thomas Hardy, from a letter in The Humanitarian, from 1910 also believed that Darwinism should lead to better morality. He wrote:

> 'Darwinism logically involved a readjustment of altruistic morals by enlarging the application of the Golden Rule from the area of mere mankind to the wider animal kingdom.'[28]

But does nature follow a Golden Rule? Jesus appealed to the Golden Rule, of 'do unto others as you would have them do unto you', *(Matthew 7:12)* as a summation of the Law of Moses and the teachings of the prophets. This concept for good ethics was a common phrase, perhaps borrowed from Greek sources, but also existing in the Jewish tradition.[29] When we try and apply the Golden Rule to Darwinism we find a subtle change in the rule, which can best be described as 'do unto others *before* they do unto you', and Hardy is wrong to ascribe the Golden Rule to evolutionary thinking, which is based on 'survival of the fittest'. Perhaps in a human competitive system, like a football, or boxing match, both sides agree by the rules of 'winner takes all', but this does not provide a loving ethic for society as a whole where the weak should be protected. The Golden Rule implies that we consider other people's interest to be at least equal with our own. Nature indeed cannot obey the Golden Rule because it requires abstract thought that remains the preserve of humanity. It is highly questionable whether any predator, such as a polar bear or lion ever has any remorse for killing its food, and such an animal would not think twice before even eating the last antelope, seal or deer. In fact male lions will kill a lioness's young so that she is ready to mate again. Wild animals are driven by basic instincts to feed and reproduce, and there are many organisms that lead largely solitary lives.

Darwin developed many of his ethical ideas from David Hume, and William Lecky's book, *The History of Human Morals from Augustus to Charlemagne* (1869). Lecky saw an evolutionary development of improving ethics from first century Roman times to the ninth century and beyond. Augustus represents the tyranny of the Roman Empire, with Charlemagne helping to establish the more acceptable Holy Roman Empire in later centuries.[30] Emperor Constantine had though become a Christian by the fourth century, so it is surely the Christian church that can legitimately claim to be the reason for the improvement of civilised ethics with a change from a rather brutal brand of paganism to gentler more disciplined monotheism. As an example of the positive effect that Christians have made in society through the years, we may point to the Christian William Wilberforce who campaigned tirelessly for the abolition of the extremely profitable slave trade.

Incidentally Wilberforce may have made the church many enemies by destroying this profitable, but miserable trade, and it is rather ironic that it is his son Bishop Samuel Wilberforce who finds himself against the forces of godless progress in the shape of Thomas Huxley in June 1860. Whether we can attribute any conspiracy theory to this is highly questionable, but it is worth bearing in mind that it is the African who finds himself degraded by both the greed-ridden slave trade and evolution. Part of the justification for slavery was based on the idea that other races were somehow less human than Western civilised people, and this together with loss of slave income, may have partly encouraged the acceptance of Darwinian 'survival of the fittest'. Although Christianity may have had a rather paternalistic view of the African 'noble savages', its main motive in seeking to open up Africa in the first place was to spread the message of Jesus Christ, and to a lesser extent to bring commerce and civilisation. Many Africans readily accepted the new faith because Jesus Christ enabled them to overcome the fear of evil spirits that was endemic within their traditional animistic faith. Sadly though, unscrupulous traders wanted to include human traffic as part of the process, therefore corrupting the missionaries' idealised African civilisation of faith and commerce.

Although it was possible for William Wilberforce to remove man's shackles by Act of Parliament, the rule of law could never force people to view each other as equal citizens created in the image of God. This failure is also shown by the futile attempts of present day politically correct thought police to control people's attitudes to each other. To show how deeply ingrained these racist assumptions are in evolutionary thinking, we may ask why researchers have been looking for the earliest humanoid fossils in Africa and other third world countries all along? The recently found Flores remains have regretfully been ascribed a separate human species as well by some evolutionists.

The African people were viewed as being sub-human, and they then became a simple resource for use by industrialists to make money, in the same way as industrialists decimated whale and penguin populations for the sake of collecting oil and cared little for health and safety issues in factories and mines. These same callous thoughts informed people like Herbert Spencer who promoted the logical brutality of evolutionary ideas. This is the corrupting legacy of evolution, taught by progressive thinkers, Victorian industrialists and researchers, and later by fascists and communists alike. It will be considered later whether Christianity, with its concept of mankind's dominion over nature gave any endorsement to this rape of humanity and nature, or whether the forces of godless progress are to blame.

Whereas amiable, but naive Darwin, with all the charm and character of his observed bumble bees thought that evolution would lead to better morality, others such as Herbert Spencer saw the simplistic logic of the struggle for existence, or as he called it, 'survival of the fittest'. Spencer was a Social Darwinist and believed that the highest morality was simply survival. He taught that there should be no social provision for the poor, and that the suffering and death of the weak was a necessary evil.[31] It was as well Darwin's Cousin, Francis Galton who developed the concept of eugenics, believing that humans should be bred selectively to build a better race. In America at the end of the nineteenth century many considered social provision for the poor morally wrong as a result of Spencer's theory.

With this in mind we must begin to look deeper, to the reason why we need the traditional Judeo-Christian code of human and environmental ethics, and what the basis for those ethics are. To question whether it is possible to build an ethical system without reference to God, or any other religion for that matter, and also to look at why the church is largely ignored today on the issue of morality. We will begin to see later that trying to build a system of ethics without a spiritual dimension, is like trying to plot a point on a piece of paper or in space and time, without reference to a relevant coordinate system. Imagine for instance asking, which way is 'up' in the universe, without reference to the Earth's poles, or plane of the solar system, or the background of stars. In the same way, it is necessary to have a spiritual coordinate system in life to provide coherent dimensions on which to base ethical standards.

While most Christians are likely to agree with the ethical

importance of the arguments for Christianity and creation, it still leaves open the question of why we should believe in a recent creation as opposed to an ancient one. For all the arguments over evolution verses creation this debate may only take us back to a form of deistic natural theology, and the successive catastrophes of Buckland and George Cuvier. This is still some way from literal creationism, and some of the theological arguments presented by young earth creationists as to why we should accept the Genesis account literally may at face value appear rather weak to some.

There is of course some important theology in the Genesis account, such as the fall and death of mankind, but a progressive creationist or theistic evolutionist may still claim to accept the theology by viewing the account as only allegorical. The main argument presented by young earth creationists is that the concept of pre-Adamic races, or the gap theory with re-creations after each catastrophe, requires death before the fall, which then undermines the very purpose and work of Jesus Christ. This therefore means that creation as revealed in Genesis 1-3 was not good and that sin did not come through one man, which takes away from the need for a saviour, and man's responsibility.

Appealing to theistic evolution has further serious theological implications. If God created biological life through survival of the fittest, then there is a major problem with our understanding of God's character, and how we approach Him. This is the justice of God problem, or *Theodicy* problem, and belief in natural selection implies that God did not create everything perfectly, in which case he would not be worthy of worship, either for his goodness or omnipotence. Trying to bridge this gap is a major problem for those who believe in theistic evolution.[32] The only apparent solution to this problem would be to find an evolutionary fall from grace, but this would violate natural selection itself. While these arguments against theistic evolution are perfectly valid, they clearly do not appeal to many evangelical Christians who have not really thought through all the issues that belief in theistic evolution entails.

An old universe of billions of years also has superficial appeal to some Christians, as it produces a sense of wonder in the same way that the sheer spatial size of the universe invokes a sense of wonder and worship among all Christians. However, the downside is that it tends to remove God to a distant and powerless place. The idea of an on old universe, perhaps billions of years old, also helps some Christians come to terms with understanding God's purpose on the earth and within the universe, when set against eternity. But what is 15 billion years compared to eternity? In simple logical terms 15 billion years set against eternity is no different than 6000 years set against eternity. Of course 15 billion years is a more remote figure and harder to envisage than 6000 years, which makes it look closer to infinity and easier to digest.

There is a need for a deeper understanding of the roots of a belief in progressive creationism or theistic evolution, and why young earth creationism has such little appeal. The reason young earth creationists fail to engage in the broader reasons why belief in a recent creation matters, is I believe because of confusion over what constitutes fundamentalism. As has been shown, one of the pioneers of fundamentalism, B.B. Warfield, believed in evolution and continued to deny the miracles in the church age, along with previous cessationist Calvinists. Warfield's fundamentalism was for a large part deistic in nature, but viewed as orthodox. It is too easy for Christians to embrace and accept a fundamentalist position in the name of orthodoxy, without really examining the basis for that fundamentalism. Not only was the fundamentalist Christian B.B. Warfield a believer in evolution, but it must be questioned how much influence the Social Darwinist Herbert Spencer and other evolutionary forces have had on Christian fundamentalist thinking in the West and especially America. What appears to be orthodox fundamental Christian belief may in fact be underpinned by extreme right wing political and evolutionary philosophy, and not based on Christian values at all. On the other side, many fundamentalist young earth creationists are also wary of the full implications of recent theism, because it may be seen as leading to charismatic experience, which is viewed by many fundamentalists as being part of the post-modern New Age movement and therefore rather dodgy in theological terms.

The reason why the arguments for a recent creation are important can be summed up as the immanence and imminence of

Jesus Christ. Whereas the deist has a vague belief in the existence of a god, the theist believes in a God who both dwells within, *immanent*, and is close to the believer in space and time, *imminent*. The God of the theist is one who creates, who has relationship with, and who also imparts revelation to the believer, perhaps even working miracles along the way. This can be summed up with the word Emmanuel, meaning *God with Us*. The God of the Apostle Paul was a God who worked in the present with dynamic power, the Christian Gospel being described as the *dunamis* of God. (*dunamis*, for instance in *Romans 1:15* is the Greek word for power from which we get dynamite, dynamic, dynamo, etc.). The god of the deist is weak, powerless and distant, not being concerned with a relationship with mankind at all. By rejecting a recent creation, the modern Christian, perhaps even charismatic in theology, unwittingly undermines theism, and undermines the immanence of Christ and the faith of other believers.

It would seem that one of the main reasons why charismatic Christians, such as Forster and Marston continue to reject a recent creation is because they appear to accept the underpinning philosophical assumptions of gradualism without question. This is wrong in my view because gradual evolution can only be considered correct if the underpinning assumptions are correct. There are, however, very strong reasons to reject gradualism, not least because practically every fossil tells a tale of rapid burial. The uniformitarian assumptions are widely believed in an urban age that has become increasingly detached from nature. This also ties in with widespread materialism today, where people do not have time for spiritual thought. McGrath shows how urban detachment from nature has led to a rather romantic view of the environment among biocentric environmentalists. While this may also be true of many urban Christians who have become somewhat detached from nature, some of the leading Christians of the nineteenth century lived much closer to nature yet still rejected a recent creation. This is likely a result of deistic thought that was endemic in Western education during the later Enlightenment period. William Buckland for instance, was constantly undermined by Charles Lyell who appeared to be working to a different agenda behind the scenes to deliberately destroy belief in the Mosaic account of the deluge.[33]

Buckland was a major contributor to the Christian apologetic work 'The Bridgewater Treatise'. He was born in Axminster, East Devon in 1784 and took a keen interest in the natural world of birds and their nests, and also the rock layers from the local quarries around the town, and towards Lyme Regis. He was educated in Tiverton, and Winchester where he was able to continue amateur studies of the chalk layers to add to childhood studies of the Dorset Lias. He obtained a scholarship from Oxford in 1801 and became a fellow in 1809, and in the same year entered Holy orders. In 1813 he was elected reader in Mineralogy at Oxford, became reader in geology in 1819 and Dean of Westminster in 1845. During this time he enjoyed close friendships with Mary Anning, and the diluvialist Rev. William D. Conybeare, vicar of Axminster for a number of years. Both scientists shared a belief that the land was shaped by catastrophic flood events, and were intimately acquainted with the geology of Devon and Dorset. However, Buckland's views of the rock layers were close to Cuvier with successive catastrophes, followed by divine re-creations, and he later finds himself in confusion and madness where his only solace was to clutch a large Bible. Buckland appears to have died of a tuberculosis infection in the brain.

Although Buckland and Conybeare, and perhaps even Cuvier, tried to uphold belief in the Noahic Flood, admittedly with previous successive catastrophes, they were surrounded by deistic Enlightenment thought, which had been informing geological assumptions for many previous decades. There is also evidence that through the Enlightenment, those seeking political and social change manipulated Western thought towards deism, supported revolution in America and France, and it would seem that they were acting in concert. By gaining positions of power, these often secretive groups were then able to promote friends and relations and exert greater influence in political and religious thought. Erasmus Darwin, who developed an early theory of evolution, was for instance a member of the Birmingham Lunar Society and supporter of the American Revolution, and the deist Voltaire was involved with the French Revolution.

However, it needs to be recognised that the main problem for belief in a recent creation is not the rock layers, or whatever underpinning assumptions are put into dubious dating methods, or whether there has been manipulation by deistic orders. There is in fact more than ample evidence that the rock layers were laid down under catastrophic circumstances, for those willing to look closely with an open mind. Both Conybeare and Buckland, who knew the geology well, would have agreed with this, not least because there are millions of pelagic squid-like organisms buried under and within massive layers of terrogenous sediment. When such animals die today they are eaten or decay quickly without leaving a trace in the sediment. This death and burial could only happen via a catastrophic event perhaps requiring global extent.

But perhaps the main problem that a creationist faces is not the geological evidence, which is easily accounted for by a global flood, but the problem of the speed of light and distant starlight. It would appear that light is arriving from stars that would take millions of light years to arrive on earth. How can we account for this in a recent creation? With the development of the Big Bang theory, and rejection of the steady state theory of Fred Hoyle, it is believed that the universe is some 10 to 15 billions years old or around 10^{18} seconds. Of course this suits the evolutionist because it gives some time for evolution to occur in an expanding universe, although when this number is compared with the number of permutations in human DNA ($4^{3,000,000,000}$ which approximates to $10^{1,800,000,000}$) it is small indeed.[34]

However, there are problems with the Big Bang theory. It assumes an expanding spatial universe, a constant speed of light and a broadly linear progression of time (although the Einstein de Sitter model suggested the universe is two thirds its apparent age). However, bearing in mind the disagreement among cosmologists over what metric should apply to an expanding universe it seems that it is only the dogma of evolution that causes scientists to insist on this broadly linear progression of time. Why should time progress broadly linearly in an expanding universe and not be curved as space appears to be? Special and general relativity allow for spatial contraction and time dilation depending on the frame of reference of observers moving relative to each other, or for that matter particles moving rapidly through space.

This idea of time dilation in fact forms the basis for a book by Dr Russell Humphreys *Starlight and Time*.[35] Humphreys's 'White Hole' cosmology offers a rival to the gap theory or pre-Adamic race ideas for harmonising scientific evidence with Scripture. As an example of how this might work, an illustration of general relativity is given in cosmology textbooks. Consider two astronauts orbiting a black hole. One remains in the spacecraft and observes while the other enters the black hole. The first astronaut sees his colleague become frozen in space as he approaches the spatial and temporal anomaly, while the astronaut who enters the black hole is crushed and ripped apart almost instantly by the massive object. Humphreys proposes a similar temporal anomaly when we view distant starlight, with the idea of the observable universe being inside a white hole and time slowing down through spatial expansion. The earth may therefore be only 6000 years old, while the stars appear billions of years old. Both observations may be true, and time is seen as being relative to the frame of reference of the observer. Christians who reject a young earth should give serious thought to this idea as a new and novel mechanism for harmonising science with the Genesis account.

A number of cosmologists have also recently toyed with the idea that the speed of light is not constant, but slowing down with time, and indeed there may also be some observational evidence for a slowing of light despite Forster and Marston's criticism of the work of Norman and Setterfield.[36] A slowing speed of light may account for the horizon and homogeneity problems identified with inflation theory in the early period of the Big Bang, as this appears to be a rather artificial device to account for the smoothness of space. A speed of light that is reducing with time may also account for the observed red shift. While it is recognised that this is all somewhat speculative, and to some extent it moves away from the ethical debate, it points to the fact that in cosmology there is still much to play for, and Christians should not reject the Genesis account on the basis of popular scientific thinking that is dominated by the dogma of gradual evolution. Evolutionists may also want to reconsider their assumptions about the broad linearity of time, in view of general relativity and our lack of knowledge of cosmology.

As a general conclusion it would seem that belief in evolution was pioneered by those whose enthusiasm for godless progress clouded their judgement, both in terms of scientific discovery and ethics. Science, it was thought, would solve all mankind's problems, with the scientist, especially Thomas Huxley, raised to the level of a Comtist high priest. Such attitudes still inform science today as can be seen from the *Humanist Manifesto* and from scientists like Richard Dawkins. This religious devotion to materialistic science then informs ethical decisions on genetic engineering and embryonic stem cell research for instance, where pressure for progress comes from godless attitudes in the scientific community working in concert with the forces of capitalism. Ironically today, many politicians who claim to be both Christian and socialist, appear willing to allow these questionable practices that have more in common with fascism and atheism. All of this is allowed in the name of progress and profit.

For too long Christians have given up their own ethical ground to science, largely as a result of the evolutionary rhetoric of Darwin, Huxley and their followers. Christians have compromised their faith by accepting claimed scientific evidence without calling the scientists' bluff and examining the evidence for themselves with open minds and without the scientists' *a priori* godless philosophical assumptions. For too long Christians have allowed their faith to be treated with disrespect, and God's position sidelined. When we as Christians begin to rebuild faith in a powerful God who is very close in time and space we will begin to see a greater respect for the natural and the human social order as ordained by God.

Notes and References

[1] Forster, R., Marston, P., *Reason, Science and Faith*, Monarch Books, Lion Hudson Plc., Crowborough, East Sussex, UK, p. 309, 1999.

[2] Bowden, M., *The Rise of the Evolutionary Fraud*, Sovereign Books, Bromley, Kent, UK, pp. 112-113, 1982. See also: Irvine, W., *Apes, Angels, and Victorians*, Weidenfeld and Nicolson, p. 183, 1956.

[3] Colling, A., *Science Matters: Discovering the Deep Oceans*, Open University, p. 31, 1995. Correspondence from Huxley to Haeckel, (nd).

[4] Ibid.

[5] Huxley, T.H., *The Scientific Aspects of Positivism,* Lay Sermons, Addresses and Reviews, London, pp. 129-130, 1870. <http://aleph0.clarku.edu/huxley/UnColl/Rdetc/Posit.html>, Accessed March 2006. Also in: The Fortnightly Review, (Trollope, A., et. al.), (n.s.), 5, pp. 653-670, 1869.

[6] Ibid., Lay Sermons, Addresses and Reviews, p. 133.

[7] Ibid., Lay Sermons, Addresses and Reviews, p. 130.

[8] Huxley, T.H., *Science and Religion*, The Builder, Vol. 17, Museum of Geology, p. 35, January 1859.

[9] Zacharias, R., *Jesus Among Other Gods*, Word Publishing, Nashville, Tennessee, p. 64, 2000.

[10] Huxley, T.H., op. cit., *Science and Religion*.

[11] Colling, A., op. cit., p. 29. Acknowledgement is also given to Angela Colling for the story of Bathybius.

[12] Huxley, T.H., *On the Educational Value of the Natural History Sciences*, Address delivered at St. Martin's Hall, London, 1854. In: Huxley, T.H., *Collected Essays*, Vol. 3, *Science and Education*, London, p. 46, <http://aleph0.clarku.edu/huxley/CE3/EdVal.html >, Accessed March 2006. Also in: Colling, op. cit., p. 32-33.

[13] Huxley, T.H., *Owen's Position in the History of Anatomical Science.* In: Owen, Rev. R., *The Life of Richard Owen*, vol. 2., pp. 273-332, John Murray, London, 1894. (The author was the grandson of Richard Owen). See also: Foster, M., Lankester, E.R., (eds.), *The Scientific Memoirs of Thomas Henry Huxley*, vol. IV, p. 682, Macmillan & Co., London, 1898-1903, <http://aleph0.clarku.edu/huxley/SM4/Owen.html>, Accessed March 2006.

[14] Lubenow, M.L., *Bones of Contention*, Baker Book House, Grand Rapids, Michigan, pp. 86-119, 1992.

[15] Bowden, M., *Ape-Men: Fact or Fallacy?*, Sovereign Books, Bromley, Kent, UK, 1981; also: Bowden, op. cit., *The Rise of the Evolutionary Fraud*.

[16] Bowden, op. cit., *The Rise of the Evolutionary Fraud*, p. 38.

[17] Huxley, T.H., *Collected Essays*, Vol. 9, *Evolution & Ethics and Other Essays*, London, p. 80, 1894, (*Evolution and Ethics*, The Romanes Lecture, 1893), <http://aleph0.clarku.edu/huxley/CE9/E-E.html>, Accessed March 2006.

[18] Ibid., p. 12, (*Evolution and Ethics: Prolegomena*, 1894), <http://aleph0.clarku.edu/huxley/CE9/E-EProl.html>, Accessed March 2006.

[19] McGrath, A., *The Re-enchantment of Nature*, Hodder Headline, London, 2003, p. 167.

[20] Ibid.

[21] Huxley, T.H., op. cit., *The Scientific Aspects of Positivism,* Lay Sermons, Addresses and Reviews, pp. 129-130.

[22] Lewis, C.S., *Miracles*, no ref. Quoted in Dembski, W.A*., The Intelligent Design Movement*, Cosmic Pursuit, Spring 1998, <www.leaderu.com/offices/dembski/docs/bd-idesign.html>, Accessed March 2006.

[23] Ferngren, G.B., Numbers, R.L., *C.S. Lewis on Creation and Evolution: The Acworth Letters, 1944-1960*, Perspective on Science and Christian Faith, 48 (1), March 1996. Personal letter from C.S. Lewis to Bernard Acworth dated 13th September 1951. (Letters by C.S. Lewis copyright © C.S. Lewis Pte. Ltd. Reprinted by permission)

[24] Huxley, J., *Record of the Chicago Centennial Celebration of the Publication of the Origin of Species*. (paraphrased comments by Julian Huxley), 1959. In: Tax, S., (ed.), *Evolution after Darwin*, Vol. 3, 1960.

[25] Simpson, G.G., *The World Into Which Darwin Led Us*, Science, Vol. 131, pp. 969, 973-974, 1st April, 1960. In: Whitcomb & Morris, *The Genesis Flood*, p. 443.

[26] Le Fanu, J., *Of Mouse and Man, and a New Sense of Wonder*, Review, Sunday Telegraph, UK, p. 4, 22nd December 2002.

[27] Open University, Wye College, University of London, *Darwin and Moral Philosophy*, Environmental Ethics, Block A, Part 3.2, 1997.

[28] Hardy, T., From a letter in The Humanitarian, 1910. Sourced from: Wynne-Tyson, J., *The Extended Circle: An Anthology of Humane Thought*, Sphere, London, 1990.

[29] Barker, K.L., et. al., (eds.), NIV Study Bible, footnotes to Matt 7:12, Hodder & Stoughton, 1987.

[30] Open University, Wye College, London, op. cit.

[31] Ibid., Box 3.2.

[32] Southgate, C., *God and Evolutionary Evil: Theodicy in the Light of Darwinism*, Zygon, Vol. 37, No. 4, pp. 803-824, Dec. 2002.

[33] Bowden, op. cit., *The Rise of the Evolutionary Fraud*, pp. 92-99.

[34] The timeframe of 10^{18} seconds for the age of the universe can be multiplied by the possible number of molecules in the observable universe (10^{80}) if it were full of organic soup of amino acids, and multiplied by the highest frequencies of gamma rays (10^{20} per second) to give the total number of possible events in the universe (10^{118}). This number can then be compared with the number of permutations in human DNA at the amino acid level ($20^{1,000,000,000}$ or approximately $10^{1,300,000,000}$). In fact just one essential protein such as hexosaminidase A contains 529 amino acids with 20^{529} permutations (or 10^{688}). The mismatch between the level of complexity in DNA and possible events in the universe is staggering.

[35] Humphreys, D.R., *Starlight and Time*, Master Books, Green Forest, AR., 1994.

[36] See for instance:
• Magueijo, J., *Faster than the Speed of Light*, William Heinemann, London, 2003.
• Norman, T.G., Setterfield, B., *The Atomic Constants, Light and Time*, Invited Research Report of the Stanford Research Institute / Flinders University, 1987. (Unofficial report, see Bibliography).

Chapter 5

Natural Theology, Rights and Duties

Now all has been heard; here is the conclusion of the matter:
Fear God and keep his commandments,
for this is the whole duty of man.
(Ecclesiastes 12:13)

What are we to make of an ethical theory based on rights in an atheistic or humanist worldview? Is it possible to construct an ethical standard based on rights in a universe where survival, fitness and probability are all pervading? Although it is claimed by evolutionists that we do indeed live in such a universe, it may be argued that rights cannot have any meaning in a place where ultimate meaning is itself denied. However, it must be noted that we actually live in an age when everybody demands their *rights*, from women's rights, to animal rights, to men's rights, to the end to slavery and racism, and to rights for all sorts of other minority groups. How are we to understand human rights in this godless context, and what does this inbuilt demand for human rights say about humanity, or say about our human origins? Do such demands for human rights in fact undermine the godless or atheistic assumptions and point to a more meaningful universe? This chapter will try to answer these points.

It may at first be recognised that for every right there is also a duty. This forms the basis for rights theory, and is sometimes called the *deontological* ethic, from the Greek word for duty. One person's right to be treated with dignity and respect gives another person the duty to act in a respectful manner to that person. The first person also has a duty to treat others with that same dignity and respect. There is, if you like, an equality of rights and duties across the board if we as human beings are born equal. But what happens when one person's rights conflict with another? Does a woman's right to an abortion conflict with the right of an unborn child to enjoy many years of life? And where do rights and duties come from? In trying to find a logical basis for ethical standards based on rights and duties, we need to answer these questions, and assess where the solid foundation for those rights is to be found. Are rights given to all from above through divine grace and command, or are they derived from some sort of social contract that might exist in a state of nature? Have rights been debased to a point where people only consider their own selfish interest?

It was John Locke (1632-1704) towards the end of the seventeenth century who tried to provide a foundation for a system of ethics, based on rights. He claimed that mankind has rights that are not derived from human political power and authority, but come from a higher source. Locke was to some extent concerned with the abuse of political power that he saw carried out during his lifetime, and his writings had some influence on revolution in France and America with great social change in England following too. He pointed out that rights exist as a sort of social contract between people in a 'state of nature', and many humanists promote Locke's suggestion that rights exist in a state of nature without acknowledging God because it suits their own belief. However, Locke appeared as a Christian writer, and believed that it is God who confers basic rights on mankind. According to Locke it is God who gives rights and obligations to mankind as a result of the existence of a divinely given law of nature.

> 'The state of nature has a law of nature to govern it, which obliges every one; and reason, which is that law, teaches all mankind who will but consult it, that, being all equal and independent, no one ought to harm another in his life, health, liberty, or possessions. For men being all the workmanship of one omnipotent and infinitely wise Maker - all the servants of one sovereign Master, sent into the world by his order, and about his business - they are his property whose workmanship they are, made to last during his, not one another's pleasure, and being furnished with like faculties, sharing all in one community of nature, there cannot be supposed any such subordination among us, that may authorise us to destroy one another, as if we were made for one

another's uses, as the inferior ranks of creatures are for ours. Every one, as he is bound to preserve himself, and not to quit his station wilfully, so by the like reason, when his own preservation comes not in competition, ought he, as much as he can, to preserve the rest of mankind, and not, unless it be to do justice on an offender, take away or impair the life, or what tends to the preservation of the life, the liberty, health, limb, or goods of another.' [1]

Locke derived much of his thinking from the idea of *natural law* [2] believing that in the absence of divine revelation, natural law provided sound reason for obeying its ethical precepts. The idea that natural law points to God as designer without the need for divine revelation provided a foundation for the later rise of deistic thought. Natural law and the idea of *rights* can also be found in the American Constitution.

'We hold these truths to be self-evident, that all men are created equal, that they are endowed by their Creator with certain unalienable Rights, that among these are Life, Liberty and the pursuit of Happiness...'

This concept had passed into the thinking of the early church through Thomas Aquinas (1225-1274), who blended the thoughts of Aristotle from the fourth century BC with the teaching of the Roman Catholic Church. Aquinas, it would seem, was a rather large boy and a slow learner, and although he originally acquired the nickname of the 'Dumb Ox', he later gained considerable respect in public debates, and trained in Paris and Cologne under Albert the Great. He was also very pious and was determined to enter the Dominican Order despite the displeasure of his rich family who kidnapped him and tempted him with a prostitute. They also offered to buy him the position of Archbishop of Naples if he would agree to marry. Aquinas became a prolific writer and developed the twin themes of reason and divine revelation. His ideas were that human philosophy and knowledge about the world could only come from the five senses of man, but theology comes through revelation and logical deduction from that revelation. This led to his 'five ways' in which he sought to prove God's existence through reasoning from the natural world.

The Natural law tradition, also known as the *teleological*

tradition asserts that without divine revelation there is a law of nature that informs our conduct as human beings and gives us a purpose to live. St. Paul, the Greek thinking former Pharisee and Christian convert, writing in his book to the Romans also claims that nature gives mankind moral guidance.

> '... since what may be known about God is plain to them, because God has made it plain to them. For since the creation of the world God's invisible qualities - his eternal power and divine nature - have been clearly seen, being understood from what has been made, so that men are without excuse.' *(Romans 1:19-20)*

Natural law originally came down to Aquinas from Aristotle, although it may be argued that the Greek thinkers borrowed heavily from Jewish sources and especially Solomon who also developed the idea that the study of nature should lead to good personal conduct. One example of natural law from the study of nature is the lesson that ants give to the lazy, but this is an example taken from Solomon. Aristotle considered that in order to understand an object it was necessary to understand it in a number of different ways, or *causes* of its being. These are the *material, formal, efficient* and *final* causes. The *material* cause of an object is its substance, what it is made of, while the *formal* cause explains how a material object exists. The *efficient* cause explains why a material object exists in different forms, while the *final* cause explains the purpose of the object. Aristotle considered that it was not possible to fully understand an object until he understood its final purpose or function. This is the *teleological* understanding of nature from the Greek *telos*, which means purpose. From this he derived an ethical basis for society, and saw ethics and science as being more closely bound than we perceive them today. One example of this for instance is that the biological psychology of our brains affects the way we behave in an everyday manner. All natural objects were accordingly seen as being good. Although Aristotle believed in an original unmoved mover as the cause of all life, he saw in life subsequently a grand process of evolution, and as such did not see the brutality of nature as part of a broken perfection as the Judeo-Christian tradition teaches.

Aristotle also sub-divided natural objects into those that are alive and those that are not. For the many different living organisms, these were also sub-divided and considered living at different levels. Plants for instance have only a nutritive soul, able to feed, grow and reproduce. Animals on the other hand have the ability to feel sensation as well as nutritional abilities, but it is only mankind that is able to think as well as possessing the other two faculties of nutrition and sensation. The study of nature to discover the mind and character of God became known as natural theology, although different emphases developed in the Greek thinking East to that in the Latin West. Thomas Aquinas attempted to rework the ideas of Aristotle with Roman Catholic thinking. Joseph Des Jardins for instance notes that Aquinas developed Aristotle's scientific and ethical teleology by appealing to evidence of a divine purpose that was operating in nature. Accordingly, natural entities act out their God given plan in the world, and because God's purpose observed in nature is seen as being good, then the natural order itself can be equated with a good ethical order. As well as natural entities displaying God's plan, Aquinas believed that the harmoniously functioning natural ecosystem itself displays the goodness of God's purposes, and therefore nature itself provides regulations, or natural laws, that ought to be followed. Because this knowledge of personal conduct from nature is divinely inspired, Aquinas argued, then fulfilling this ethical obligation is of the highest calling for an individual. While this natural theology of Aquinas has many attractions, it doesn't take into account the apparent brokenness and brutality that may also be observed in nature.[3]

There are also a number of secular objections to the idea that moral or ethical standards are to be based on natural law. Firstly it is claimed that living entities have no characteristic function or purpose, they just exist. What is the purpose of a cat or dog for instance, or more importantly, what is the purpose of a man or woman? Did God really create the dog to become man's best friend? St. Francis of Assisi saw in each object a lesson in theology. The ant is a preacher to the lazy for instance, but is this really why God made the creatures? Perhaps in part yes, but rather it may be argued that each creature performs a small part in a larger divinely created ecosystem, often existing in symbiotic relationships with other creatures, and this is its major function. Each small part fulfils a small niche in the divinely created order as a small cog fulfils a critical function in a larger watch or clock. The cat for instance catches birds, which in turn eats the bumble bee, which gathers nectar and pollinates the flower, etc., in a grand cycle of life, although this observational response must be qualified in terms of God's original plan for creation as noted above, and which is described more fully below.

Secondly it is objected that not all natural entities are good. As already mentioned in Chapter 2, this is known as the naturalistic fallacy and is an important point to address. Is the guinea worm that burrows into the face of a child for instance good, or the HIV virus that leads to AIDS? Incidentally many of these harmful disorders, viruses and bacteria are mutant forms of less harmful types. Bird flu viruses mutate in overcrowded marketplaces, sickle cell anaemia develops as a mutational response to the high death rate from the malaria virus. Thomas Malthus too described the actions of diseases which gain a foothold as a result of overcrowded population, and considered this to be natural, but it may instead be considered a function of the fall. In fact, with reference to Scripture, the main answer to this is that nature has been subject to a fall from grace that occurred within the perfect Garden of Eden that God originally declared was good. Nature has fallen from perfection to a more brutal and unkind state because of the rebellious actions of human beings. Animals are now carnivorous whereas before they were vegetarian. This theme is partially echoed in the minds of many radical environmentalists, who see mankind's activity in the world as destroying a more perfect natural ecosystem. If nature has fallen from grace, then it may legitimately be argued today, that not every part of nature is fulfilling its original purpose. According to Genesis for instance God made mankind to be vegetarian, not meat eaters, and it would seem that the carnivorous animals were also part of that vegetarian perfection.

The guinea worm and HIV may therefore be considered aberrations in nature, and from a Christian perspective the elimination of such entities may be considered part of God's initial great commission to rule over the earth and subdue it. Although this original great commission was given before the fall, the commission remains valid even to the present day except that the fall made the task of subduing nature harder and more complex. The theological and ethical implications of this are controversial and worthy of much greater consideration. What of lions that eat antelope, for instance? Isaiah for his part sees a return to the Garden of Eden perfection where the lamb lays down beside the wolf and lion.

> 'The wolf will live with the lamb,
> the leopard will lie down with the goat,
> the calf and the lion and the yearling together;
> and a little child will lead them.
> The cow will feed with the bear,
> their young will lie down together,
> and the lion will eat straw like the ox.
> The infant will play near the hole of the cobra,
> and the young child put his hand into the viper's nest.
> They will neither harm nor destroy
> on all my holy mountain,
> for the earth will be full of the knowledge of the LORD
> as the waters cover the sea.' *(Isaiah 11:6-9)*

The final objection to the natural law tradition is the one given by Darwin with his theory of evolution. It takes away the reason why organisms exist and claims that they are just the product of probability and accidents. There is no purpose or *telos* to nature. Animals and plants just are. Mankind just is. If Darwin is correct, then natural law is fatally undermined and our whole basis for ethics based on natural law or rights is undermined and replaced by a different law of nature, based on utilitarian survival instincts instead.

Des Jardins argues that modern neo-Darwinism significantly challenges the natural law tradition of Aquinas, perhaps insurmountably. It is claimed that evolutionary processes involving natural selection, acting on random mutations within a changing environment, can account for the appearance of design and order seen in nature without appealing to teleological arguments. As a result, nature itself is reduced to mechanistic physical processes, involving hundreds of millions of years of random, meaningless change. As such, nature has no ethical dimension and can neither be described as being good or bad, it just is.[4]

If nature just 'is', derived by chance from evolution in a godless system, then it would point to a worrying conclusion that the concept of rights does not in fact exist, and we are without purpose. This point needs an effective response. We may not find much purpose in the animals and plants around us, except of course that we enjoy eating some of them, but what happens to our whole belief system when we deny any purpose for our own existence? We may also ask what happens to nature when we deny it any purpose except how it might benefit us in the short term. Is our purpose to 'eat, drink and be merry for tomorrow we may die', or is it as the Westminster Shorter Catechism[5] states, 'to glorify God and to enjoy Him for ever'? The denial of purpose and rights, that atheism and Darwinism imply, is a most fatal flaw in those twin godless ideas.

Of course Christians may not agree with all the teachings of Aristotle, and prefer Aquinas or Locke's Christian response to Darwin's challenge. It must be acknowledged as well that natural law and natural theology on their own are weak substitutes to divinely revealed Scripture, and looking for purpose in nature may be over-stepping the mark when the artist behind creation may simply have painted for pleasure. The basic appearance of design, evident in nature, points to the existence of a designer and should lead to a sense of wonder and worship. The beauty, perfection and diversity found in nature also points to the idea that we should take pleasure in enjoying the wonders of creation along with an apparently absent or distant landlord. It is the very character of the natural world that points to the character of the artistic Creator, who incidentally may be found closer than originally thought when we begin to love humanity and creation.

However, with regard to the Darwinian challenge, the basic point is worth emphasising. What Darwin and his promoters managed to do was to overthrow the long held belief that nature provides mankind with a natural law for good ethical conduct based on rights and duties, and therefore undermined the purpose of life. As Aquinas and Locke showed, in the absence of divine revelation, natural law gives insight towards a loving rights-duties based ethical standard for society. Nature had been seen as good in its original creation, but now in overthrowing the natural law tradition, Darwinian evolution instilled a different law of nature, without reference to God. Herbert Spencer called it the 'law of life' or 'survival of the fittest'. Adolf Hitler called it the 'iron logic of nature'. This is the new naturalistic law of survival of the fittest, which in a godless context may be seen as being amoral, but in a Christian context is seen as brutal and an offence to humanity and nature itself.

What does this new law teach us? That one man's misfortune, suffering or death is purely accidental, or even a product of someone else's competitive will, which steals from another without recourse. As a result there is no need to care for the weak or the disabled, and a callous disregard for the poor becomes acceptable. Not only is there a callous disregard for others, but also the need to survive is the overwhelming ethical compulsion, even at the expense of others. Not only does Darwinism overthrow the natural law tradition, it also undermines ethics based on rights because it seeks to do away with the Creator who upholds rights and who expects everyone to do their duty to others. Under Darwinism, mankind no longer has a responsibility towards anyone but him or her self. But as can be seen, ordinary people have an inbuilt understanding that it is right to protect their own and other's rights, and this is more than a simple desire for selfish survival. Darwinism and any ethical standards based on rights are incompatible.

Finding a basis for good ethics, without reference to God, is at the heart of the contract theory of rights, and was perhaps best described by Thomas Hobbes (1651). Hobbes described a primitive state of war that would exist in a purely natural state where law did not exist. This would mean that every man was enemy to every man, but the horrors of such a state of war would encourage people to flee from it and introduce laws and a law enforcing government. A state of war provides no basis for work, for starting a family, for prosperity or for developing culture. As a result, people form a mutual agreement not to harm one another and seek to introduce a government to compel people to agree to ordered rules. Accordingly, people then agree to these certain standards because there is some beneficial return. One person agrees not to steal from another, if the second person agrees not to steal from the first. I agree not to hit you if you agree not to hit me. This is the basis for Hobbes morality, which is in fact based purely on self-interest. Hobbes comments that:

> 'Whatsoever therefore is consequent to a time of war, where everyman is enemy to everyman, the same is consequent to the time wherein men live without other security then what their own strength and their own inventions shall furnish them withal. In such condition there is no place for industry, because the fruit thereof is uncertain, and consequently no culture of the earth; no navigation, nor use of the commodities that may be imported by sea; no commodious building; no instruments of moving and removing such things as require much force; no knowledge of the face of the earth; no account of time; no arts; no letters; no society; and, which is worst of all continual fear and danger of violent death; and the life of man, solitary, poor, nasty, brutish, and short. To this war of every man against every man, this also is consequent; that nothing can be unjust. The notions of right and wrong, justice and injustice, have there no place. Where there is no common power, there is no law: where no law, no injustice.' [6]

The view of Hobbes's state of war is later echoed in the Darwinian concept of survival of the fittest. Hobbes looks back to a time when every man was at war with every other man, but as even Darwin pointed out, competition for survival in a state of nature would mean that some limited affections would exist to help one family or tribe compete against another. Even for the atheist, it is recognised that there was never a time when every man was against every man, and in nature generally symbiosis is as common as predation.

To critique Hobbes idea of a contract of rights we must first assume that warfare exists at a family or tribal level, in which case some limited altruism would already exist. John Mackie[7] expanded Hobbes's egoism and suggested that although people are not interested in other people's lives, they are interested in the lives of close family and friends, and they also agree to act with restraint because it may bring personal indirect benefit. This concept is known as limited altruism, and may be considered similar to Darwin's parental and filial affections. A person within a population may not benefit directly by restrained actions, but if enough people agree to restraint then the population may benefit as a whole, which then indirectly benefits the individual.

However, this concept of limited altruism may be better described as prudence, and it does not give rise to a basis for morality because as may be seen through history it has never been applied consistently. In fact, just like the Darwinian weak affections, limited altruism is still based on the idea of self-interest, even at a group level, which does not provide for a truly altruistic morality. A desire for affection within families, or within a tribe does not stop conflict between families and tribes, or even within families.

For Hobbes and later contract theorists, there is a fundamental problem, in that the idea of law and justice is merely of human construction, being based on personal or group self-interest. A person's right to justice is therefore dependent on the will of the majority population, or the will of governmental powers to maintain order. One group may indeed prudently conclude that cooperation with other groups will bring benefit, while other groups may conclude with equal prudence that conquest over other groups will bring benefit. This is akin to a sort of 'do unto others before they do unto you' mentality. Determining which is more prudent, conflict or cooperation, therefore requires a calculus based on unknown quantities. Is it more beneficial to agree peace with another tribe when trust is uncertain, or go to war and defeat them before they have a chance to do the same to you? As we may observe across the world, tyrannical regimes get into power where the will of a powerful minority is often established over a weaker majority. Sometimes the majority population denies human rights to minorities within a state. If it is possible for a contract of rights to be constructed to enable everyone to live better, it may be clearly seen that it does not work in practice. Power corrupts, and absolute power corrupts absolutely.

A small but powerful clique of extended family or tribe, within a population, may indeed conclude that to end a state of war, a powerful dictatorship must be constructed to keep the masses down. This dictatorship is then held in place to maintain privileges for the minority. Human rights are then dictated from human powers, and the maintenance of order is often given as the main justification for its legitimacy. The judicial legal powers then exert control and dispense law for the benefit of the ruling classes. By rejecting a divine plan and purpose, an increasingly secular state becomes more and more legalistic, not less, but it is mankind who establishes these laws with God's ideal rejected. Human made laws no longer seek to reflect a divine order where rights and duties are established from above, but laws are simply put in place to control the conduct of others, and this is where a purely secular state will end up. In this sense human made laws themselves become a poor substitute for God.

However, it is widely recognised that human rights exist at a much deeper level than mere human legality or will. If slavery and apartheid are wrong today, then they must also be considered wrong everywhere and throughout all times, and changes in human law cannot make them right. Indeed there is a deep instinct, sometimes hidden deep within each of us, that knows when our own, or even someone else's rights are being denied. Human rights cannot therefore be conferred from humanity to have legitimacy, whether they have developed through a state of war or not.

In other words the state of war, even at a tribal level, that people are so keen to flee from, cannot work in a Darwinian context because competitive advantage for the sake of survival remains paramount. A Darwinian modification to Hobbes's view is that one tribe will seek to gain ascendancy over another, especially if resources such as food and water are scarce. Such conflicts are observed in human affairs throughout history and even in the present day. It may be recognised that people do grow weary of the brutality of warfare, but that doesn't stop wars breaking out often, and in many countries.

It may also be noted that rational people often fail to act rationally, but act out of irrational passions. In fact it is often these irrational passions that start disputes and wars in the first place, even when basic resources are plentiful. Male hormones and other irrational emotions often drive tribes to fight war against other tribes, even when there is no competition for female affections, or for scarce resources. Such irrational emotions include xenophobia, pride, feeling insulted or slighted and a desire for revenge, or just acting out of sheer aggression. Neither Hobbes's contract view, nor one modified by weak Darwinian affections are able to provide any basis for a loving and coherent morality, especially when people are driven by such irrational fears. But even if Hobbes's contract theory could be made to work to provide human rights for those able to enter rationally into a contract, it cannot apply to those unable to agree to that contract. The unborn, mentally ill and animals cannot agree a contract, but they too must surely have rights.

John Rawls[8] attempted to take contract theory one step further and reworked Immanuel Kant's concept that people should be seen as ends in themselves, and not a means to an end. However, Rawls does not attempt to address the foundational existence of morality. Rawls sees people as starting out as moral, which does not help the atheist looking for a naturalistic basis for morality.

Immanuel Kant, for his part, claimed that all rational beings are ends in themselves, and as such have rights based on their own *intrinsic* value. Philosophy progressed through the Enlightenment from the time of Bacon, Descartes and Locke with an increasing emphasis on deism; that is, that the natural world followed the original God given laws of nature, with the interventionist God of the Bible relegated to a very distant sideline. Deism is in many ways a throwback to Aristotle's original, but distant 'unmoved mover'. However, Kant and later German philosophers moved to develop an increasing anthropocentric philosophy with each man the arbiter of what is right or wrong, with knowledge limited to the material time and space. The following represents Kant's view of rights based on intrinsic value.

'Now I say man, and in general every rational being, exists as an end in himself, not merely as a means for arbitrary use by this or that will: he must in all his actions, whether they are directed to himself or to other rational beings, always be viewed at the same time as an end. All the objects of inclination have only a conditioned value; for if there were not these inclinations and the needs grounded on them, their objects would be valueless. Inclinations themselves, as sources of needs, are so far from having an absolute value to make them desirable for their own sake that it must rather be the universal wish of every rational being to be wholly free from them. Thus the value of all objects that can be produced by our actions is always conditioned. Beings whose existence depends, not on our will, but on nature, have none the less, if they are non-rational beings, only a relative value as means and are consequently called *things*. Rational beings, on the other hand, are called persons because their nature already marks them out as ends in themselves - that is, as something that ought not to be used merely as a means - and consequently imposes on that extent a limit on arbitrary treatment of them (and is an object of reverence).' [9]

Kant believed that in human relations each one of us has rights based on our intrinsic value. Human beings as rational beings must be treated with dignity as ends in themselves, and not as means to an end. Therefore, for instance it would be wrong to defraud and deceive someone in a business transaction because the other person would be denied the opportunity to make a rational choice and share in the rational decision making process. The other person, if deceived into entering into a fraudulent transaction, would not be making a choice based on reason. However, Kant only considered this moral question to be between rational beings, and therefore excluded future generations of people, unborn children, and animals. Animals, to Kant, were to be considered non-rational and therefore only 'things'. As such they may be treated as a means to an end. While animals may never become rational beings, the unborn and future generations will one day be able to make rational choices if they are given the opportunity. Kant does not answer this question. Also if we are to base the idea that mankind has intrinsic value on ability for rational thought, then it takes away from the concept that intrinsic value is given from above by God. It is only rational human beings who are able to enforce their rights. This concept of rights forms part of the basis for morality today.

Kant did in fact leave a small place for religion because it provided a basis for morality for the simple and uneducated. However, educated people may rely on their own reason to provide a basis for good ethical standards. Therefore mankind himself could decide on what constitutes ethical standards, and people should not rely on God, and Jesus himself is given the place of a good moral teacher. While some moved towards a deistic view of God, other

German philosophers moved towards pantheism. Friedrich Schleirmacher for instance became a Lutheran preacher and believed that God could only be known through religious experience. Georg Wilhelm Friedrich Hegel on the other hand developed the idea that God exists as a worldly Absolute Spirit. The world is therefore a manifestation of God, and Jesus is seen as the human form of the divine Spirit. Ludwig Feuerbach later moved this on one step and proposed that this spirit should be identified with nature itself. As such, the knowledge of God became the knowledge of one's self. Another student of Hegel, Karl Marx was not satisfied with reality being based on the purely human understanding of the spirit of the world or nature, and suggested that all nature was no more than the material. While this is just a brief discussion of the German philosophers, it highlights an increasingly man centred understanding of ethics, where God is eventually removed altogether under Darwinian and Marxist thought. Rights under a purely material worldview can only be anthropocentric, and the mind of each man becomes the arbiter of morality.

Most people today, if asked, would tend to disagree with Kant's idea that only rational beings have rights, and superficially believe that everyone, including future generations of people, must be treated as rational beings and ends in themselves on the basis of equality. Animals too should not be treated as simply things, but as sentient beings that are not there for our sadistic pleasure. Fox hunting or badger baiting is greatly disliked because it abuses animals for the sake of human pleasure.[10] Even though the animal is non-rational it would seem that modern people view them as more than things, and not to be treated as a means to an end for someone else's pleasure.

However, when we look a little deeper into the beliefs of modern Western society, we find the issues have not been thought through, and foxes are gaining more rights than unborn human babies. The West has adopted Kant's view that unborn children, because they are unable to make rational choices, can be treated as a means to an end. Babies facing abortion are not given the opportunity to make rational decisions about whether or not they should be denied life and terminated. The opinion of the medical profession, and the feminist mantra of 'a woman's right to her own body', means that unborn babies are treated as non-rational beings and therefore a means to an end, often carelessly conceived by men and women for the sake of short term pleasure. Of course women should be free to make a choice whether to become pregnant or not, and the life of a mother should be saved even if that sadly means the loss of an unborn baby if complications seriously threaten the mother's life, but so many abortions are carried out for social reasons alone, and sex is treated simply as a pleasurable activity with little thought for the consequences. Compare this with the negative way society views cruelty to foxes for the sake of pleasure.

Another more recent philosopher, the American Tom Regan, believed that subjects of a life, such as animals and young children, should be considered to have *inherent* value. According to Regan, subjects of a life who are not rational moral agents, and therefore unable to make rational choices, should be considered moral patients with their inherent value recognised and rights protected. To Regan, the criterion for assessing whether someone has rights and value is more than simply asserting their ability to make rational choices as Kant had done. Regan considered that individuals who could not make rational choices still have rights based on their inherent worth. Both moral agents and moral patients have inherent value and rights. Unborn babies and children may not be able to make rational choices, but that doesn't mean they do not, or should not have rights, as Kant's position would suggest.[11]

It is increasingly recognised that human rights, and even animal rights, exist at a much deeper level than godless evolutionary forces would have us believe. People and animals in fact have inherent value, and therefore rights that cannot be dismissed. In this post-modern age people are beginning to seek spiritual answers to questions of rights, but have not yet returned to the full understanding of rights and duties that exist in the Judeo-Christian tradition as outlined by Thomas Aquinas.

Appeals for rights today are very much tied up with single-issue pressure groups, often competing against each other in Darwinian fashion with little regard for the rights of others. Human rights are given to those who shout loudest. Secular states become more and more controlling where human made laws replace the God given respect for life. However, for society to be truly free and fair it must be recognised that rights and duties exist in an equal setting, and at a much deeper level than pure survival instincts suggest. Western society needs to return to the natural theology and natural law tradition, where the appearance of design in nature points to a God given plan. This would restore people's understanding that they have duties towards others as well as rights, and elevate Western values above those allowed by purely Darwinist philosophy. We must recognise that a truly ethical society must protect the rights of the weak and powerless as well as the strong.

Notes and References

[1] Locke, J., *Second Treatise of Civil Government*, Chapter 2: *Of the State of Nature*, Section 6, 1690; Reprint: *Two Treatises of Civil Government*, Dent, Everyman ed., London, 1953.

[2] The term *natural law* is used here to describe an ethical concept. It can also be used in a scientific context, as in the "regularity of natural laws", see page 39.

[3] Des Jardins, J.R., *Environmental Ethics: An Introduction to Environmental Philosophy*, 3rd ed., Wadsworth Group, Thomson Learning Inc., Belmont, USA, p. 24, 2001.

[4] Ibid., pp. 25-26.

[5] Church of Scotland, General Assembly, *Act Approving the Shorter Catechism*, (Agreed upon by the Assembly of Divines at Westminster), Session 19, Edinburgh, Question 1, 28th July 1648. <www.epcew.org.uk/wsc/>, Accessed March 2006.

[6] Hobbes, T., *Leviathan*, 1651; Reprint: Oxford University Press, 1996.

[7] Mackie, J.L., *Ethics: Inventing Right and Wrong*, Harmondsworth, Penguin Books, pp. 105-124, 1977.

[8] Rawls, J., *A Theory of Justice*, Clarendon Press, Oxford, pp. 11-17, 1972.

[9] Kant, I., (trans. Paton, H.J.), *Groundwork of the Metaphysic of Morals*, Chapter 2, Hutchinson University Library, London, 1948.

[10] Whether or not fox hunting with dogs is the most organic and least cruel way of controlling foxes to maintain biodiversity is another question, but the 'sport' element of fox hunting should rightly be condemned.

[11] Regan, T., *The Case for Animal Rights*, Routledge, London, pp. 241-243, 1984.

Chapter 6

The Error of Epicurus

As the Father has loved me, so have I loved you. Now remain
in my love. If you obey my commands, you will remain in my
love, just as I have obeyed my Father's commands and remain
in his love. I have told you this so that my joy may be in you
and that your joy may be complete. My command is this: Love
each other as I have loved you. Greater love has no one than
this, that he lay down his life for his friends. You are my
friends if you do what I command. I no longer call you
servants, because a servant does not know his master's
business. Instead, I have called you friends, for everything that
I learned from my Father I have made known to you. You did
not choose me, but I chose you and appointed you to go and
bear fruit—fruit that will last. Then the Father will give you
whatever you ask in my name. This is my command:
Love each other.
(John 15:9-17)

In the eighteenth century the sceptical agnostic and empiricist
thinker David Hume proposed that the *Principle of Utility* provided
grounds for people to accept qualities that they believe to be good.[1]
In this sense utility may be considered more than simple usefulness
for a purpose, with an emphasis instead on the presence of pleasure
or happiness, and absence of pain and unhappiness. In ancient
Greece, Plato (in Protagoras) showed Socrates judging his decision-
making on the consequences that those actions had in terms of
pleasure and pain. An action may be deemed right if it gives the
greatest happiness or pleasure to the greatest number of people, and
wrong otherwise. The Epicureans too based ethical decision-making
on the idea of happiness, and the philosophy of Epicurus forms the

basis for Hume's own work and indeed much of modern thinking.

Epicurus believed that friendship provided the basis for a happy life, although this became linked to a denial of the existence of God as well. Epicurus and his followers believed that ethical conduct could be explained in humanistic terms alone from the pleasure we gain from love and friendship, although it may be noted that the observation that joy is derived from loving friendship does not demonstrate that it derived by chance. The quote from *John 15* above shows that joy, love and friendship are gifts of grace from God. However, the Epicureans of Jesus and Paul's time had reduced their concept of happiness from friendship to short term sensual pleasure. It may be noted that a similar trend has occurred in the West today where godless ethics are again based on Epicurean philosophy which has given rise to hedonistic personal pleasure seeking, and it may be argued that this is the natural effect of Epicurean ethical philosophy. In fact Paul, from observations of pagan Roman and Greek culture, seems to allude to this outcome in *Romans 1*.

Jeremy Bentham also promoted the principle of utility in the eighteenth century.[2] Bentham was concerned with finding a rational basis on which to make sound legislation. This has become known as the *Principle of Utility*, or *Principle of Greatest Happiness*, and is a means of determining which actions are correct in terms of happiness and pleasure, or reducing pain and unhappiness. John Stuart Mill also later reworked and refined Bentham's writings.[3]

For David Hume, sympathy was the overriding sentiment that could guide us in our moral conduct, and as noted, Epicurus too found pleasure in friendship. Each of us knows what it is to experience pleasure and pain, and as such we may wish those around us to experience the more pleasurable side of life, although incidentally it may be observed that the human condition is more complex than this. Hatred and wishing misfortune on others are powerful emotions that can take control of individuals and society, and are often as common as love or wishing someone else well. However, Hume seems to go further than this, and denies the objective reality of good and evil and places such ideas in the subjective sympathetic mind of an observer.

So this ethical tradition, which sees ethics centred on human sentiment, stretches from the Epicureans to David Hume and Adam Smith, through Jeremy Bentham, John Stuart Mill and Charles Darwin to environmental ethicists such as Aldo Leopold.[4] Although sentiments include such things as attitudes and feelings of happiness or sadness, emotions of love and affection, for Hume, sympathy for others was of overriding importance as an ethical sentiment, even providing the origin for ethics itself. Therefore, according to Hume, the 'oughts' of ethics comes from facts about us, and do not come from facts about the natural world as Aquinas claimed. For Hume, moral evil lies within the individual who sees such things as murder and rape as being an offence against an internally disapproving sentiment. Although Hume claimed that evil really exists, he believed that the evil lies within the observer, not in the object of suffering.[5]

However, this does not answer the question of why we should say that pleasure is better than pain, love better than hate, or happiness better than unhappiness, in a material universe without ultimate meaning. How can we objectively determine what is good and evil in a godless universe, especially when Hume identifies good and evil with the subjective opinion of the observer, and not with the object of suffering itself? It is of course a correct observation that people prefer blessings to curses today, but this only informs our present continuous state, and it cannot answer why pleasure and happiness exist, or why such concepts should guide our moral conduct towards others. Hume also opens himself up to all sorts of counter arguments. Does something cease to be evil if the observer or oppressor has no sympathy, but instead hates his victim? Is the action of a murderer good because he does not have sympathy for his victim? What if subjective observers disagree over who should be the object of sympathy. Which one is right?

It was Hume who most clearly identified the fact that 'is' should not necessarily imply 'ought'. An observation of facts does not imply that an action is morally correct, nor that something is good simply because it is natural. It may be argued, for instance, that facts are independent of human judgement whereas values are dependent on human judgement, although it may be noted that the interpretation of facts themselves are underpinned by philosophical assumptions. Fox hunting, for instance, may have a long history, and people gain pleasure from it, but that doesn't mean people ought to hunt foxes for pleasure. However, in trying to find a basis for morality based on the human observation of sympathy, Hume seems to base the 'ought' of ethics on the 'is' of one human sentiment instead of another.

The argument suggests that sympathy exists, therefore it is a natural part of humanity, and we must follow its lead. But while sympathy clearly does exist, it does not provide a sound basis for morality. There are other powerful sentiments, and we need an objective way of determining, which ones are valid for a particular time or circumstance. They may inform our conduct, but something has to be right at a deeper level to have objective meaning in terms of right and wrong. Sympathy and sentiment on their own may therefore be considered extremely shallow bases for morality. As an example of this shallowness, the main objection to fox hunting seems to be that the fox is a cute furry animal with large pretty eyes, and a sly grin. We may label this sentimental sympathy as the 'cute, furry animal syndrome', and show little sympathy for the unseen chickens and rabbits that are eaten by the fox. These are sometimes killed by the fox's survival instincts alone without a pressing need for food. What is more is that an unborn baby that is hidden from view in the womb gains less sympathy when aborted, even though it may objectively be argued that abortion is a greater wrong than fox hunting.

Des Jardins makes similar comments, and observes that human sentimentality provides an unstable foundation on which to construct an ethical system, noting that for every example of human cooperation, sympathy or affection, there are other examples of hatred, competition or selfishness. The challenge for Hume's ethical system is that we need reasons to offer positive instead of negative sentiments, as human psychology is just as capable of offering hatred and division, instead of love and cooperation. Des Jardins uses as an example the destruction of rain forests by poor farmers, who are driven by positive moral sentiments to provide for their families, as they see no ethical or pressing reason to protect the ecosystem. This problem is an echo of Immanuel Kant's objection to Hume's ethical system. Kant noted that human psychology and sentimentality can only offer hypothetical and subjective imperatives, whereas an objective system of ethics requires categorical imperatives or obligations that rational people must follow.[6]

While Hume considered that the sentiment of sympathy provided a basis for good ethical conduct, Bentham, and later Mill, developed an alternative to the utilitarian ideal. Accordingly, an action may be considered good if it tends towards happiness rather than unhappiness or reduces pain or brings greater pleasure to the greater number of people. While this may at first appear superficial it may be argued that the role of the Christian church on earth is to increase the general happiness and well-being of humanity and nature. A simplistic rejection of utilitarianism would therefore be wrong. However, there are serious problems with the principle of utility when we use it to construct a godless basis on which to build ethical standards.

According to classical utilitarianism, an action may be considered right or wrong, only in terms of the overall consequential outcome. In this context, traditional ideas of morality do not exist. However, there are many actions that might give short term beneficial happiness, but cannot be stated as being moral. It is often said, for instance, that 'revenge is sweet', but revenge may be considered morally unacceptable. This is especially apparent when we observe groups of people, for instance, taking the law into their own hands in the formation of lynch mobs, and finding a sense of self-righteous satisfaction. Often this leads to indiscriminate violence, which goes on to work greater evil, than was ever done in the first place. An eye for an eye will leave everyone blind. Lying, murder, adultery and abortion may all have short term pleasurable or beneficial consequences for some, but this does not make them morally right, and indeed these actions have long term negative consequences and cannot be said to increase the overall happiness. A search for personal happiness may indeed encourage people to seek a hedonistic or selfish lifestyle, with little regard for the happiness of others.

Some people fill their bodies with illicit drugs for short term pleasure, but it is clearly not good for them in the long run. People demand abortion, but this does not allow the unborn child to make a decision as to what is good for itself. Should utility be extended to the unborn and future generations, assuming we might know what they want? Some people also gain pleasure from fox hunting or the exploitation of others such as slaves. Should their pleasure be allowed? Such questions continue to arise. How should we value people in other countries? How should we value future generations? Should we extend utility to sentient animals, or even non-sentient plants? Utility clearly has many unanswered questions.

We must also question the quantity and quality of pleasure and pain. How is the quality and quantity of pleasure or absence of pain to be measured? In order to achieve this it would be necessary to set up a calculus of pleasure and pain. But are the pleasures of ten people worth the pain and suffering of one? If we consider, as Bentham did, that utility must be equal, then each person must count as one, but do people make rational choices in deciding what is good for them? Is it possible to reduce morality to an arithmetic calculus? It may of course be argued that uneducated people lack the necessary tools to decide beforehand what is the best outcome for them, but it must also be recognised that even the most highly educated in society fail to accurately gauge beforehand the negative consequences of failed political decisions. Trying to determine what is right and wrong, based on an unknown future consequence, is problematic in the extreme.

If The *Principle of Utility* were to provide the basis for a sound moral framework, then we would quickly end up in selfish dispute and confusion. Yes, people do make many decisions on the basis of happiness, such as a walk along the beach, eating chocolate ice cream, or a trip to an art gallery, but these are not moral decisions. In fact, on a wider point, the *Principle of Utility* is one of the weaknesses of democracy. People often vote for their own self-interest, and not the good of others, or necessarily the long term good of the country. Some people might vote for tax cuts, when tax rises are needed to provide for essential services and pay off debt. Others might choose to exploit the social welfare system by not working and living a reckless, carefree life. Decisions made on the basis of utility are littered with difficulties, and do not give the firm objective foundation needed for a strong and stable civilisation. There surely has to be a system of rights and responsibilities.

Having said that, many decisions can be made on the basis of utility. Trying to predict the long term benefit of certain policies forms the basis for a lot of political decisions, where there is no clear distinction between what is right and wrong. In anthropocentric terms, therefore, utility may be seen as filling in the gaps between ethics based on rights and duties. Choosing which holiday to take, for instance, may be considered morally neutral and based on personal preference. And as has already been pointed out, it may legitimately be argued that increasing the overall happiness of humanity and nature forms much of the Christian church's mission on earth. However, utility cannot provide a foundational basis for that Christian mission in human terms.

Attempts to find a foundation for ethics and human rights outside of a religious framework are problematic in the extreme. If an independent divine evaluator is not the one determining right from wrong, then rights merely become the preserve of human will, or weight of human opinion. According to Locke, people will agree to put an umpire in place to judge on behalf of everyone, as without it people must agree their own legal boundaries. The case for a contract of rights as a basis for a compassionate ethic may seem good, but as Locke claimed, human rights are derived from an omnipotent and loving God as part of the natural law tradition. The role of judge is to interpret law for the sake for humanity, and Locke's idea of morality in a state of nature, was to find a moral basis for sound human government, not to undermine God's position. Locke's position does not give comfort to those who want to find a godless basis for good ethics. Phillip Johnson has summarised these issues well, commenting that each non-supernatural source of ethical authority is only temporarily convincing. He notes that human authority forms the basis for all alternatives to supernatural authority, and of course human authority remains subject to personal opinion.[7]

Here is the basis of the argument, that whatever foundation we look for on which to construct an ethical standard without reference to a supernatural authority must rest on human authority. But human authority is dependent on individuals or groups of people, and each person has an equal vote in determining what is right and wrong. Each person may give the common retort, 'what gives you the right to decide what is good for me?' This problem, of finding a source of morality based on natural law and rights in a secular context, has been described by Johnson as the 'modernist impasse'.[8] On the one hand it would seem that modernists want to be free to make laws according to their own agenda, but on the other hand they want laws to stop others infringing their own liberal idea of what is right and wrong. Johnson comments that modernists struggle to justify the imposition of restraining obligations on others, although they are more than able to proclaim liberties.[9]

Johnson, at the beginning of his article, sets out the background with reference to a dispute of what constitutes natural law in the United States Supreme Court. It would seem that on the one hand the liberals want to determine what is right and wrong according to human standards, without reference to any higher authority, but in believing that there is no higher power to determine right from wrong, they move towards nihilism without realising the outcome. Johnson highlights this dispute by quoting from a notable lecture by Arthur Leff. Leff points out that all of us are keen for others to obey laws that we ourselves would put in place, but at the same time we desire personally to live outside of law. As an example, in the UK the common cry is that laws should exist to stop others using their cars, the reason being that room should be freed up on roads to allow us to drive freely. It is perhaps ironic that so called liberals often have a propensity to make laws for others to follow, becoming in the process legalistic control freaks. This attitude, that may be latent in each of us, shows the desire to control others while allowing oneself to be free, but in rejecting supernatural authority we are unable to find an objective basis for ethics.[10]

Leff observes that when we remove God from our worldview we are left searching for an objective means of evaluating ethics, which he calls the 'unjudged judge' or the 'uncreated creator of values'. He comments that we cannot make progress until we recognise our need for the Lord, although he remained unwilling to accept this logical outcome. Secularism has not only removed God from his place, it has also removed any objective, authoritative and coherent framework on which to build an ethical or legal system.[11] Johnson suggests that each one of us has become a 'godlet', with an equal right to set laws as any other little godlet.[12]

When we look at secular Western society today we find an inconsistent application of ethical standards across the board. As Leff says, each of us demands that our own rights are respected, but we also demand the right to live our own lives as we please, often with little respect or regard for the rights of those around us. This then gives people the right to live out a life in utilitarian, hedonistic pleasure. We demand the right for pleasure without considering our duty towards our fellow humanity. This can clearly be seen over the issue of abortion where a casual attitude to sex means that there is an increase in unplanned pregnancy. Today in Britain a woman can even have an abortion to take a holiday, but is an unborn child worth less than a week in the sun? It would seem that babies in the womb gain little sympathy being so clearly out of sight. There is no consideration of Regan's appeal that those who are not moral agents, such as unborn babies for instance, should be treated as moral patients with intrinsic value, and abortion is carried out under Kantian, or even utilitarian thought that only rational beings have rights or moral standing. People demand their own rights to do as they please sexually with little regard for the object of their passions or the impact on society, nor for the impact on any potential child. As for the objects of passion, they may later suffer the consequences of sexually transmitted diseases or HIV/AIDS from whatever sexual arena they live in.

The reason for mentioning abortion and homosexuality as ethical issues here is that both are contrary to the logic of Darwinian survival of the fittest, as well as being contrary to traditional Judeo-Christian standards. Abortion cuts across the natural reproductive process, whereas homosexuality does not even engage in natural reproduction. How could a true gay gene for instance ever reproduce itself? If it could, it must be questioned whether it was ever gay in the first place. What does this tell us about Darwinism? That in overthrowing God, Darwinian ethics do not reduce mankind to the level of the animals, or necessarily mean the rigid application of survival instincts, but places each of us in the place of God where we decide our own ethical conduct. Once again, we follow the sensual hedonistic ethics of the Epicureans, when we adopt the atheistic philosophy of Epicurus on which Darwinist ethics are based.

Today, most rational beings are able to stand up for their own rights, based on intrinsic value, and as such much of our ethical basis follows a sort of contract of rights. However, this doesn't answer the question of how we should treat people who are not rational beings. This includes, for instance, the mentally ill, the unborn and animals. A true ethic based on rights and duties would recognise, as Regan did, that moral patients should have rights extended to them because they are subjects of a life.

Hitler seemed to set himself up as a god and demanded obedience to the fascist cause, denying others the right to life, but rational people who wanted their rights protected eventually overthrew him. As Leff and Johnson suggest, we have now become our own little 'godlets'. Western society rejected Hitler's rigid application of survival of the fittest, and many of us now demand the right to live according to our own desires and passions with little regard for others.

The other main drive in ethics today is really a throwback to Hume's idea of sentiment and sympathy. If a person wants to have their rights recognised by other rational beings, it helps to gain public sympathy. Many successful pressure groups use arguments based on sympathy to uphold or gain 'rights' for people or even animals. A woman gains more sympathy than the unborn baby, a gay young man gains sympathy by appealing to sentiment and applying a feminine demeanour, and a fox gains sympathy by having a cute face and a fur coat. In the British House of Commons today, at the start of the 21st Century, a majority of MPs favour a ban on fox hunting while maintaining a woman's right to have an abortion up to 24 weeks, this despite increasing photographic evidence of the humanity of the unborn child even at 12 weeks. It is likely though that the increasing sentimental aspect of this will restrict later abortions in coming years. But is a fox really worth more than an unborn human child?

Appeals to sympathy cannot determine whether something is

right or wrong at a much deeper level. When we view other people and nature as part of God's creation, it informs us how we should treat each other. A return to the natural law tradition as developed by Thomas Aquinas would greatly improve our society and civilisation in ethical terms. Each of us as people, and indeed animals, do have rights, but these are conferred by God and not given just because of ability for rational thought as Kant proposed, or from gaining sympathy. There is a need in legal and ethical matters to return to a more coherent ethical standard based on rights and duties that are given by God. But how should we balance utilitarianism with rights in a Judeo-Christian context? There are indeed many decisions that may be made in terms of preference, according to some sort of principle of greatest happiness. Who we marry, which holidays we take, where we work, etc. These are largely morally neutral decisions.

Holmes Rolston[13] has also challenged the naturalistic fallacy of Hume because the consequential materialism gives an inadequate basis on which to base ethics. Ethical humanists are limited to consider that the ecosystem only has value as far as it can contribute to man's experience. The phrase *naturalistic fallacy* is now used more widely to imply that it is fallacious to equate any values with facts. Moore in 1903 attempted to show that the concept of good defies definition, both in natural and empirical terms of happiness and survival of the fittest, in which case materialistic ethics become amoral.[14] Rolston disagrees with the materialistic basis for ethics and observed that a purely scientific evaluation cannot provide a basis for ethics, and instead there is a need for a metaphysical or philosophical response. He comments that this is not strictly science, but what he terms meta-ecology. He suggests that there is something within each one of us that should delight in seeing the biotic community thrive, in the same way we should consider it good to take pleasure in the success of family and friends. Rolston asserts that when we consider environmental ethics from a study of nature we move from *is* to *good*, and then to the *ought* of ethical conduct, although in order to do this we must leave pure science behind. He goes on to suggest that for some, *ought* is discovered simultaneously with *is*, and notes that this is puzzling. While this has a lot of appeal, it is very much a subjective appeal to the sentiments of environmentalists. It cannot provide a consistent and objective ethic for those who do not share his love of nature, as many people today do not.[15]

Rolston leaves open the question of what metaphysics should apply, but he continues to accept the process of evolution, and asserts that the ecosystem has more value than the individual. *coaction in adapted fit* is preferred to survival of the fittest, which allegedly distorts the truth of the reality of evolution. However, it may be noted as a valid point that simply because something is natural does not make it good, as the case of HIV/AIDS or the Guinea worm demonstrate. Rolston's rejection of the Genesis 1-3 account of a *good* creation followed by a *fall* from grace runs into the theodicy problem as described by Christopher Southgate.[16]

While Christians do recognise that the ecosystem itself has rights, and therefore Christians have a duty of care towards it, an observation from an individual's own experience is that ethics exist at the level of the individual, and not at the level of the community as Rolston claims. Denial of the fact that rights exist at the level of the individual formed the basis for abuses of human rights by communists and fascists alike, and Tom Regan warns us of the dangers of developing a theory of environmental fascism by denying individual rights for the sake of some greater good.[17] While it is recognised that the ecosystem has value, and that optimised biodiversity is good, we must also recognise that individuals have intrinsic values too. Behind the eyes of the fox, hunted for pleasure by man, is a real animal being, but there is also a real being behind the eyes of the rabbit that is hunted by the fox. There is a real child behind the eyes of one affected by the guinea worm, or infected with HIV/AIDS. An observation of nature is that symbiotic relationships are generally good, nectar gathering by bumble bees is good, fruit eating by fruit bats is good, but there is something broken and not so good about the fox that eats the rabbit, or the lion that eats the antelope. It would seem that the *naturalistic fallacy* is not altogether false and God's good creation appears broken as if fallen from perfection.

Whereas Regan tried to develop a basis for ethics on the idea that moral patients as well as moral agents as individuals have rights, Peter Singer adopted the idea that the principle of utility should help us understand which individuals have equal moral standing. Singer agrees with Bentham, that the notion of rights is meaningless, and based his philosophy of ethics on the ability of a person or animal to suffer pain or enjoy happiness. He therefore seeks to make the case that sentience is sufficient to decide which beings should have their interests considered and protected. Using this criterion, Singer goes on to claim that to deny animals their equal moral standing with sentient humans is in effect equal to sexism or even racism. He calls this *speciesism*, and his views helped to inspire various animal liberation movements.[18] While this may have superficial appeal, Singer developed the idea further until non-sentient humans, such as the mentally handicapped, the old or even new born babies were considered to be without moral standing, and therefore considered to have less standing than fully sentient animals. Through Singer and others, godless ethics based on utilitarianism can be seen to descend into environmental fascism, and today many people care more for the welfare of animals than they do for the welfare of humanity. Today, legislation is moving in the direction of protecting animals from harm while moving to take away the rights of human beings who do not yet have, or have lost the ability to defend their own cause as rational beings. Godless utilitarianism does not therefore lead to equality or justice, but instead leads to a degradation of ethics based on intrinsic rights and values, and ultimately leads to a form of environmental fascism.

We may go one step further in seeking to understand utilitarianism in Christian terms and ask another question; of whether we should reject utilitarianism altogether, or is there a place for it in a Judeo-Christian scheme of ethics? If we consider the principle of utility in theocentric terms, then it would appear that it forms the basis for God's very purpose in creation. If God initially created all things good for his own pleasure, then our place in it must be subordinate to that purpose. Under this understanding, utilitarianism may form the fundamental basis for ethical conduct, but it can only do so in union with a God of love, and a love for humanity and nature. Law exists for those who do not know how to love. The main objection to such a theocentric ethical basis is that it is based on faith, and not pure rational thought, but that doesn't take away from the sheer beauty of it, or from the beauty of nature that points to it. As Pascal pointed out, 'The heart has reasons for which reason knows nothing.'

But how are we to know what our place in creation is? The answer may be given in terms of the Law of Moses, and the book of nature. The Law of Moses may be seen as a sort of health and safety legislation to maintain order within God's overall utilitarian purpose. Legal rights and duties theory therefore exists as a function of God's pleasure to maintain order in His creation. However, the Mosaic Law should not be applied in strict legalistic terms, and instead we must live out the heart of the law, which is love itself. But how should law be applied in a loving Judeo-Christian context? The Apostle Paul presented a detailed argument in the book of Romans that pointed back to pre-Mosaic times. Basically this is the law of grace, which is lived our in faith and love.

> 'For in the gospel a righteousness from God is revealed, a righteousness that is by faith from first to last [or from faith to faith], just as it is written: "the righteous will live by faith." '*(Romans 1:17)*

> 'Therefore, there is now no condemnation for those who are in Christ Jesus, because through Christ Jesus the law of the Spirit of life [Law of grace] set me free from the law of sin and death [law of liberalism]. For what the law [Law of Moses] was powerless to do in that it was weakened by the sinful nature, God did by sending his own Son...' *(Romans 8:1-3)*

The summation of the legal Mosaic Law is based on a utilitarian argument of loving one's neighbour, and also expressed in *John 15*. This is selfless love and faithful service to others, which leads to joy for the giver. This type of love is much more than sentiment and sympathy, but a love that is costly in terms of self-sacrifice. However, by living by this love we find ourselves no longer under a strict legal code, but find joy in giving to others. Such depth of love can only be lived out in terms of faith. The Law of Moses may be summed up as 'love thy neighbour' as taught by Jesus Christ and later by St. Paul.

However, we may ask, as Jesus pressed the Pharisees, who is my neighbour? It would seem that to some degree the law of love should be extended to the natural world of animals and plants as well. After all, the whole of nature is part of God's creation, and love of creation has formed part of the experience and mission of many faithful saints, preachers and missionaries, including St. Francis of Assisi, the Celtic saints living in remote places, and even to Albert Schweitzer.

In the secular West, people who live without reference to God find themselves coming up against the law of sin and death. This may be observed, for instance, over the issue of HIV/AIDS and a casual approach to the sexual health of others. However, according to Paul, God does not wish people to live according to a strict legal code in order to escape the law of sin and death, but wishes people to live according to the law of God's Spirit, who brings the joyful loving life of Christ into the believer. By putting on the glasses of Christ, people begin to see each other and nature as He sees them. Not as lustful objects for abuse, but as people and natural entities with intrinsic value. Here again in Romans we find the twin books of Scripture and nature referenced. The problem for those who follow Epicurus is not their love for friendship, but their denial of the grace of God that supports love and stops people from reducing ethical conduct to short term hedonistic pleasure.

As we have seen already, St. Paul appeals to nature as giving a moral voice, as does McGrath who suggests that a reawakening of a sense of love and wonder for the natural world should inform our ethical conduct.[19] Paul, after setting out his gospel in the first eight chapters of Romans, shows how the Christian, having accepted the gospel of Jesus Christ should go on to liberate and care for creation.

> 'The creation waits in eager expectation for the sons of God to be revealed. For the creation was subjected to frustration, not by its own choice, but by the will of the one who subjected it, in hope that the creation itself will be liberated from its bondage to decay and brought into the glorious freedom of the children of God.' *(Romans 8:19-21)*

A utilitarian argument may therefore form the basis for a Christian environmental ethic by extending the law of 'love thy neighbour' to the realm of animals and plants as well, but this must be in harmony with the grace of God to be effective. For the Christian, the whole of nature and humanity are part of God's creation and therefore worthy of respect. God Himself created for His own pleasure. This law was expounded by Jesus Christ and recorded in *John 15*, and by St. Paul in the book of *Romans*. Those who live by the law of love find themselves fulfilling the legal code of Moses without it appearing burdensome, but instead it becomes a pleasure. However, the argument presented by Jesus, and later by Paul, does not mean that others do not have rights within the Law, but that people should live by the spirit of the Law. In this way, respect and rights are given to others as they are recognised as being part of a divine order in creation. We may also recognise that unborn children have rights as moral patients, as well as preserving the beauty, integrity and stability of the world for future generations. In this way we begin to return to the natural law and natural theology argument of Aquinas and become good stewards of creation. But seeking to build a utilitarian morality outside of the Judeo-Christian faith system leads to all sorts of contradictions and fails to provide any sort of foundation for loving ethical standards, but instead leads to a denial of human rights and leads to a form of environmental fascism. We must also recognise that rights and duties exist at the level of the individual, but that the ecosystem, as part of God's creation, also has rights that Christians must respect.

Notes and References

[1] Open University, Wye College, University of London, *Utilitarianism, Ethical Theory and Environmental Values,* Environmental Ethics, Block B, Part 1, p. 7, 1997.

[2] Bentham, J., *An Introduction to the Principles of Morals and Legislation,* first published 1789.

[3] Mill, J.S., *Utilitarianism,* Longman, Green and Co., London, 1863.

[4] Leopold, A., *The Land Ethic*, in Part IV of: *A Sand County Almanac*, Oxford University Press, New York, 1949. See also: Callicott, J.B., *In Defense of the Land Ethic*, p. 79, State University of New York Press, Albany, 1989.

[5] Des Jardins, J.R., *Environmental Ethics: An Introduction to Environmental Philosophy*, 3rd ed., Wadsworth Group, Thomson Learning Inc, Belmont, USA, p. 24, 2001.

[6] Ibid., p. 203.

[7] Johnson, P.E., *Nihilism and the End of Law*, First Things, 31, pp. 19-25, March 1993, <www.firstthings.com/ftissues/ft9303/articles/pjohnson.html>, Accessed March 2006. See also: C.S. Lewis Society, <www.apologetics.org/articles/nihilism.html>, Accessed March 2006.

[8] Ibid.

[9] Ibid.

[10] Leff, A., *Unspeakable Ethics, Unnatural Law*, lecture given at Duke University, 1979. Quoted in Johnson, op. cit.

[11] Ibid.

[12] Johnson, op. cit.

[13] Rolston III, H., *Challenges in Environmental Ethics*, In: Cooper, D.E., Palmer, J.A. (eds.) *The Environment in Question: Ethics and Global Issues*, Routledge, London, pp. 135-146, 1992. (Holmes Rolston is known as "Rolston III" because he shares the names of his father and grandfather).

[14] Moore, G.E., *Principia Ethica*, Cambridge University Press, 1903.

[15] Rolston III, op. cit.

[16] Southgate, C., *God and Evolutionary Evil: Theodicy in the Light of Darwinism*, Zygon, Vol. 37, No. 4, pp. 803-824, Dec. 2002.

[17] Regan, T., *The Case for Animal Rights*, University of California Press, Berkeley, pp. 361-362, 1983.

[18] Singer, P., *Practical Ethics*, Cambridge University Press, pp. 48-59, 1979.

[19] McGrath, A., *The Re-enchantment of Nature*, Hodder Headline, London 2003.

Chapter 7

Christianity and Respect for Nature

Farewell, farewell! But this I tell
To thee, thou Wedding Guest!
He prayeth well, who loveth well
Both man and bird and beast.
He prayeth best, who loveth best
All things both great and small;
For the dear God who loveth us,
He made and loveth all.[1]

A number of recent environmental writers have claimed that through the centuries the Christian church has not cared for the environment as well as it might. Christianity, it would seem, has too often focused on sound doctrine and upholding political power, largely ignoring the call to care for God's creation. What are the reasons for this?

Lynn White wrote a well-known paper in 1967, entitled *The Historical Roots of our Ecologic Crisis*.[2] This paper highlighted the point that Christianity has often been seen to give approval to the idea of the *domination* of nature from the Genesis account. White comments that:

'The victory of Christianity over paganism was the greatest psychic revolution in the history of our culture. It is fashionable today to say that ... we live in "the post Christian age." ... Our daily habits of action, for example, are dominated by an implicit faith in perpetual progress ... It is rooted in, and is indefensible apart from Judeo-Christian teleology. The fact that communists share it merely helps to show what can be demonstrated on many other grounds: that Marxism, like Islam, is a Judeo-Christian heresy.'

'... Christianity inherited from Judaism ... a striking story of creation ... Man named all the animals, thus establishing his dominance over them. God planned all of this explicitly for man's benefit and rule: no item in the physical creation had any purpose save to serve man's purposes.'

'Especially in its Western form, Christianity is the most anthropocentric religion the world has seen.' [3]

White sees the rise of the natural theology tradition of Aquinas as the beginning of a slippery slope that seeks to exploit nature. While Aquinas and those who saw in creation a divine plan and purpose, and law for good ethical conduct, Lynn White sees this as the beginning of the progressive technological age. White comments:

'By revelation, God had given man the Bible, the Book of Scripture. But since God had made nature, nature also must reveal the divine mentality. The religious study of nature for the better understanding of God was known as natural theology. In the early Church and always in the Greek east, nature was conceived primarily as a symbolic system through which God speaks to men ... This view of nature was essentially artistic rather than symbolic. While Byzantium preserved and copied great numbers of ancient Greek scientific texts, science as we conceive it could scarcely flourish in such ambience. However in the Latin West by the early 13th Century natural theology was following a very different bent. It was ceasing to be the decoding of the physical symbols of God's communication with man and was becoming the effort to understand God's mind by discovering how his creation operates.' [4]

Christianity came under a great deal of attack from many environmentalists as a result of White's paper, partly because it appeared to support the very rejection of Christianity that they were looking for. However, it was not White's intention, as a churchman himself to attack the Christian faith for the sake of it, but instead point it in another direction. According to White, many industrialists in the eighteenth and nineteenth century took up the concept of domination found in Scripture, and wedded it to a belief in the inevitability of scientific and technological progress, believing it acceptable to exploit nature without regard. They gained moral permission for exploitation from a misreading or misunderstanding of the Biblical concept of dominion. While some churchmen may have corrupted the love of God for the love of money and progress, it would be wrong to see this as officially sanctioned by the teachings of Christianity's founder, Jesus Christ, or by its more pious followers. However, it may be admitted that the Church has often upheld political power, whether Catholic or Protestant, to maintain its own place in society, and as a result some ethical compromises have been made in the past towards this end.

As an aside, it would seem that once again true Christianity took the blame for the work of other less scrupulous individuals, in the same way that Christianity often gets the blame for witch-hunts. However, it is usually those with little religious faith who carry out acts of revenge in the name of self-righteousness, or other dubious motives, but revenge is not a Christian virtue. Pandering to popular hatred and encouraging a lynch mob mentality, it would seem, also sells newspapers.

The witch finder general, Matthew Hopkins also made a good financial living by uncovering witches while preying on the superstitious and ignorant mindset of the time. Hopkins later disappeared in unknown circumstances after putting to death a local, aged preacher. As an example of the actions of the church to develop a more intelligent response to the occult, the Spanish Inquisition in 1538 sent Valdeolitas to Navarre to stop popular witch-hunts, and explain to local people that failed crops were actually due to bad weather, not witches. By 1611 Alonso de Salazar found no evidence of witchcraft, and the Inquisition became a model of the Enlightenment. The Inquisition was not as violent as atheistic revisionism makes out, but quickly reformed itself. This was at a time when Isaac Newton believed in alchemy, and forces of godless political power tortured people in the name of revolution.[5] These examples highlight that there is a deep-seated antipathy towards Christianity in modern society, born largely out of Enlightenment philosophy, which moved progressively in a godless and purely materialistic direction.

With regard to the environment, White believed that modern science was equally to blame for exploiting nature, by providing the necessary tools for Western society to use in its endeavours at exploitation and domination of nature, and White found some crumbs of comfort for Christians. In his paper, White went on and promoted the radical ideals of St. Francis of Assisi who lived a simple, humble life in harmony with nature, and believed that this could form the basis for a new ethic. Accordingly, mankind must take his place in creation alongside the animals in worship and fellowship towards God. White shows how St. Francis saw in nature, and inanimate objects, a glorification towards God with even the ants and fire being our brothers and sisters in a grand partnership with mankind for the praise and glorification of the Creator.[6] White concludes with regard to St. Francis of Assisi that:

> 'His view of nature and of man rested on a unique sort of pan-psychism of all things animate and inanimate, designed for the glorification of their transcendent Creator, who in the ultimate gesture of cosmic humility, assumed flesh, lay helpless in a manger, and hung dying on a scaffold.'[7]

The issue of dominating nature by Christians for the purpose of exploitation that White raises is a real one and needs to be addressed by Christians. Is it true that evangelical Christians have joined in and exploited nature in the belief of technological progress, or a false view of domination and failed in their duty to care for God's creation as well as they might? Could it be that even some rich and powerful Christian evangelicals exploit nature for profit, and fail to do all they can to protect God's creation for its beauty, stability and integrity? Are we doing all we can to turn from an oil economy, through the use of renewable energy, or do the oil profits mean more to us than oiled sea birds and rising global carbon dioxide levels? This is a serious point, because if we don't address the issue, then our Christian witness to the world is compromised. Does nature exist to be exploited by mankind, or does man exist to care for nature as good stewards and bring glory to God?

Having said that, there is much in White's writing that may be criticised from a Christian perspective, and McGrath for one considers it fundamentally flawed. Although White praises the Roman Catholic St. Francis of Assisi for his love of nature, with regard to Celtic Christianity he comments that legends of Celtic and Irish saints had told stories to show human domination over other creatures.[8]

McGrath responds to this by stating that it seriously misrepresents the true nature of Celtic Christianity, which had real love for and passionate concern for the environment. McGrath suggests that White was forced to take this view because of his preconceptions about Christianity and its relationship with nature. Instead, McGrath shows how the Celtic saints, who lived close to nature saw it as God's gift to humanity, to be celebrated and honoured, and this reverence offers a model for a modern ecological movement.[9]

Celtic Christianity finds its roots in the doctrine of John the evangelist and his gospel. It was the disciple John, for instance, who records Jesus saying that the relationship between God, himself and mankind was comparable to the relationship between a vine, the branches and the gardener. It is both in the interest of the branches the vine and the gardener to produce healthy fruit, and this could only be achieved by the branches remaining in the vine.

> 'I am the true vine, and my father is the gardener. He cuts off every branch in me that bears no fruit, while every branch that does bear fruit he prunes so that it will be even more fruitful ... Remain in me, and I will remain in you. No branch can bear fruit by itself; it must remain in the vine. Neither can you bear fruit unless you remain in me.'
> *(John 15:1-4)*

This theme is later reflected in the hymn of St. Patrick, sometimes known as The Deer's Cry or St. Patrick's Breastplate where Patrick confesses that 'Christ is with me, Christ before me, Christ behind me, Christ in me, Christ beneath me, Christ above me...'[10]

For the Celtic Christian, often living alone in cliffside caves or stone dwellings with only the sea otters, porpoises and gulls for company, there was something very real about the natural world, which demonstrated very vividly a close spiritual reality behind everything. The awesome crashing waves and the brilliance of the night time starlit heavens invoked in them something of the wonder of creation. They found strength and courage by confessing faith in the Creator of creation. There was seen as well a very close relationship between the God of love and His creation of people and nature, for which he cared deeply. In return, mankind was expected to remain in Christ, the one true vine, with an expectation for a similar response from humanity towards God and other people and nature. McGrath suggests that the Celtic Christians' experience and sense of wonder at the natural world provides a strong basis for a caring and considerate Christian environmental ethic. This is in contrast to the assertion by White that Christianity gives credence to the abuse of nature by technological progress.

It would appear that White's attempt at placing the Irish saints with the forces of exploitation is a result of his view of an East-West split in Christendom. As noted though, Celtic Christianity has very early origins and roots in the Middle East, and in many ways these saints share the more artistic view of natural theology with the Eastern Church. It would be more accurate to speak of an early-late divergence of natural theology instead of an east-west split. The more scientific approach to natural theology was derived as a later enterprise, with churchmen seeking to understand the mind of God through a closer examination of nature. Whereas the early Christian saint might observe the behaviour of ants and find a sense of wonder and worship, later natural theologians were more likely to dissect the ant to find the wonder of creation and the mind of God from within the organism.

Other environmental philosophers, such as John Passmore in *Man's Responsibility for Nature*[11] also considered White's view of the domination of nature found in the Judeo-Christian faith, and claimed that this view was not really widely held. Passmore highlighted two other Christian traditions regarding mankind's relationship with the natural world. The first saw mankind's role as a *steward*, and the second saw mankind as having a role to *perfect* nature. Passmore saw the stewardship role of the Judeo-Christian tradition as a rather weak one, with stewardship being more to do with church life, and not nature. He claimed that the stewardship role that mankind has towards nature, arose sometime in the seventeenth century. However, when it came to the view that mankind has a duty to perfect nature, he believed that it provided a strong basis to build a new environmental ethic. Passmore quotes the seventeenth century Chief Justice, Sir Michael Hale.

'The end of man's creation was that he should be the viceroy of the great God of heaven and earth in this inferior world; his steward, villicus [farm manager], bailiff or farmer of this goodly farm of the lower world.' '... invested with power, authority, right, dominion, trust and care, to correct and abridge the excesses and cruelties of the fiercer animals, to give protection and defence to the manuete [tame] and useful, to preserve the species of divers vegetables, to improve them and others, to correct the redundance of unprofitable vegetables, to preserve the face of the earth in beauty, usefulness, and fruitfulness.' [12]

In fact, contrary to White and Passmore, when we look at the general theme of the Biblical great commissions given to Adam, Noah, and by Jesus to the disciples, it is one of fruitful stewardship and restoration towards an original perfect state through disciplined action. Both a restoration towards perfection and careful stewardship are part of the Christian's responsibility towards creation.

'Be fruitful and increase in number; fill the earth and subdue it ...' *(Genesis 1:28)*

'Be fruitful and increase in number and fill the earth ...' *(Genesis 9:1)*

'... go and make disciples of all nations ... teaching them to obey everything I have commanded you.' *(Matthew 28:19-20)*.

This idea of stewardship and perfecting is also seen in the idea of the gardener in *John 15* with God tending the vine to make it even more fruitful. Robin Attfield with *The Ethics of Environmental Concern*[13] went further than Passmore, and believed that the stewardship tradition is as old as Christianity itself, and widely taught. Attfield also noted, from works by John Baillie[14] and John Bury,[15] that a belief in progress could be seen as a Christian heresy, and believed that stewardship could form the basis for a more complete environmental ethic. In fact, today the stewardship role of mankind's relationship to nature has been widely adopted around the world by governments, the United Nations and conservation groups alike.[16] People have perhaps misunderstood the concept of domination as well. Christianity in its purest form has seen the concept of a servant king, a domination which uses power to serve others and nature. The Creator God is seen serving His creation. This is best illustrated by the picture of Christ as Creator God, sacrificing Himself on the cross on behalf of His own human creation.

There is great scope for Christians to rediscover their duty towards nature and promote the traditional ethic of disciplined stewardship and service. This rule is not to be seen as tyrannical, but as a properly ordained act of service to all creation. Even the act of subduing nature, as stated in Genesis, can be viewed as limiting the natural tendency of nature to survive by crowding out opposition. This subduing can be seen, for instance, through the controlled culling of a top predator, for instance the magpie, if the population grows too large, in order to maintain biodiversity as a whole. Magpies are accused of eating the young of songbirds with numbers in decline. Sadly, such actions are regrettable when set along side God's original good creation, but are necessary as a result of man's fall from grace. Death is a constant reminder of man's rebellion against God. But even without the fall, Adam was expected to act as gardener, and as any gardener knows, some plants grow quicker than others and need to be pruned to allow slower growing shrubs to survive. As Genesis states:

> '… let them rule over the fish of the sea and the birds of the air, over the livestock, over all the earth, and over all the creatures that move along the ground.' … 'Be fruitful and increase in number; fill the earth and subdue it.' *(Genesis 1:26-28)*

Fruitfulness or prosperity may also be seen as a Christian environmental ethic. The image is of the gardener tending the vine in *John 15*, with the vine and the one who tends the vine living in perfect harmony. Much of the language of the Bible is written in terms of fruitfulness towards God. Christianity is at heart theocentric despite claims of anthropocentricism, and Christians should make no apology for this. Mankind is seen as being both part of creation, and elevated above it to have managerial responsibility towards it. As long as mankind is acting in submission to God, then it remains God centred, but as soon as mankind starts acting outside of God's commands, then he moves towards anthropocentricism. Note in the following passage that *creation* as a separate entity is to be liberated by the *children of God*, as mankind, in submission to God's rule.

> 'The creation waits in eager expectation for the sons of God to be revealed. For the creation was subjected to frustration … in hope that the creation itself will be liberated from its bondage to decay and brought into the glorious freedom of the children of God. We know that the whole creation has been groaning as in the pains of childbirth right up to the present time.' *(Romans 8:19-22)*

So to some extent, part of the Christian church lost its way with regard to the environment, from the Middle Ages, through Enlightenment thinkers to the industrial revolution, by accepting a view of progress, which then led to the exploitation of nature. However, this is by no means the majority position, and many of White's assertions are incorrect, with the Church's basic message seen in terms of restoring God's creation to an original perfect state.

Another argument presented by Stuart Burgess, is that the appearance of design in nature suggests that God has deliberately designed some animals for mankind's use. Burgess points to the horse with its suitable size, shape and strength, which makes it an ideal form of transport.[17] The dog is also often known as man's best friend, and canine characteristics, such as a social nature, pack hunting instincts and a keen sense of hearing make it ideal for use as a trained sheep dog, working as a team with the shepherd. Does this argument mean that the Judeo-Christian tradition encourages an anthropocentric exploitation of nature? In fact, this argument points to designed symbiosis, not exploitation. Both horse and dog gain benefit from relationship with mankind, enjoying the company of human beings, finding security and ready provision of food. Designed symbiotic relationships also exist in non-human areas of nature, with for instance clover providing food for bumble-bees, which in turn pollinate the flower.

Darwinian evolution has thrown up its own confusion with evolutionary ethics. It is rather perplexing to see popular nature presenters promoting evolution through natural selection, or survival of the fittest, which supposedly brings about progressive adaptation to species, and then hearing them explain how dreadful it is that mankind as a product of this process, goes on to cause death, destruction and extinction. This may be a slight over-simplification, but in general, natural history presenters adopt this approach, appealing to popular sentiment. On the one hand the historic change process of the environmental destruction of species is seen as good, but the current process of the environmental destruction of species is seen as bad. Presumably, if a South American farmer can raise more children by cutting down more rain forest trees with loss of biodiversity, then that is all well and good as far as the Darwinian ethic of survival of the fittest is concerned, but this is surely not acceptable as far as the Christian stewardship ethic is concerned. As noted previously, Des Jardins comments that moral sentiments that are based on Hume's ethical system and used by Darwinian natural selection provide no incentive to protect the ecosystem and maintain biodiversity.[18]

Of course the Darwinist may claim that mankind gains other benefits from preserving something of the beauty, stability and integrity of the countryside that has evolved over millennia, but such ability for environmental concern requires abstract thought, which is lacking from all other animals. In fact many societies, both tribal and civilised, have learnt too late that destruction of the environment leads to unpleasant consequences, but once the mistake is learnt it is possible for people to develop complex mitigation strategies. If a society cuts down a rain forest, they may find that they suffer degradation of the top soil, and then find their towns, villages and crops destroyed by flash floods. Animals too may learn to avoid danger once encountered, but they lack the far greater capacities of mankind to think, and are unable to respond well to unfavourable changes in circumstances. There are indeed symbiotic benefits that help preserve biodiversity within nature, but once again the idea that this evolved this way is not proved. Once again, the Christian may easily reply that this was part of God's plan of creation all along.

The deep or romantic environmentalist's dilemma, that seeks to preserve nature on the one hand while upholding a belief in destruction through survival of the fittest on the other, is itself born out of Darwin's attempt to relegate mankind to the level of the animals and deny his role in stewardship, and deny God's place as the one who created and sustains. If mankind is relegated in this way as the Darwinists believe, then any talk of anthropocentricism is misguided, as every part of the ecosystem becomes biocentric including mankind. In this way everything man does, whether good or bad environmentally, should be viewed as biocentric, and even to question the consequences becomes meaningless because according to Darwin, survival is paramount. It is precisely the ability to understand and make value judgements that separates mankind from all other animals.

In a purely materialistic world, utilitarianism becomes the only objective ethic in a godless system when deciding what action to take, but as we observe, the consequences are often unpredictable and negative. Very often the romantic or deep environmentalist finds such utilitarianism an anathema and they have a deep-seated idea that something spiritual is at stake when nature is destroyed, although often this is expressed in pagan terms. However, pure Darwinian natural science cannot answer such spiritual desires that are within people. This has led to a rejection of scientific modernism in recent times, although not a return to Christianity itself. The observed level of environmental destruction and change that mankind causes, and the level of concern shown by environmentalists, demonstrates that mankind cannot be viewed as being just part of the bio-community. Mankind has the ability to make choices over what happens to the environment based on abstract thought, intelligence and wisdom, which no other animal has. Mankind also has spiritual needs and an inherent knowledge of right and wrong, that modernism cannot answer. These observations, that mankind has the capacity for conscience, conscious thought, understanding and comprehension, which are not found in any other animal or plant, calls for a spiritual answer to environmental concern, and the reality of mankind's capabilities challenges both Darwinism and biocentrism. However, these capacities must not be allowed to run unchecked, but must be harnessed by submission to a strong and loving Christian faith system by upholding the moral conscience that lies within each of us. Sadly, some suppress their moral conscience and choose to work acts of wickedness that are clearly seen to be wrong by their peers.

Darwin tried to claim that nature had some sort of filial or parental affection on which to build a new ethic, but this is not always born out in reality. If a lion killed the last gazelle in Africa, he would neither know nor care, although the lion would be a little concerned when he fails to find his next meal. The observation that parental and filial affection exists in nature does not prove that it evolved that way. It may be asserted that a loving God created life to enjoy parental protection and the warmth and company of others, although as we have seen, many organisms and human cultures do not follow its lead, preferring conflict to love.

Huxley suggested that some animals prefer the company of others, often flocking together for a desire for community, and to protect from predatory danger. As an example, rooks will flock together in the search for food, but the crow on the other hand is a solitary bird, living largely on its own. However, these two birds are very similar, and it is virtually impossible to tell the difference between a crow and rook in flight. Huxley believed that fear of exclusion through anti-social behaviour may play a part in building an ethical standard, but this can be shown to be flawed logic. There may indeed be fear of exclusion from a group, especially in survival terms, but this does not lead to loving ethics, only to grudging obedience. Are we to love, simply because of fear of exclusion from a group?

As an example from nature, it may be asked whether the crow is less ethical than the rook because it doesn't flock together? A desire for community living does not exist in many animals, but that doesn't make these solitary animals less ethical than their more friendly cousins. What is more is that many people who engage in anti-social and unethical behaviour even prefer the company of others, sometimes living in large extended families, or small tribal groups. The football hooligan is a classic example of this, loving his own kind, and flocking together for protection, but trashing and abusing those of a different team. A desire for community living has nothing to do with good ethical conduct. In fact it is the ability to choose to love even one's enemies, or the naturally unlovable, that is the mark of true morality. This is the exact opposite of survival instincts, which can only seek personal advantage. It also seems that once again, evolution wants it both ways. Some organisms have evolved to utilise symbiosis, or the herd instinct, or parental and filial affections because it gives benefit in survival, whereas others have not because it gives benefit to survival. A case of heads I win, tails you lose.

In an essay on evolution and ethics, Huxley preferred to discuss the evolution of ethics, rather than the ethics of evolution, and seems to follow Hobbes ideas. Huxley recognised the difficulties in bridging the ethical gap in an evolutionary paradigm, although as usual his main line of attack was to discredit traditional Christianity. He focused on the traditions of the Greeks and Indians, and suggested that good and bad come to all men without regard for each person's goodness or worth, suggesting that it is all the work of accidents of nature. He also expressed his belief that one day people will come to understand how ethics evolved outside of a religious framework.

'The propounders of what are called the "ethics of evolution," when the 'evolution of ethics' would usually better express the object of their speculations, adduce a number of more or less interesting facts and more or less sound arguments in favour of the origin of the moral sentiments, in the same way as other natural phenomena, by a process of evolution. I have little doubt, for my own part, that they are on the right track; but as the immoral sentiments have no less been evolved, there is, so far, as much natural sanction for the one as the other. The thief and the murderer follow nature just as much as the philanthropist. Cosmic evolution may teach us how the good and the evil tendencies of man may have come about; but, in itself, it is incompetent to furnish any better reason why what we call good is preferable to what we call evil than we had before. Some day, I doubt not, we shall arrive at an understanding of the evolution of the aesthetic faculty; but all the understanding in the world will neither increase nor diminish the force of the intuition that this is beautiful and that is ugly.' [19]

This failure reveals an unbridgeable gap that, although Huxley believed would be crossed by evolution, has not been closed in the hundred or so years since Huxley spoke. It cannot explain the much greater capacity for moral thought that mankind has over all other animals, and it cannot explain the very knowledge of good and evil itself, nor how we should determine which actions are good and which are bad. Huxley also recognises that mankind has a desire and need to subdue and civilise nature, and not allow it to run out of control.

'Let us understand, once for all, that the ethical progress of society depends, not on imitating the cosmic process, [evolution] still less in running away from it, but in combating it. It may seem an audacious proposal thus to pit the microcosm against the macrocosm and to set man to subdue nature to his higher ends; but I venture to think that the great intellectual difference between the ancient times with which we have been occupied and our day, lies in the solid foundation we have acquired for the hope that such an enterprise may meet with a certain measure of success.' [20]

In both regards, of recognising the reality of good and evil, and the need to subdue nature, Huxley is merely acknowledging what Genesis records from the beginning. That mankind chose to partake of the knowledge of good and evil in defiance of God, and that mankind's purpose was, and is, to fill the earth and subdue nature, or more simply to work against survival of the fittest instincts and maintain biodiversity. However, explaining these in evolutionary terms is impossible. The promotion of evolution by Huxley and others, and failure to find an ethical basis for mankind from evolution, allowed others to push the more logical 'survival of the fittest' concept with terrible consequences in later decades. Huxley's rather weak argument was that 'survival of the fittest' should really mean 'survival of the best', with smaller animals sometimes better able to cope with the competition for food and resources.

'Men in society are undoubtedly subject to the cosmic process. As among other animals, multiplication goes on without cessation, and involves severe competition for the means of support. The struggle for existence tends to eliminate those less fitted to adapt themselves to the circumstances of their existence. The strongest, the most self-assertive, tend to tread down the weaker. But the influence of the cosmic process on the evolution of society is the greater the more rudimentary its civilization. Social progress means a checking of the cosmic process at every step and the substitution for it of another, which may be called the ethical process; the end of which is not the survival of those who may happen to be the fittest, in respect of the whole of the conditions which obtain, but of those who are ethically the best.' [21]

According to Huxley, 'survival of the best' then leads to an improving civilisation, although here Huxley is playing with words again. Huxley replaces 'fittest' for 'best', and then changes 'best' to mean best ethical conduct with utopian undertones. This is an illogical premise, that nature progresses through survival of the fittest, but now mankind progresses socially by setting aside survival of the fittest for those who have the best ethical conduct. Does greater civilisation mean better able to survive in evolutionary terms? It doesn't work that way for all other animals so why should it suddenly change for mankind in evolutionary terms?

However, it is the Christian who is called to live by faith and trust that God will provide, while setting aside one's own immediate interest for the sake of others. In doing so a strong and loving civilisation is constructed because of God's faithfulness to bless those who give. The classic example is Abraham who let his nephew Lot choose the best pastureland, while Abraham raised sheep in a desert. As the story turns out it was faithful Abraham who prospered. This principle of faith and trust bringing benefit can only work in theistic terms if the meek are really going to inherit the earth. As St. Paul points out:

'He [Abraham] believed God, and it was credited to him as righteousness. Understand, then, that those who believe are children of Abraham. The Scripture foresaw that God would justify the Gentiles by faith, and announced the gospel in advance to Abraham: "All nations will be blessed through you." So those who have faith are blessed along with Abraham, the man of faith.' *(Galatians 3:6-9)*

Of course some benefit in terms of survival does come from leading a disciplined life, but discipline by its very nature requires training, and as may be observed in the West, people's natural inclination is to reject the discipline that comes from faith. Huxley is entirely wrong to try and ascribe the observed beneficial consequences of faithful Judeo-Christian service to evolution.

It is rather ironic that although the official naturalistic science community has such a low regard of Christianity, Christianity is seen by many biocentric environmentalists as being part of that same official scientific establishment that pursues scientific progress at the expense of everything else. As has been shown in a previous chapter, it was in fact Huxley and his supporters who promoted science as a positivist substitute for religion, and turned it into the progressive 'master of the world' able to answer all the problems of life. As we have seen, Lynn White tried to place at least part of the blame on Christianity, but the wide acceptance of White's idea reveals a bias against Christianity, which can only be explained in part by White's paper. The overriding scientific paradigm of Huxley, which places materialism above everything else, must take the wider blame. Huxley was skilled at passing life's ills onto Christianity. Incidentally this skill in passing the blame is shared by Darwin's and Huxley's supporters and followers, and Christians continue to face criticism from godless forces that are more culpable for much of the wrong in the world.

It is materialistic Darwinian philosophy that most powerfully promotes the inevitability of technological progressive change, whereas Christianity has only occasionally flirted with the idea, despite White's accusations. In the ex-Soviet countries where the material creed of atheistic socialism and natural science asserted a belief in godless progress without question, we find greater damage to the environment than in the West. Marxism is at heart a materialistic creed derived from a belief in evolution. Another creed to come out of Darwinian materialism is 'greed is good' capitalism, which also exploits nature for selfish ends.

The deep biocentric environmentalists therefore accuse Christianity of giving moral authority to technological progress, while unwittingly upholding the basis for technological progress through the acceptance of the brutal, materialistic concept of Darwinian survival of the fittest, which forms the theological foundation for belief in godless progress. McGrath comments that as a result of the pretentious intellectual systems that have dominated Western society over the past 200 years we have lost touch with nature and instead developed our own worlds. As a result of this decoupling from nature, people neglect the environment and fail to recognise their dependence on the countryside, whereas for previous generations care for the land was of vital importance. McGrath comments that it is technology and urbanisation that have separated modern humanity from nature, and Christianity should not be implicated. As a result of this separation from nature, some have exploited it without regard, while others have romanticised it with fictional nostalgia.[22]

It is the move towards materialistic, atheistic humanism, with its religious devotion to science as the answer to all life's problems, that most powerfully upholds and pursues technological progress that then leads to environmental damage. Technology and urbanisation have also led to a lack of connection to the land among ordinary people. Deep biocentric environmentalists fail to see where the real blame lies and often become pagan or neo-pagan as a result, rejecting the founder of Christianity, Jesus Christ. Biocentric environmentalists should instead consider rejecting unfettered survival of the fittest if they are genuinely concerned for the environment, and adopt the Judeo-Christian stewardship position instead.

However, this has not yet happened, and many extreme biocentric environmentalists want to reduce the human population, and some even promote extreme ideas close to those of Spencer, Galton, Haeckel and later Hitler, to preserve the environment and animal rights. There is flawed logic in the evolutionary deep biocentric view of nature, which actually undermines the very idea of animal rights. If mankind is reduced to the level of animals, as Darwin asserted, then everything mankind does, as being part of the great natural unknowing struggle to survive and increase, is surely acceptable. The logic of the biocentric argument absolves mankind from having civil responsibility to care for nature, because mankind becomes another beast of the field.

Extending parental or filial affection to the whole of nature including mankind is absurd, because the raising of more young would override everything, and according to Darwin inter-tribal or inter-species competition is part of his evolutionary paradigm. Darwinian affections are in fact limited, haphazard and partial. Wherever biocentric environmentalists get their deep concern for nature from, it does not come from being just another beast in the field, or through weak Darwinian affections, and this deep environmental concern invalidates biocentricity itself. If animals and plants are to have any rights at all by extending civilisation to nature, they do not derive from Darwinism, but from a loving Creator.

There is a much deeper urge in humanity to protect nature, which is at heart a function of a spiritual reality, and that spiritual reality finds its most consistent and loving heart in the Judeo-Christian Scriptures. Mankind is the only natural entity that cares, or can care for the wider environment in which we live. When we damage the environment, we have the capacity to know what we have done, and work out ways to change our behaviour in the future. Deep environmental and biocentric scientists accept and promote evolution, even though it is this same popularised view of evolution, the more logical survival of the fittest view, which gives credence to the concept of scientific progress, which damages the environment and not true Christianity. Spencer's, and more especially Hitler's view of the 'Iron Logic of Nature' became the reality of evolution despite weak protestations from Darwin and Huxley.

> 'When man attempts to rebel against the iron logic of Nature, he comes into struggle with the principle to which he himself owes his existence as man.' [23]

> 'How ... can man reverse the law of life?' [24]

Although Huxley rejected Spencer's more brutal view of evolution when it came to sociological human affairs, survival of the fittest is in reality the only Darwinian view as far as nature is concerned. Much of Spencer's social Darwinism has declined, except that in business it is still maintained by a powerful capitalist force.

Huxley was also the one who promoted Comte's scientific positivism, which is the overriding paradigm today in the capitalist

West, although Huxley thought that he had rejected Comte's idea of setting up a scientific clergy. Huxley seemed to favour a non-conformist view of positivism, without scientific priests and bishops, but in reality a positivist clericalism has developed, with the word of the natural scientist considered almost divine. Darwinism has become a religion, with Huxley and Darwin seen as positivist equivalents of Paul and Peter. Positivist science and the naturalistic scientific community wedded to big business have become 'Catholicism *minus* Christianity'.

> Nothing can be clearer. Comte's ideal, as stated by himself, is Catholic organization without Catholic doctrine, or, in other words, Catholicism *minus* Christianity.' [25]

> 'Rightly or wrongly, this was the impression which, all those years ago, the study of M. Comte's works left on my mind, combined with the conviction, which I shall always be thankful to him for awakening in me, that the organization of society upon a new and purely scientific basis is not only practicable, but is the only political object much worth fighting for.' [26]

In attempting to account for everything in purely natural terms, evolutionary science has overthrown the accountability that mankind has towards God through the traditional ideas of natural law and natural theology. Once again, Huxley hated this tradition, and it is the logic of unfettered survival of the fittest and godless progress which damages the environment, not true Christianity. Although survival of the fittest is observed in nature, the injunction given to mankind was to *subdue* the earth, or more simply to limit the extent of survival instincts within nature and among people. Mankind has been called to live by faith, not a grasping, selfish survival instinct. But Huxley commented:

> 'Now let me tell you quite frankly, that I almost think it beneath the dignity of my calling, as a man of science, to listen to such objections as these. If it be *really* true that science is opposed to religion, all I can say is, so much the worse for religion. If science is *really* opposed to traditions, the sooner the traditions vanish and are no more seen or heard of, the better. For science, and the methods of science, are the masters of the world.' [27]

The blend of Spencer's view of unrestrained capitalism, with Huxley's scientific 'masters of the world' is best illustrated with the debate on genetically modified crops. The main drivers for change are global companies who want to use science and technology to make money for their shareholders, and scientists want to pursue their technology without moral restraints. Without the restraint that comes from viewing nature and humanity as being sacred, there is no moral objection to altering God's creation. This is because nature is viewed in only material terms, believing that genes just evolved from one species to another through a process of random mutations. However, the Christian view is that we should be very careful in fiddling with genes because it may legitimately be claimed that God has placed certain genes in certain species for a reason. The Mosaic Law *(Leviticus 19:19)* forbids the mating of different kinds of animal. Genetic modification, which mixes up the gene pools from different animals in a similar way, is in effect breaking this law. Of course Christianity has moved away from a strict legalistic interpretation of the Mosaic Law, and believes instead that the Law of Moses provides a broad framework for maintaining personal, social and environmental health. As an aside, selective breeding does not violate the law because it is bringing out genes within created kinds of the same type of animals, which is permissible.

History is littered with technological disasters because mankind abused the created order. BSE or Mad Cow Disease came about because scientists deemed it acceptable to turn cows into cannibals, by putting protein from dead bovines back into cow feed. When we change the glory of creation to genetic accidents in time, then we reduce nature to mere objects to be tampered with according to human will. It is ironic that this is called progress. However, Christianity is not responsible for giving moral authority to the abuse of creation in this way, but Darwinism most definitely is because it has sought to overthrow the Christian basis for ethics, and has in effect turned mankind into gods. It is a humanistic approach to science that gives rise to the accusation of 'playing God'. Darwin believed that his theory would place mankind among the animals, but in reality it has worked to place him on God's throne. Huxley also set up the 'X Club' with other like minded scientists, with the purpose of pursuing science without recourse to 'religious dogma' and also worked to instil a sense of conflict with religion in order to undermine it.

The Christian stewardship role of mankind is to govern wisely and subdue the earth, which is to mitigate the excesses of survival of the fittest and to live in harmony with nature. Most people view the extinction of various species as being morally wrong, and indeed it is surely a Christian duty to protect vulnerable species from extinction where possible and maintain bio-diversity, because all are part of God's creation. A purely logical Darwinian view would say that extinction is part of the progressive change process so that new and better species can survive and come to the fore.

To highlight the work of one Christian environmentalist and humanitarian, it is worth looking briefly at a more recent pioneer in this area, the German Albert Schweitzer. Schweitzer worked as a missionary in Africa and paid for his work through musical recitals in Europe. He believed that all life was sacred and worthy of respect and developed an ethic based on *reverence for life*. Schweitzer says that there should be a compulsion to help and protect others, that every moral person should feel within himself or herself. To uplift and protect life is seen as good, but the desire to destroy, repress or injure life is evil. This, to Schweitzer, is a fundamental ethical principle and he places it almost as a definition of good and evil.[28]

While we may assert that this is good, it may be argued that Schweitzer overstated his case because he includes such things as tearing a leaf, or plucking a flower, or even crushing an insect as being evil. However, we all have to eat, even if fruitarian, and sometimes it is necessary to crush a mosquito or step on a nettle to protect a child. But Schweitzer was presenting a general principle that remains valid, that causing unnecessary suffering to animals through a callous disregard for their welfare is wrong. Schweitzer recognised the need to protect people, and sometimes to kill animals for food and clothing, although he hated using insecticide and would sooner save the life of a mosquito than kill it. However, the need to kill for food should always be done responsibly with careful, conscious thought. Schweitzer developed his idea based on the German *ehrfurcht vor dem leben* (reverence for life), which implies an attitude of awe and wonder.[29] For Schweitzer, reverence for life was more of an attitude of who we are as Christians, than a moral law to follow religiously. In many ways reverence for life appears to extend the teaching of Jesus, of 'love thy neighbour' to the realm of nature as well. Alister McGrath, with *The Re-enchantment of Nature*, has also proposed that a sense of wonder of the natural world should inform our ethical conduct as Christians.[30]

So many of the environmental and human centred ethical controversies we find today are caused by the assumption that scientific progress is inevitable, and that it should be pursued by pushing back or denying the boundaries of traditional Christian based ethics. However, it was Francis Bacon who believed that a combination of 'sound reason and true religion' would mean that human power over nature would be exercised in a responsible fashion. On the Utility of Science he commented:

> 'But if a man endeavor to establish and extend the power and dominion of the human race over the universe, his ambition (if ambition it can be called) is without doubt both a more wholesome thing and a more noble than the [desire for personal or political power]. Now the empire of man over things depends wholly on the arts and sciences. For we cannot command nature except by obeying her. ... If the debasement of arts and sciences to purposes of wickedness, luxury, and the like, may be made a ground of objection, let no one be moved thereby. For the same may be said of all earthly goods; of wit, courage, strength, beauty, wealth, light itself, and the rest. Only let the human race recover that right over nature which belongs to it by divine bequest, and let power be given it; the exercise thereof will be governed by sound reason and true religion.' [31]

Many environmentalists have accused Bacon of effectively endorsing the rape and torture of the natural world. However, McGrath defends Bacon and believes that he encouraged science to act only in line with Scriptural injunctions. Bacon's language is closer to the idea of harnessing fire or the wind for useful service than images of rape and torture, and Bacon promoted the twin books of God's Word and God's Works. McGrath comments that Bacon's words, claiming the need to 'hound nature in her wanderings' so as to 'lead and drive her', cannot be taken as deploying images of rape or torture, but are instead a description of developing controlled experiments with the aim of enabling scientific experimentation.[32]

However, it is godless man who wants to take total control of nature without a moral conscience, whether it is genetic engineering, human cloning, embryo research, the never ending encroachment of concrete over green field sites, or the endless march of technology without ethical boundaries. This then begs the question. How should Christians view progress? Do we accept the assumptions of perpetual progress, or do we favour a stewardship role in the world, or do we see our role as one of restoring the natural world to its Edenic perfection? In many ways, Christians should see their role as one of rebuilding, or re-establishing the world under God's government, with Christ as the enthroned King, Creator and Saviour. This is certainly the view of many Evangelical Christians, with the development of the Restoration movement in the twentieth century,[33] which has many similarities to traditional views on millenarianism. It is also the view of the Roman Catholic Church, with the Pope seen as Christ's representative on earth, and most Anglicans take a similar view.

However, do Christians also see the inevitability of progressive change? There does seem to be times of wild optimism and overwhelming pessimism as events unfold, as Saint Augustine of Hippo would have observed. The South Sea Bubble, and the boom and bust of successive stock market bubbles, perhaps best highlights this swing in sentiment. However, knowledge is built upon knowledge, and technology and scientific know-how increases over the years, but the question of how that knowledge is used determines whether we live in a moral society or not. Simply because it is possible for us to do amazing things with science, does not mean that we should do those things. It is the traditional Christian faith that should provide the ethical voice in our world and give moral guidance to research scientists involved in technological change. Scientists and industrialists who seek to make moral judgements are stepping outside of their own competencies.

In the Biblical account of creation, the perfect Garden of Eden was ruined by the sin of the first human beings. Eve disobeyed God, when she took the fruit from the forbidden tree, although it was a man who carried out the first violent act when Cain killed Abel, and God placed the blame on Adam for eating the fruit. This story introduces the two theological concepts of the fall from perfection, and original sin. However, later the Bible goes on to show how it is God's long term plan to rebuild the Edenic perfection, under His authority. Christians believe that it is the function of the church to govern and restore the world, to be salt and light.

A vision by Daniel perhaps illustrates this point more clearly, recorded in Daniel chapter two. Daniel interpreted Nebuchadnezzar's dream of a large statue, and saw a rock fall at the feet of the brilliant idol which represented a number of godless human empires. This rock destroyed the idol and grew into a great mountain and covered the earth. Incidentally, atheistic humanists are deeply troubled by the book of Daniel, because it points to the coming of Christ, even though it predates Christ by many centuries. Christ even quoted from the book. The vision of the rock though highlights how the Church of Jesus Christ, filled with God's Spirit, and representing God's Kingdom on earth, will ultimately triumph in humility over proud and unprincipled humanistic empires. This battle will finally be won when Christ returns.

Earlier in Genesis, we find the first sign of God's plan of restoration, when He appears to Abraham and promises to bless the whole world through his seed. This story also introduces the concept of fruitful prosperity for obedience, which is repeated in the Law of Moses, where God sets before the Israelites a blessing and a curse. Blessing for obeying God's commands, and a curse for rebellion. In fact we find this right through the Bible. 'Cursed is the ground because of you' were God's words to Adam and Cain. Noah had to endure the ultimate oceanic catastrophe through others' sins. However, Abraham received blessing for his obedience. He prospered, and grew rich through the rearing of sheep in what had been a desert because he obeyed God. The Apostle Paul, some two thousand years later, states that this blessing passed to the Christian church, to those who live by faith. *(Galatians 3:14)*. So Christianity should view its role in the world as one of restoring nature to perfection through humility, discipline, obedience and working with

God's grace, and therefore heralding in the Government of Christ on earth. This leads to a fruitful life in submission to Christ, in harmony with creation. Christians also believe in an increase in fruitful prosperity for this obedience.

This idea of fruitful prosperity is not about gaining material wealth for selfish motives, but it ties in with giving to others, and contributes towards the health and well-being of the land, which for instance goes on to flow with milk and honey, and provides grazing for cattle and sheep. There is both an environmental and social aspect to fruitful prosperity. Prosperity is about the divine economic laws of sowing and reaping, and is part of the environmental principle of stewardship, and the principle of compassionate social provision for the poor. If we sow good seeds we will reap a good harvest, but if we sow bad seeds then we will reap a poor harvest. It is in the interest of all of us, and especially Christians, to care for the land.

> 'The desert and the parched land will be glad; the wilderness will rejoice and blossom. Like the crocus, it will burst into bloom; it will rejoice greatly and shout for joy.' *(Isaiah 35:1-2)*

So the Christian's view of progress and ethical concern should be in terms of careful stewardship, restoration and fruitful prosperity, working with God's grace and under His Sovereignty, managing the present through effective stewardship and working towards the restoration of a perfect creation under Christ's authority. But this is not the same as the humanistic ideal of progress, or the cult of scientific modernism, which desires to use scientific knowledge and power outside of a spiritual and moral dimension. In fact the vision interpreted by Daniel shows how godless humanistic systems will all ultimately fail, as was the fate of Stalinist and Leninist materialistic systems, and Hitler's fascist state. In the end, Christ will prove triumphant over all godless systems. It was also Nebuchadnezzar's proud boast that he did not need God's grace. His proud comment condemned him to seven years of madness, eating grass like the wild animals.

'Is not this the great Babylon I have built as the royal residence, by my mighty power and for the glory of my majesty?' *(Daniel 4:30)*

According to tradition, Satan's pride also caused him to lose his place in heaven, when he tried to ascend to the throne of God. *(Isaiah 14:12-17)* But there is fruitful blessing for humility and obedience, to live in harmony with nature as stewards, working with God to bring the whole of creation back to a most perfect state under Christ's authority.

Notes and References

[1] Coleridge, S.T., *The Rime of the Ancient Mariner*, 1798. Various revisions: <http://etext.lib.virginia.edu/stc/Coleridge/poems/Rime_Ancient_Mariner.html>, Accessed March 2006.

[2] White, L., Jr., *The Historical Roots of our Ecologic Crisis*, Science, Vol. 155, No. 3767, pp. 1203-1207, 10th March 1967.

[3] Ibid., p. 1205.

[4] Ibid., p. 1206.

[5] Kenny, A., *Down with Superstition*, Spectator, pp. 14-15, 20th March, 2004.

[6] White, op. cit., pp. 1206-1207.

[7] Ibid., p. 1207.

[8] Ibid., p. 1207.

[9] McGrath, A., *The Re-enchantment of Nature*, Hodder Headline, London, p. 32, 2003.

[10] St. Patrick's *The Deer's Cry*, (trans. Meyer, K.), Selections from Ancient Irish Poetry, 1928. In: Adams, D., *The Cry of The Deer*, Triangle/SPCK, London, pp. 3-5, 1987.

[11] Passmore, J., *Man's Responsibility for Nature*, 2nd/3rd editions, Duckworth Publishing, 1980.

[12] Ibid., p. 30.

[13] Attfield, R., *The Ethics of Environmental Concern*, University of Georgia Press, 1991. (Second Edition © 1991 by the University of Georgia Press, Athens, Georgia 30602)

[14] Baillie, J., *The Belief in Progress*, Oxford University Press, London, Glasgow, Toronto, 1950.

[15] Bury, J.B., *The Idea of Progress*, Macmillan Press, London, 1920.

[16] Open University, Wye College, University of London, *Religion and Environmental Values, Christian Stewardship*, Environmental Ethics, Block A, Part 2, Section 3.2, Box 3.2, 1997.

[17] Burgess, S., *Hallmarks of Design*, 2nd ed., Day One Publications, Leominster, England, pp. 157-158, 2004.

[18] Des Jardins, J.R., *Environmental Ethics: An Introduction to Environmental Philosophy*, 3rd ed., Wadsworth Group, Thomson Learning Inc, Belmont, USA, p. 203, 2001.

[19] Huxley, T.H., *Collected Essays*, Vol. 9, *Evolution & Ethics and Other Essays*, London, pp. 79-80, 1894, (*Evolution and Ethics*, The Romanes Lecture, 1893), <http://aleph0.clarku.edu/huxley/CE9/E-E.html>, Accessed March 2006.

[20] Ibid., p. 83.

[21] Ibid., p. 81.

[22] McGrath, op. cit., p. 186.

[23] Hitler, A., *Mein Kampf*, 1933, (trans. Manheim, R.), p. 260, Hutchinson, UK, 1969. [USA copyright © 1943, renewed 1971 by Houghton Mifflin Company, all rights reserved.] Reprinted by permission of the Random House Group Ltd. and Houghton Mifflin Company.
See also: Nevard, A., *Hitler's Debt to Darwin*, Daylight No. 29, Autumn / Winter 1999; Reprint: Creation Science Movement, Pamphlet 329.

[24] Attfield, op. cit., p. 76. (Attfield comments on Spencer's view of survival of the fittest in *Social Statistics*, 1851).

[25] Huxley, T.H., *The Scientific Aspects of Positivism,* Lay Sermons, Addresses and Reviews, London, p. 133, 1870.
<http://aleph0.clarku.edu/huxley/UnColl/Rdetc/Posit.html>, Accessed March 2006. Also in: The Fortnightly Review, (Trollope, A., et. al.), (n.s.), 5, pp. 653-670, 1869.

[26] Ibid., Lay Sermons, Addresses and Reviews, p. 130.

[27] Huxley, T.H., *Science and Religion*, The Builder, Vol. 17, Museum of Geology, p. 35, January 1859.

[28] Schweitzer, A., Lemke, A.B. (trans.), *Out of My Life and Thought*, Holt, New York, p. 131, 1990.

[29] Des Jardins, op. cit., p. 136.

[30] McGrath, op cit.

[31] Bacon, F., *On the Utility of Science*, 1620. From the Instauration Magna (Great Renewal). In: Presky, M., *Mike's World History*, July 2003, Galileo Library, <www.galileolibrary.com/history/history_page_138.htm>, Accessed March 2006.

[32] McGrath, op. cit., p. 103.

[33] Walker, A., *Restoring the Kingdom*, Hodder & Stoughton, London, 1985.

Chapter 8

Progress, Deism and the Faustian Pact

'Even the humble trilobites … had eyes of extraordinary complexity, some species having at least four hundred lenses fixed on the surface of the cornea. 'This is utterly inexplicable … [without] the same Intelligent Creative power.' [1]

Robin Attfield[2] has shown that a belief in progress can be viewed as a Christian heresy despite accusations from Lynn White that Christianity has given approval to the idea of technological progress and the exploitation of nature over the years. Attfield partly based his writings on earlier works by John Baillie[3] and John Bury.[4] The rise of evolution was also influenced by progressive and deistic philosophers, and formed part of a general move away from Biblical Christianity. To counteract deistic and atheistic thought from the time of David Hume, natural theology was reworked and developed by the well-known proponent William Paley with his book *Natural Theology on Evidences and Attributes of Deity*. This chapter will look in more detail at how a belief in progress and deism developed as a move away from the traditional Christian teaching and divine grace, and therefore should be viewed as being alien to Christianity itself.

McGrath has also suggested that the rise of a belief in scientific progress, with mankind attempting to control nature, and people without need of God's grace, is akin to a Faustian pact. In this science fiction story, Dr Faust cannot gain the controlling power he desires over nature and humanity from God, so instead he makes a pact with the devil to gain that control. McGrath comments that this Faustian pact, with desire to gain power over nature, forms part of a fundamental longing in the human soul that has not been given sanction by God. He notes that throughout the twentieth century many individuals, governments and corporations were willing to enter into such a pact to gain independent power and control. Accordingly, Faustian progress is defined in terms of technological advance with little concern for the moral implications or the quality of the environment. McGrath notes that human progress can be seen through the development of weapons of war, from bows and arrows to nuclear missiles, and ultimately such progress threatens the whole of nature and humanity.[5]

The concept of natural theology held progressive godless forces at bay for many years, but Darwinian evolution argued against the main claim of natural theology, that biological organisms were designed by an intelligent being. Without sufficient evidence, the Darwinian claim was widely accepted, and this acceptance made it possible to overthrow the need for a creator and law giver, and therefore also overthrow Christian-centred ethics. However, science has moved on, and today the appearance of design in nature is being reawakened with, for instance, the immense complexity of the cell now becoming known. It is increasingly apparent that Darwin's theory is flawed, and the ethical basis is again being challenged. This challenge does not only come from Christians, but also from other faiths, who also reject the idea of perpetual scientific progress without reference to some sort of spiritual value. To Darwin, the cell was just a black box, but today enormous complexity is apparent, with an increase in knowledge of the cell's internal structure and genetic code.[6] Natural theology is reasserting itself as the *Intelligent Design Movement*,[7] and the need for Christian based ethics is once again coming to the fore. This is especially important as genetic engineering is throwing up tremendous ethical challenges for this and future generations.

With respect to natural theology, Lynn White states that the early church, especially in the Greek East, saw nature as primarily having symbolic importance, with the ant providing a sermon to sluggards and the flames being symbols of the soul's aspiration. As we have seen, White went on to point to St. Francis of Assisi's view, which saw the ant and the flame praising God together with mankind. According to White, by the 13th century natural theology had turned into an exploration of creation itself to discover the mind of God as a way of thinking God's thoughts after him.[8] As such, modern science grew out of Christian theology, with religious devotion inspiring it and the *creation* account giving *science* direction and impetus. White comments:

> 'If so, then modern Western science was cast in a matrix of Christian theology. The dynamism of religious devotion, shaped by the Judeo-Christian dogma of creation, gave it impetus.' [9]

But what are we to make of nature? What role does natural theology play in true Christianity? Does it give mankind symbolic lessons as sermons from ants, or does it help us to explore the mind of God, or is it as St. Francis of Assisi saw, our fellow nature brethren praising God together with mankind? St. Paul saw nature as pointing to the existence of God, and showing His 'invisible qualities [of] eternal power and divine nature.' *(Romans 1:20)* This accordingly highlights God's Holy character, which calls for an obedient response from mankind. Nature therefore should inspire worship of God, but mankind falls into idolatry and worships created things instead of the Creator. In this sense, nature does play the role of preacher towards mankind. Christians also see nature as being a provider of food, warmth and shelter.

However, Christianity has through the ages also seen nature as being in a partnership of praise towards God, much as St. Francis of Assisi would have wished. The trees of the fields for instance 'shall clap their hands', and the songbirds sing out the glory of God in their dawn chorus. In this sense, the natural world and mankind are created for God's own pleasure. Mankind therefore has great responsibility to care for the world in which we live.

The Bible clearly sets out consequences for sin. However, the theological concept of original sin, expounded by Saint Augustine, has been questioned over the centuries. Philosophers such as John Locke, in *The Reasonableness of Christianity*, believed that the concept left mankind totally incapable of self-improvement, and therefore totally dependent on divine grace.[10] Locke believed that education could allow people to become more moral, although he perhaps did not fully understand the theological concept of grace, or human nature. The Judeo-Christian tradition has always believed that training and education are the ways of overcoming the rebellious human will, working with God's grace, and the role of teacher was ranked alongside pastor and apostle by St. Paul. *(Ephesians 4:11)* However, Augustine's view of original sin was perhaps over-stated, and many Christians have attempted to balance the doctrine with personal responsibility. Original sin was atoned for by Christ's sacrificial death on the cross, and therefore mankind must cooperate with divine grace, and is capable in partnership with God of improvement through education and discipline. It is clear from Scripture that we have responsibility and will be held accountable for our own actions.

The twin themes of future hope and past history have captivated minds over the centuries. On the one hand people are looking for a progressive improvement, or hope in the future, and on the other hand they are looking over their shoulders and scrutinising the past. The Bible gives both an historic account of past events and moral conclusions, and points to a better future if we will learn from past mistakes and worship God faithfully. The Pagan Greeks and Romans had a rather more tragic view of their past, with no overall hope. St. Augustine had originally criticised those Christians who believed that the world would just get better over time, and also spoke against the more cyclical pagan view of history. Today, when we consider the issue of evolutionary origins, we must carefully consider how the theme of progress throughout history has helped to give rise to molecule to man evolution and the natural atheistic belief system in the West.

Attfield goes on to show how the modern view of the inevitability of progress grew out of France after the revolution.[11] In the seventeenth century, Bacon and Descartes began to promote the idea that the pursuit of scientific knowledge would enable mankind to gain power over nature and natural forces, although they did not see this as inevitable, but as a result of a conscious effort, working under God's grace. The twelfth century philosopher Joachim of Flora also believed that it was God's providence that human development should be progressive. He saw a coming millennium age of love and justice under the Holy Spirit.[12] Throughout later centuries, others began to believe that increasing scientific knowledge from the likes of Newton, Copernicus and Galileo, would lead to greater human happiness. Influential writers on progress included Turgot, Leibniz, and Fontenelle. Gottfried Wilhelm Leibniz for his part was also an influential theoretician of geology and attempted to blend his progressive ideas into the geological evidence and so give an historic account of the earth.

It was a contemporary of Fontenelle, Abbe de Saint Pierre, who believed that an inevitable increase in scientific knowledge would lead to continued social and moral progress. For him it was human well-being that was the reason behind divinely inspired progress.[13] These ideas led to discontent with the status quo, and pressure for reform at a time when the state of France under Louis XV believed in the authority of the divine right of kings. Later, Chastellux and Condorcet began to build the history of progressive change. Condorcet taught that there were nine ages of progress and the nations were about to enter a tenth age of equality, health and virtue.[14] However, many of these writers continued to rely on divine grace to lead the world to its ideal state. Kant also agreed with Joachim, that God's grace was necessary for progress, although Kant also believed that mankind's revulsion of violent struggle would cause people to seek peaceful ways of progressing. Kant's pupil Johann Herder went on to derive laws of history, one of which was that the destructive powers of nature would one day be withered away by maintaining powers. Other German philosophers, such as Johann Fichte, Friedrich Schelling and Georg Hegel, began to construct the history of sociological development without reference to divine grace, believing that mankind had, and would continue to shape his own moral development. This is very much a humanistic view of development, but it becomes clear that the philosophical ground was laid for the theory of naturalistic evolution to rise to the fore.[15]

Hegel too developed his dialectic view that a thesis must be opposed by an antithesis. In the middle, people tend towards the centre ground, which he called a synthesis. He taught that a society could be moved towards a thesis by exerting pressure over a period of time. In doing this, it is possible to establish a new synthesis closer to the desired thesis. Revolutionary forces have used this process, as can be seen for instance with the struggle between capitalism and Marxism representing a thesis and antithesis. Politically correct secular forces continue to seek to undermine the Christian church in the present day in the same way, by seeking to set a new consensus or synthesis over for instance the issue of gay marriage and gay clergy, this away from traditional Christian values.

At the same time as the belief in progress was on the rise in Europe, others began to question Christian theology more directly. The philosophy now known as deism developed as a broad church, with some promoting a form of pantheism while others could be considered Christian deists. At its most simple, deists believe in the 'absentee landlord' view of God, or more simply that God created everything and then left the universe to run according to divinely preset natural laws. God is seen as being both distant and powerless to act, either being unable or unwilling to intervene in the natural realm that He set in motion. One pioneer of deism who promoted a pantheist view of nature was the Dutch Jew Baruch Spinoza.[16] Holland at this time was a relatively tolerant place for intellectuals, and Spinoza's parents had migrated to this small state where they felt safe. However, Spinoza's most controversial writing, *Tractatus Theologico-Politicus*, published anonymously in 1670, set him against both his own Orthodox Jewish faith and the Roman Catholic Church.[17] He was expelled from the synagogue and his book officially banned by the Dutch state and the Roman Catholic Church after four years. Spinoza, like many Jews, found himself living as an alien and migrant, wandering around Europe with no homeland and an apparently distant God who no longer seems able to hear the prayers of the faithful Jew. Bearing this in mind, it is perhaps understandable that he should have developed the deistic view of God that he did.

Spinoza believed that God was to be found everywhere within nature, and accordingly claimed that everything we view as nature was in fact of one substance, which he considered God. He saw Christian and Jewish faith as simply the blind and uneducated following of tradition and human priests. He claimed that the Holy

Scriptures were corrupted by man, and denied miracles as the simple understanding of ancient people. For instance, he asserted that Ezra had written the Torah and the books of the pre-exile period from Genesis to I and II Kings.[18] Spinoza was a rationalist, and believed that he was trying to place hermeneutics, the study of Scripture, on a more scientific footing. Accordingly, miracles simply could not happen either, as they would violate natural laws, and as we have seen, Spinoza's view was that nature and God were one and the same, and so God would be violating himself in working miracles.[19] This was indeed controversial. However, not all rationalists were deistic in their view, G.W. Leibniz for instance was a German protestant and honoured by the Royal Society in London.[20]

One flaw in the rationalists' argument was that they denied the need for empirical evidence, believing that reason alone was enough to understand everything. However, a number of British empiricists, such as John Locke, continued to assert the need for experience in knowledge. Locke believed there was good reason to believe the resurrection and other miracles, because these were in themselves the experiences of Christian faith, and as such, miracles were accorded a place above reason. However, David Hume later blended Spinoza's deistic view with the empiricism of Locke. Incidentally, Hume's father Joseph spent time in Holland where Spinoza had once lived. After impregnating a servant girl outside of marriage, Joseph Hume fled to Utrecht in 1702 where he studied law for three years to escape the family dishonour.[21]

David Hume believed that the only reality was that which can be experienced personally, and he doubted the evidence and testimony of miracles found in the Bible.[22] Hume's view though may be considered far too narrow, as there is a lot of scientific empirical evidence that we simply have to take on trust. We do not have, for instance, time to carry out all experiments for ourselves and must trust those who carry them out to tell the truth. This is no different to the trust placed in Christian witnesses to the resurrection and the other miracles of Jesus, in believing that the truth has been recorded accurately. The Apostles were, after all, willing to die for their belief that Jesus Christ was raised from the dead.

Following Spinoza's work, deism, and his views of higher

Biblical criticism, spread across Europe both in France and Germany, and to some extent in Britain as well. Spinoza himself lived an apparently good life and this attracted others to his views, and the beliefs of the deists were in many ways not that far from Christian doctrines. They believed in a benevolent deity who dispensed some grace, with reward and punishment for good and bad conduct. They saw the value of repentance, good ethical conduct, and worship, but what they rejected was the authority of Scripture and the power of God to work miracles in the past, present and future. They viewed miracles as unscientific because they were not generally observed. Accordingly, God was seen as being the initial great designer and law-giver, who now allows people to work out their own lives as they see fit.

A number of early English deists, such as Lord Herbert of Cherbury (1583-1648), viewed their own ideas as a search for finding a rational explanation for Christian faith without recourse to Biblical revelation.[23] They saw faith as reasonable because of the evidence of nature, and their work was not an attempt to denigrate the traditional faith that they valued. This line of argument was virtually the same as the natural theology of Aquinas. However, later writers such as John Toland, in *Christianity Not Mysterious* (1696), and Matthew Tindal in *Christianity as Old as Creation* (1730), took this one stage further and saw Christianity as a natural religion, with the miraculous aspects seen as mere superstition. Anthony Collins, in *Discourses of Free Thinking* (1713), attacked Old Testament prophecy, claiming that it did not accurately predict the ministry of Jesus. Thomas Woolston, with *Discourses on the Miracles of our Saviour* (1727-1729), disputed the miracles of Jesus and His resurrection. Woolston was later fined for blasphemy and imprisoned because he could not find the money to pay.[24]

As a result of this trial, and Woolston's fate, and also general religious revival, deism went underground in Britain and one leading Bishop, Thomas Sherlock, writing in *The Trial of The witnesses of the Resurrection* (1729), argued that the evidence from eye witness accounts for the resurrection of Jesus would stand up in a court of law. A few years later Joseph Butler in *Analogy of Religion* (1736) asserted that evidence for a supernatural Christian faith could be seen from both nature and the testimony of Christian faith itself.[25] Anyone wanting to write about deism in the latter part of the eighteenth century and early nineteenth century tended to hide their views in the philosophy of natural theology, a more acceptable and safer path to follow, even if somewhat ambiguous. This was the case with James Hutton. Deism and higher Biblical criticism, also known as neology, that was popular in parts of Europe, was also held at bay in Britain, and there was a reaction against the revolution in France. The Anglo-Saxon world was experiencing an awakening of faith through the preaching of men like John Wesley, George Whitfield, and Jonathan Edwards, and also by other high church Bishops such as Samuel Horsley, and William Van Mildert.

When we look a little deeper, we can find the root of Darwinian theory firmly planted in the Scottish Enlightenment of David Hume, James Hutton, Adam Smith and Erasmus Darwin, among others.[26] Hume, Smith and Hutton lived in Edinburgh at the same time, and were acquainted with each other, sharing mutual friends, and of course Erasmus was Darwin's grandfather who had proposed his own theory of evolution. Erasmus Darwin later set up the Birmingham Lunar Society and encouraged Hutton and others to join. Charles Darwin later borrowed heavily from the work of others to construct his theory. As we have seen, Hume promoted his own brand of atheism, while Hutton worked on gradual geology, and Smith developed the concept of unfettered capitalism as the most natural and efficient way of ordering the economy and for selecting who should succeed. Some saw progressive improvement in Adam Smith's theory of economic growth through laissez faire capitalism and private enterprise.[27] Charles Lyell was profoundly influenced by Hutton's work, and Darwin himself studied in Edinburgh and found Lyell's arguments fascinating while aboard *HMS Beagle*. All of these ideas find their way into Darwin's thinking. It is ironic that the city of Edinburgh was once home to John Knox the fiery Scottish preacher.

In France, Jean Jacques Rousseau and Francois Marie Arouet, better known as Voltaire, were concerned with social institutions and both became deists. Rousseau believed that existing institutions such as the state and church were responsible for all the problems he saw around him, and wrote the *Social Contract* in 1762, believing that a society is governed by a secular social contract and not by some divine right given to kings. This question did not arise so clearly in Britain, as the Magna Carta treaty had much earlier placed kings under the rule of law, and England had developed a stronger parliament system, partly through Anglo-Saxon culture and an earlier English revolution. Rousseau believed in a divine Being, but thought the mystery of God beyond human reasoning. Voltaire also believed that God should be served and worshipped, but was a major critic of organised religion, believing it to be corrupt and deceitful.[28]

The later British deists were responsible for passing the views of Spinoza and higher Biblical criticism to Germany. Although deism went underground in Britain, Germany continued the work of higher Biblical criticism. Gotthold Lessing was both a writer and dramatist and published the works of Hermann Reimarus, called *Fragments*, following his death in 1768. This book poured scorn on the Old Testament and New, and claimed that the resurrection was a fraud carried out by the Apostles who wanted an easy life, although this is difficult to sustain, bearing in mind both Jewish and Roman enemies of the early church. Reimarus had been in England for a time during the eighteenth century and had studied the work of the deists closely. Lessing tried to defend Reimarus' work, but his arguments appear both contrived and confused, and many other German scholars took up the theme of higher Biblical criticism none the less. This cast doubt on the authorship and authority of the Bible, which has continued through to the present day. Kant also leaned towards deism towards the end of his life.

The higher Biblical criticism, or neology of the deists was hidden in Britain for many years, but later became more and more apparent towards the middle of the nineteenth century. A number of writers tried to counter this rise and noted that deism was in fact endemic in the British Church, even though very few professed it openly. Many deists in Britain and Europe may also have belonged to the highly secretive society of freemasons. William Irons, in the *Whole Doctrine of Final Causes* (1836), wrote 'a large portion of what passes as Christianity is but Deism in disguise', and noted the ambiguity of natural theology and deistic thought.[29] Others, who were concerned about the rise of deism and radical political thought, included John Pye Smith with *Scripture Testimony to the Messiah* (1821), Hugh Rose on *The State of Protestant Religion in Germany* (1825) and Edward B. Pusey with his book entitled *Historical Enquiry into the Probable Causes of the Rationalist Character Lately Predominant in the Theology of Germany* (1828).[30]

On close investigation it becomes clear that deistic philosophy, possibly even gnostic or pagan in nature, has influenced the rise of gradual geology and evolution. James Hutton and Abraham Werner were certainly deistic in thought, although at a superficial level Charles Lyell showed some religious belief when it suited,[31] and sometimes appeared troubled by evolution because of its affront to Christian theology.[32] However, Lyell's real motivation is not entirely clear, and his statements often appear contradictory, seemingly manipulating people and thoughts behind the scenes, even encouraging Darwin to write *Origins*.[33] When trying to piece together a person's life, it is usually possible to follow a consistent lead between actions and written statements. Sometimes people change their views, but this is usually a consistent and well sign-posted change, as for example St. Paul's conversion on the road to Damascus. But for Lyell there is great inconsistency between public statements and private actions throughout his life.

Lyell resurrected the work of the deist Hutton in his book *The Principles of Geology*, and Lyell's book went on to influence Darwin while aboard *HMS Beagle*. Later, Lyell befriended the young Darwin who found the attention flattering and emotionally rewarding. Darwin had a troubled childhood, with an overbearing and cold father, and at first seemed to want to live a carefree life of leisure. Following the voyage of the Beagle, Darwin was drawn into a different world by his new found friends. According to Bowden, Lyell was crafting the acceptance of gradualism behind the scenes, in a carefully thought out strategy to destroy the 'Mosaic Systems', encouraging Darwin to write, while avoiding public arguments over his ideas until the time was right.[34] At other times, Lyell seemed to reject ideas of progressive organic change within the rock strata, because he feared evolutionary ideas would challenge his superficial Christian belief and damage his cause.[35] In a private letter to a close geologist friend, Lyell reveals that he is working to a long term disguised strategy of twenty to thirty years to undermine Christianity.

> 'I am sure you may get into Q.R. [Quarterly Review] what will free the science from Moses...'
>
> 'If we don't irritate, which I fear that we may (though mere history) we shall carry all with us. If you don't triumph over them, but compliment the liberality and candour of the present age, the bishops and enlightened saints will join us in despising both the ancient and modern physico-theologians. It is just the time to strike, so rejoice that, sinner as you are, the Q.R. is open to you. If I have said more than some will like, yet I give you my word that full half of my history and comments was cut out, and even many facts; because either I, or Stokes, or Broderip, [close friends of Lyell] felt that it was anticipating twenty or thirty years of the march of honest feeling to declare it undisguisedly.' [36]

Although Darwin appeared sick with worry over the implications of his writing, he was willing to follow the deceitful methodology of Lyell to attack Christianity. This is revealed in a couple of letters in his later life.

> 'Lyell is most firmly convinced that he has shaken the faith in the Deluge far more efficiently by never having said a word against the Bible, than if had acted otherwise ... I have lately read Morley's Life of Voltaire and he insists strongly that direct attacks on Christianity ... produce little permanent effect: real good seems only to follow the slow and silent attacks.' [37]

> '... yet it appears to me ... that direct arguments against Christianity and theism produce hardly any effects on the public, and freedom of thought is best provided by the [gradual] illumination of ... minds, which follow from the advance of science.' [38]

Other geologists of the time appear to have been undermined by these hidden activities. Dean William Buckland and Adam Sedgwick were Evangelical in their thinking, even if they thought the earth to be much older than the traditional Biblical timescale, but they appear concerned with the rise of evolution and the implications for the degradation of ethics. Some have argued that they were in fact semi-deists, although both Mortenson, and Forster and Marston dispute this.[39] Sedgwick in fact wrote to Darwin, pointing out a link between moral conduct and humanity's view of the material world.

> 'You have ignored this link, and if I do not mistake your meaning, you have done your best in one or two pregnant cases to break it. Were it possible (which, thank God, it is not) to break it, humanity, in my mind would suffer a damage that might brutalize it, and sink the human race into a lower grade of degradation than any into which it has fallen since written records tell us of its history.' [40]

Despite Sedgwick's assertions, evolutionists managed to break this link in the minds of many, and the debasement of ethics are now all too clear. Although Sedgwick was correct that the link couldn't be broken in theological terms, evolutionists have overcome the link by simply ignoring the theology.

It is clear that some form of deistic thought and influence permeates Protestant and Evangelical Christian theology even to this day. As a result of Luther and Calvin's teaching, many Protestant Christians believed that the age of miracles ceased with the death of the Apostles. This cessationist view was undermined by the enthusiastic faith of the Methodists, and more recently by Pentecostal and Charismatic revivals, begun in Wales and Sunderland in 1904 and in Azusa Street in Los Angeles in 1906. Although the cessationist position of Protestant faith did not deny the Biblical miracles, it seems clear that deism has had a wide and subtle influence within the Church and society.

It is the simple observation of each one of us, that miracles are not our common experience, that brings deistic thoughts to the fore. However, a lack of personal experience of the miraculous cannot disprove the reality of someone else's experience, and one's personal experience is not universal, but very limited in time and space. However, today post-modernism is awakening people's appetite for greater spiritual reality, although people are tending to look to alternative faith systems rather than Christianity.

Following the revolution in France, the themes of deism, social justice, progress and its historic development came together, with a rejection of traditional Christian thought. Saint-Simon[41] taught that a

171

new physicist religion would arise and replace Christianity with a moral and social dimension, and Auguste Comte stated that the fundamental law of history consisted 'in the growing power of altruism over egoism brought about by a fusion of intelligence and sympathy.' [42] Comte, in his book *Lessons from Positive Philosophy*, promoted the inevitability of human development through history by stating that mankind passed through various historic stages. Firstly knowledge passes through a theological state where, according to Comte, mankind invented the idea of God, then a metaphysical one where people tried to discover truth through philosophical argument, to finally arrive at a scientific stage where science would provide all the answers for understanding present and historic truth. This has become known as scientific positivism, but it is flawed logic, as Karl Popper has explained with the idea of falsification. Science cannot provide answers to un-observed and unrepeatable historic events, and as such, these ideas cannot be verified through experiment. Comte sought to set up a positive religion of humanity, with himself as the high priest. Although this movement failed at the time, the basic idea has passed into present day humanist thinking in the Western world through Thomas Huxley and his supporters, and the writings of atheistic scientists such as John Dewey who wrote the first *Humanist Manifesto*, and later Richard Dawkins. It has been noted that humanist science continues to look like a religion, with the philosophy of science accepted as divine truth, and the scientist as high priest. Darwinism, despite lack of observable evidence, is taught as observed scientific fact. As Phillip Johnson comments:

> 'Mixing religion with science is obnoxious to Darwinists only when it is the wrong religion that is being mixed. … Julian Huxley's religion of "evolutionary humanism" offered humanity the "sacred duty" and the "glorious opportunity" of seeking "to promote the maximum fulfilment of the evolutionary process on the earth." … Inspired by the same vision, the American philosopher and educational reformer John Dewey launched a movement in 1933 for "religious humanism", whose Manifesto reflected the assumption current amongst scientific naturalists at the time that the final demise of theistic religions would usher in a new era of scientific progress and social cooperation for mankind.' [43]

Comte taught that society must eventually become organised according to the social sciences, and if necessary coerced in that direction. To some extent, this belief was self-fulfilling. He saw his own development towards humanistic reason, and then applied it to the world and everyone else, although it is questionable how an ethic based on sympathy can be forced on people. Humanists today continue to promote the same idea, that an ethical system can be constructed without reference to religious thought, and it is widely held in Western thinking, although it may be noted that humanism is very limited across a global stage in comparison to the size of other faith systems. The majority of people across the world still hold to religious belief with most being monotheistic.

So the idea of inevitable progress started out as a Christian idea of divinely inspired moral and sociological improvement, perhaps even with a millennial restorative edge. Progress was originally an attempt to rebuild an Edenic perfection in cooperation with divine grace, but later became a deistic, humanistic idea of natural scientific progress a century or two later, without the need for divine guidance. By the start of the nineteenth century, the inevitability of progress was widely believed, with God relegated to standing on the sidelines and watching from a distance, unable to intervene. Attfield states that:

> 'The French thinkers of the early nineteenth century put the idea of progress firmly on the map, not least by blending the German belief in inevitable temporal development with the historically based confidence of the French enlightenment that intellectual and moral improvements would continue in the future.' [44]

Ideas of equality and civilisation, through Guizot, became blended with the belief in progress, and this led to the spread of anti authoritarianism in Britain. Robert Owen and William Godwin were the first to promote this in Britain, but later Karl Marx and Friedrich Engels took up the same idea of revolutionary social progress. Western thought clearly turned away from the ideals of Bacon, and there are many examples of technological disasters in later years because mankind has arrogantly rejected divine grace and guidance.

Bacon proposed that human power should be in submission to God.

> 'Only let the human race recover that right over nature which belongs
> to it by divine bequest, and let power be given it; the exercise thereof
> will be governed by sound reason and true religion.' [45]

It is against this background of a belief in historic and inevitable progress, without divine intervention and inspiration, that evolution arose in Britain. All that was needed now was to link human development with biological development of the species, and find a mechanism to explain how evolutionary change might come about. Various anatomists working with reptile fossils provided evidence that organic life might have progressed through the geological record. Gideon Mantell, a leading fossil collector and anatomist, claimed that there had been an *Age of Reptiles*, which preceded the age of mammals.[46] Deborah Cadbury comments that this supported the views of evolutionists, that there was a progressive process of evolutionary change from simple forms to the more advanced.[47] Mantell was not entirely happy with the conclusion of the early evolutionists, and both he and others such as Dean William Buckland and Richard Owen opposed gradual biological progression on philosophical grounds. For Buckland and Owen, the evidence from observation was also a powerful reason to oppose the progressive evolutionary theories of Jean-Baptiste Lamarck, and Geoffrey Saint-Hilaire. Mantell too struggled to come to terms with this progressive interpretation of the evidence.

Geoffrey Saint-Hilaire, for his part, had claimed that the extinct fossil reptiles had progressed through a process of evolution into more recent mammals, such as the *megatherium*. Geoffrey went further and looked for *homologies*, or equivalent parts between different kinds of animals to prove relationship. He suggested, for instance, that the hard upper shell of some insects resembled the vertebrae of reptiles, fish and mammals. Accordingly, in a paper presented in February 1830 he suggested that the hard shells of some cephalopods, such as the nautilus and fossil ammonites, were equivalent to the backbone of vertebrate fish. This was highly speculative stuff, and Cuvier easily and comprehensively dismissed his ideas, calling him a *poet*.[48]

In the first part of the nineteenth century, early theories of evolution appeared to challenge the authority of the Bible, and with it the moral and social fabric of British society. Many establishment figures felt threatened that Britain might fall into the same revolutionary fervour that had gripped France, and indeed Britain was in a state of unrest. In 1832 the Reform Bill redistributed power, giving industrial towns seats in Parliament, and increasing the size of the electorate. This small reform helped to move people away from political revolution. Owen and Buckland and many other privileged scientists took up the challenge to counter the growing menace of revolutionary and evolutionary theories, and at the time it was easy to hold evolution at bay because the promoters had only primitive theories of how this adaptation might occur.[49]

George Cuvier also roundly condemned the evolution of Geoffrey Saint-Hilaire as 'pantheism' in a public speech on the 8th May 1832 at the College de France. Cuvier gave an impassioned speech, highlighting *divine intelligence* as being behind organic life, but this brave speech took its toll on him. While many in the audience were overcome with emotion, Cuvier suffered a stroke as a result and he died six days later.[50] With the death of the great George Cuvier, people looked around for others to wear his mantle. To the dismay of Richard Owen, Professor Robert Grant, an anatomist at the University of London was proposed as the next Cuvier by the distinguished paper the *Lancet*. Thomas Wakley, the editor of this respected paper, claimed that Grant was unrivalled in the British Empire, but Grant favoured Geoffrey Saint Hilaire's evolution. Many establishment clergymen viewed the University of London as a godless place in comparison to Oxford. However, Grant's lectures, in which he introduced and promoted the progressive evolutionary ideas of the Parisians, were packed. Grant believed that as the earth cooled, the changing climate caused animals to adapt and change to their surroundings, perhaps even an ape might change into a man. Evolution was gaining ground in Britain, although the highly respected Anglican scientists continued to hold it at bay for several decades.[51] The evidence from the fossils was therefore controversial and widely challenged. On the surface, Charles Lyell did not see progress in the fossil record and was a firm opponent of Lamarck's evolution,[52] although it would seem that Lyell was biding his time waiting for Charles Darwin to mould a more complete theory of gradual evolution to support his gradual geology.

The Reverend William Kirby, a respected clergyman and another writer for *The Bridgewater Treatise*, believed Mantell's assertions to be flawed. Kirby claimed that fossils of the *megalosaurus* had been found with those of the mammalian opossum, and also stated that reptile fossils had been found in various and recent strata.[53] Dean William Buckland also opposed the progressionists. In *The Bridgwater Treatise*, he tried to explain the order of burial that was found in the geological record as being evidence of a whole series of divine creations, each destroyed in successive catastrophes. After all, the *megalosaurus* and *iguanodon* displayed perfect form which was evidence of a superb designer. The fossilised animals could not therefore have progressed through trial and error. Deborah Cadbury highlights Buckland's assertions in the Bridgewater Treatise.

> "Even the humble trilobites ... [found in the Cambrian layers] had eyes of extraordinary complexity, some species having at least four hundred lenses fixed on the surface of the cornea. 'This is utterly inexplicable ... [without] the same Intelligent Creative power.' [54]

This was a powerful statement in defence of divine creation and intelligent design, and yet Buckland appears increasingly confused with his writings in *The Bridgewater Treatise*. Trying to tie together the meaning of Scripture with the geological record, and even trying to understand the evidence itself, possibly led to his later mental illness. Buckland was attempting to hold together competing geological paradigms, and also hold at bay the ever encroaching deistic and atheist theories of progressive evolution, which in turn threatened social stability through violent revolution. As far as geology goes, on the one hand he had the successive catastrophes of Cuvier, but all the while he seems increasingly influenced by the uniformitarian geology of his fellow researcher, Charles Lyell, who was subtly undermining Buckland behind the scenes. One statement in *The Bridgewater Treatise* highlights this conflict concerning the rock strata and extinct species.

'... deposited slowly and gradually during very long periods of time and at widely distant intervals.' [55]

Is it feasible that the rock strata could have been laid down very slowly over vast periods of time, and at widely distant intervals? The first part appeals to Lyell, while the second looks back to Cuvier. There is a conflict here that is still not satisfactorily resolved, even in this day, in the minds of modern scientists. Either the rock strata were laid down very slowly over long periods of time, or suddenly in catastrophic events, as the two ideas are surely mutually exclusive. However, in order to hold together the competing geological arguments and Scripture, Buckland had to stretch the meaning of Scripture and the geological evidence beyond breaking point. Although in so doing he was trying to counteract the growing progressive evolutionists in favour of an intelligent Creator, he was already confused through deistic influences, and unwittingly undermined his main line of divine defence. With regard to the meaning of Scripture in Genesis 1-3, he considered it possible that:

'Millions upon millions of years may have occupied the indefinite interval between the beginning in which God created heaven and earth, and the evening or commencement of the first day of the Mosaic narrative.' [56]

The meaning of the word 'Creation' may have been different too.

'... this by no means necessarily implies creation out of nothing, it may be ... a new arrangement of materials that existed before.' [57]

It was also Dean William Buckland who suggested to Roderick Murchison that he should look for evidence for earlier rock strata below the secondary layers among the hills of Wales. Murchison took up this challenge and ventured to the Welsh border, where he was able to examine rocks from the transition layers. These Old Red Sandstones lay beneath the carboniferous coal layers, and contained invertebrate fossils of trilobites, crinoids, and echinoids. Murchison, Secretary of the Geological Society, named the layer Silurian after an ancient tribe that had lived there thousands of years before. When

Murchison presented his findings to the Geological Society, he hinted at a progression of life found in the layers. The Primary layers were free of fossils, while the highly folded and faulted transition layers contained simple organisms. The Secondary layers contained evidence of an age of reptiles, while the Tertiary layers were full of the fossil remains of mammals. At face value, this is a compelling argument, but Lyell appeared unhappy with this stepped progressive idea because he considered the fossil evidence unreliable, and especially the *lack* of evidence from the fossilisation of vertebrate animals.[58] The main difference between the invertebrate life forms in the transition layers, and those in secondary layers, is that the former are mainly benthic or bottom dwellers, while the latter are pelagic, or free-swimming organisms. However, benthic crinoids and echinoids, and other bottom dwelling invertebrates find their way into the secondary layers too, and are still extremely numerous today. In other words, to ascribe a progression of life from simple to complex through the geological record is simply wrong, because the same level of complexity is found in each, from the trilobite to the belemnite to the present day squid. Many of those simple organisms are still with us, and the evidence from a lack of vertebrate fossils in the transition layers is not evidence at all. The highly faulted and folded transition rocks are, in effect, the fossilisation of an ancient sea bed, as most of the organisms found therein are bottom dwelling aquatic life forms. As we have seen as well, some mammalian bones, such as the jawbone of an opossum, have been found among ancient reptiles.

Richard Owen carefully studied Buckland's arguments in *The Bridgewater Treatise*, although his conclusions were somewhat different. Owen, it would seem, did not fully accept that each individual animal was specifically designed, but thought that nature may have adapted itself according to divinely given laws. However, he did accept, along with Buckland, that the ancient giant reptiles were in every part equal, if not superior to modern reptiles. Whatever the mechanism for organic change, the idea of progressive evolution was therefore wrong. He set about gathering anatomical evidence, and regularly disagreed with his competitor, the evolutionist Robert Grant.

Richard Owen married into the family of William Clift, and his career progressed rapidly to a Hunterian Professorship and council member of the Zoological Society by April 1836. The shrewd Richard Owen was now in a position to undermine Robert Grant from his respected position. He did this with characteristic efficiency and ruthlessness, by simply vetoing Grant's nomination to the Zoological Society Council.[59] Grant's access to the best fossil specimens was now denied, and as a result his career declined, followed by the decline of his once packed university lectures.

The fossil evidence is still controversial, but it does not provide evidence for biological progression, as leading scientists claim. Fossils appear suddenly in the record as fully formed, complex organisms, even in the earliest Cambrian layers, and then remain unchanged throughout the record to the present day. Atheistic thought was effectively held at bay for another twenty or so years as Owen and Buckland continued to hold sway in scientific institutions. However, as their health and judgement declined, atheistic and godless forces eventually managed a powerful counter-attack. The impetus for this was the publication of Darwin's book *The Origin of Species* in 1859, followed by the famous Oxford debate between Thomas Huxley and Bishop Samuel Wilberforce the following year. Darwin proposed a natural mechanism to account for all life forms, and with evolutionary progression asserted, his ideas offered a powerful tool for those who wanted to overthrow the God-fearing Anglican establishment.

The claim that the fossil record was progressive allowed Darwin, Spencer and Huxley to build a universal naturalistic theory, which included mankind in the great chain of inevitable gradual progressive improvement, without the need for the sustaining grace of a Creator. This was in effect the English philosophical revolution of 1859 and 1860, with the overthrow of the authority of the church. By 1864, science could boast that it was at last free of religious dogma.[60] Thomas Huxley and his friends in the X Club wanted to pursue scientific knowledge without the restraint of religious thought, and were leading figures within the Royal Society and British Association for the Advancement of Science. Scientists were now the new priests to be looked to for life's answers. Huxley portrayed theologians as being in conflict with science,[61] the enemy of knowledge, and atheistic and agnostic thinkers could now develop their own ethical standards based on the science of evolution as a great cosmic principle.

Sadly, history is full of the errors that mankind made in subsequent decades as a result, but one hundred years later, Julian Huxley still proudly boasted that the whole of life was a single process of progressive evolution, from atoms to animals to human societies, without the need or room for the supernatural.[62] Through the Enlightenment period, philosophy moved away from traditional Christian faith towards an increasingly deistic, then atheistic or agnostic faith system where the inevitability of progress was asserted. This belief in gradual and certain progress was supported by a false gradualistic interpretation of fossil evidence given by Lyell. He also carefully guided Charles Darwin to develop evolution, in a deliberately crafted plot over some thirty years or so, to undermine Christianity. The full story of this manipulation is not entirely clear, nor the scale of involvement from others, but it may be noted that Erasmus Darwin and Charles Darwin's own father Robert Darwin were freemasons. Erasmus Darwin had developed early ideas of evolution from seashells and used Rosicrucian imagery in his writing. Is it possible that the development of a belief in progress, evolution and the pursuit of materialistic science and technology have been carefully crafted by secret societies for their own religious reasons, or perhaps motivated by a desire to control wealth and power in the world? Dr Henry Morris observes that undercurrents of subversion have been evident in Europe throughout this period. Such groups, according to Morris, included revolutionary movements, Deist philosophers, Masonic syncretists, Illuminist conspirators and Unitarian theologians. Many of these groups were promoting a brand of paganism and pantheism that was previously seen in ancient Greece.[63]

Revolutionary forces have also had a powerful influence in leading people away from Christ in France, and later in Russia, China and Eastern Europe, following the deistic activities of French thinkers and German rationalistic philosophers who denigrated and ridiculed Scripture. Atheism later became more open, with the writing of Marx and Nietzsche, but it often seems that hatred of Christianity was more of a motive than atheism itself. Huxley also vehemently attacked Christianity.

It is understandable that different religions want to mould society to their own beliefs, but most do so publicly and their motives are clear, which at least leads to an honest debate. But what if secret societies that follow deistic, gnostic or even pagan religions, worshiping gods other than the Judeo-Christian one, manipulate society and science in secret? If science has been manipulated by secretive religious orders in this way, then science itself must carefully consider what has been gained and what lost by such underhand and deceitful practices. Has science itself been led up blind alleys and brainwashed in its pursuit of scientific truth, compromised by the deceitful crafting of evolution and gradualism by unscrupulous people?

By overthrowing Judeo-Christian ethics, godless science has subsequently sought to pursue technology and profit outside of any moral conscience at all. This does indeed represent a Faustian pact, whereby people seek power and wealth without submission to the Creator of all things. The next chapter will look at the fruit of naturalistic ethics following the 1860 conquest of traditional Christian-based science and ethics by the forces of godless progress.

Notes and References

[1] Buckland, W., *The Bridgewater Treatise*, (See Bibliography). In: Cadbury, D., *The Dinosaur Hunters*, Fourth Estate, London, pp. 171-175, 2001.

[2] Attfield, R., *The Ethics of Environmental Concern*, University of Georgia Press, 1991. (Second Edition © 1991 by the University of Georgia Press, Athens, Georgia 30602)

[3] Baillie, J., *The Belief in Progress*, Oxford University Press, London, Glasgow, Toronto, 1950.

[4] Bury, J.B., *The Idea of Progress*, Macmillan Press, London, 1920.

[5] McGrath, A., *The Re-enchantment of Nature*, Hodder Headline, London, pp. 82-83, 2003.

[6] Behe, M.J., *Darwin's Black Box: The Biochemical Challenge to Evolution*, The Free Press, New York, 1996.

[7] Johnson, P.E., *Darwin on Trial*, Monarch Books, Lion Hudson Plc., Crowborough, East Sussex, UK, 1994.

[8] White, L., Jr., *The Historical Roots of our Ecologic Crisis*, Science, Vol. 155, No. 3767, p. 1206, 10th March 1967.

[9] Ibid., p. 1206.

[10] Passmore, J., *The Perfectibility of Man*, Duckworth, London, pp. 212-215, 1970. In: Attfield, op. cit., p. 69.

[11] Attfield, op. cit., p. 69.

[12] Barnes, S., *Time and Progress*; Dowley, T. (ed.), *The History of Christianity: A Lion Handbook*, Lion Hudson Plc, Revised ed., p. 27; and Passmore, op. cit., pp. 212-215, 1970; In: Attfield, op. cit., p. 68.

[13] Baillie, op. cit., p. 108. In: Attfield, op. cit., p. 70.

[14] Bury, J.B., op. cit., pp. 208-210; and Baillie, op. cit., pp. 115f; In: Attfield, op. cit., p. 71.

[15] Attfield, op. cit., p. 74.

[16] Brown, C., *Reason and Unreason*; Dowley, T. (ed.), *The History of Christianity: A Lion Handbook*, Lion Hudson Plc, Revised ed., pp. 485-496, 1990.

[17] Mortenson, T., *British Scriptural Geologists in the First Half of the Nineteenth Century - Part 1: Historical Setting*, Answers in Genesis, TJ, 11(2), pp. 221-252, 1997.

[18] Ibid.

[19] Ibid.

[20] Brown, op. cit., p. 489.

[21] Repcheck, J., *The Man Who Found Time: James Hutton and the Discovery of the Earth's Antiquity*, Simon and Schuster, London, pp. 88-89, 2003.

[22] Forster, R., Marston, P., *Reason, Science and Faith*, Monarch Books, Lion Hudson Plc., Crowborough, East Sussex, UK, p. 20, p. 65, pp. 138-142, 1999.

[23] Brown, op. cit., p. 492.

[24] Ibid., p. 492.

[25] Ibid., p. 492.

[26] Repcheck, op. cit., pp. 117-143

[27] Nisbet, R., *History of the Idea of Progress*, pp. 185, 189, Heinemann, London, 1980; In: Attfield, op. cit., p. 72.

[28] Brown, op. cit., pp. 492-493.

[29] Mortenson, op. cit.

[30] Ibid.

[31] Ibid. (Mortenson suggests that Lyell's faith may have been Unitarian).

[32] Bartholomew, M., *Lyell and Evolution*, British Journal for the History of Science, Vol. 6:23, p. 266, 1973. In: Forster and Marston, op. cit., p. 331.

[33] Bowden, M., *The Rise of the Evolutionary Fraud*, Sovereign Books, Bromley, Kent, UK, pp. 92-99, 1982.

[34] Ibid., pp. 92-99.

[35] Forster and Marston, op. cit., p. 331.

[36] Lyell in private correspondence to Poulette Scrope, 1830; Lyell, C. (Ed. Mrs. Lyell), John Murray, pp. 270-271, 1881. In: Bowden, op. cit. pp. 94-95.

[37] Letter from Charles Darwin to his son George 1873. Himmelfarb, G., *Darwin and the Darwinian Revolution*, Chatto and Windus, p. 320, 1959. In: Bowden, op. cit.

[38] Letter from Darwin to Edward Aveling, Karl Marx's son in law around 1880. Herbert, S., *The Place of Man in the Development of Darwin's Theory of Transmutation*, part II, Journal of the History of Biology, Vol. 10, no. 2, p. 161, Fall, 1977. In: Bowden, op. cit., p. 98.

[39] Mortenson, op. cit., and Forster and Marston, op. cit., p. 136.

[40] Darwin, C., (ed. Darwin, F.), *Life and Letters*, Vol. 2, John Murray, p. 249, 1887.

[41] Claude Henri de Rouvroy, Comte de Saint-Simon.

[42] Ginsburg, M., *The Idea of Progress: A Revaluation*, Greenwood Press, Westport, Connecticut, p. 24, 1953, In: Attfield, op. cit., p. 75.

[43] Johnson, op. cit., pp. 128-129.

[44] Attfield, op. cit., p. 75.

[45] Bacon, F., *On the Utility of Science*, 1620. From the Instauration Magna (Great Renewal). In: Presky, M., *Mike's World History*, July 2003, Galileo Library, <www.galileolibrary.com/history/history_page_138.htm>, Accessed March 2006.

[46] Mantell, G., *The Geological Age of Reptiles*, New Philosophical Journal, Edinburgh, Vol. XI, pp. 181-185, Apr-Oct 1831. In: Cadbury, D., *The Dinosaur Hunters*, Fourth Estate, London, pp. 171-175, 2001.

[47] Cadbury, D., *The Dinosaur Hunters*, Fourth Estate, London, p. 174, 2001.

[48] Ibid., pp. 183-184. Cadbury relies on a work by Schneer, C.J., *Towards a History of Geology*, ch. 2 by Bourdier, F., MIT Press, Boston, Mass., 1967; and Rudwick, M.J.S., *The Meaning of Fossils*, Chicago University Press, 1972.

[49] Ibid., pp. 184-185.

[50] Ibid., pp. 184-185.

[51] Ibid., pp. 184-186.

[52] Forster and Marston, op. cit., p. 331.

[53] Cadbury, op. cit., pp. 174-175. Cadbury points to a book by Spokes, S., *Gideon Algernon Mantell, LLD, FRCS, FRS, Surgeon and Geologist*, John Bale and Sons and Danielson, London, p. 44, 1927; and to: Kirby, W., *The Bridgewater Treatise*, (see Bibliography), Treatise VII, Vol. I, pp. 36-42, 1835.

[54] Buckland, W., op. cit., *The Bridgewater Treatise*. In: Cadbury, op. cit., p. 194.

[55] Ibid., In: Cadbury, op. cit., p. 192.

[56] Ibid., In: Cadbury, op. cit., p. 192.

[57] Ibid., In: Cadbury, op. cit., p. 192.

[58] Cadbury, op. cit., pp. 193-194.

[59] Ibid., pp. 197-198.

[60] Jensen, J.V., *The X-Club*, British Journal for the History of Science, p. 59, pp. 63-72, p. 179, 1970. In: Forster and Marston, op. cit., p. 309.

[61] Forster and Marston, op. cit., pp. 308-311.

[62] Huxley, J., *Record of the Chicago Centennial Celebration of the Publication of the Origin of Species*, 1959. In: Tax, S., (ed.) *Evolution after Darwin*, University of Chicago Press, Vol. 3, 1960.

[63] Morris, H.M., *The Troubled Waters of Evolution*, Creation Life Publishers, San Diego, p. 59, 1980.

Chapter 9

Humanism and the Rise of Social Darwinism

On then! Value means survival-
Value. If our progeny
Spreads and spawns and licks each rival,
That will prove its deity
(Far from pleasant, by our present
Standards, though it well may be).[1]
C.S. Lewis 'Evolutionary Hymn'

By 1851, Herbert Spencer had completed his new book *Social Statistics* in which he proposed a theory of social evolution, some eight years before Darwin's publication of *The Origin of Species*. Some years later, Spencer claimed that the whole universe, both organic and inorganic, was in a continual process of evolution, and Darwin's book only added fuel to this progressive fire.[2] Spencer promoted the idea of evolution within society, and he tried to claim continuity between biological and sociological evolution through the process of survival of the fittest. This had huge moral implications, and Huxley was worried enough to try damage limitation. Huxley, and to a lesser extent Darwin, sought to tone down the inevitable logical but brutal consequences of Spencer's ideas, by finding some natural mechanism for moral conduct, although even Darwin discussed the natural evolutionary outcomes for race and eugenics in 1871 in *The Descent of Man*. Huxley had also invited Spencer to become a member of the X Club, which sought to undermine Christianity and promoted Darwinism throughout the science community.

Darwin attempted to assert that evolution should lead to a sense of kinship or filial affection within the natural world, and not a belief in unrestrained survival of the fittest, even though much of Darwin's evolutionary thinking was a biological extension of Adam Smith's economic theory of unfettered capitalism, and Malthus' work on population growth where resources are limited. Adam Smith and David Hume were acquainted, and both were concerned with finding a natural basis for ethical standards. Hume believed this was achieved without appealing to religious thought, but instead developed according to primitive sympathies that lie deep within each of us. He considered that self-love and sympathy were of equal value,[3] although it has been noted that this is a very limited and shallow form of altruism.

While some of Adam Smith's writings may be considered an accurate reflection of social reality, and indeed a constrained form of capitalism does encourage industriousness which in turn enables economic growth, the idea that extreme capitalism should progress without restraint led to many social ills in the eighteenth and nineteenth century. This included the fact that landlords and factory owners were more or less allowed to own a person's labour or tenancy with great indifference towards health and safety concerns in industrial factories, mills and mines. Accidents became commonplace, with workers often losing limbs or life to unprotected machines, and extreme capitalism also helped justify slavery among Britain's increasingly prosperous industrialists, with people reduced to the level of means to an end. Even the lack of concern for the Irish famine victims can be traced to an unhealthy obsession with the godless force of the market.

A widely held belief in *laissez-faire* capitalism meant that for many years prior to Darwin, capitalism continued along these rather brutal lines. The ideas of Adam Smith meant that in Britain and America, capitalism progressed with a callous disregard for workers' rights and their welfare. Historian Gertrude Himmelfarb noted that England was a prime breeding ground for the theory of natural selection to arise. *Laissez-faire* capitalism fitted in well with Victorian greed-philosophy and Manchester economics, and in England the basic instinct was self-interest with individuals struggling for survival. Himmelfarb noted that Darwin's book *Origins of Species* essentially applied Victorian economics to biology and had all the atmosphere of an English factory.[4]

Malthus too provided a rather fatalistic idea that nature had to compete for limited resources and the inevitability of this competition justified a grasping exploitation. He also developed an early form of eugenics, believing that the poor should be reduced in numbers through deliberate impoverishment and removal of aid, and that orphaned children for instance should be allowed to die. In his Essay on the Principle of Population he comments that:

> "Instead of recommending cleanliness to the poor, we should encourage contrary habits. In our towns we should make the streets narrower, crowd more people into the houses, and court the return of the plague. In the country, we should build our villages near stagnant pools, and particularly encourage settlement in all marshy and unwholesome situations. But above all, we should reprobate specific remedies for ravaging diseases; and those benevolent, but much mistaken men, who have thought they were doing a service to mankind by projecting schemes for the total extirpation of particular disorders." [5]

Against this backdrop of a very profitable but savage capitalism, and enslavement of people, a number of evangelicals were campaigning for better social standards. William Wilberforce worked tirelessly to end the slave trade, and eventually brought an end to this common, but unpleasant practice within the British sphere of influence. However, the business community became increasingly afraid that its livelihood would be destroyed through the introduction of workers' and human rights. With the threat of revolution declining in the latter part of the eighteenth century, as a result of some social reform, industrialists were again looking to protect their interests from further decline. Evangelicalism, especially as expressed by some troublesome Anglican priests, was seen as a threat to the pursuit of technological progress and profitable enterprise, and it is against this backdrop that Darwinian thought became established in industrial society.

For Charles Darwin and Thomas Huxley, their main interest was the pursuit of science without the perceived hindrance of religious opinion, but Huxley, and to a lesser extent Darwin, were aware of the possible negative ramifications for society of the unrestrained survival of the fittest teaching among humanity. Both therefore tried to claim that there was a discontinuity between biological and sociological evolution, although both failed to find a logical reason for it. It is likely as well that there was a desire to protect the theory of evolution from obvious flaws, possibly as a sort of afterthought. As already noted in a previous chapter, Huxley commented:

> 'There is another fallacy which appears to me to pervade the so-called 'ethics of evolution'. It is the notion that because, on the whole, animals and plants have advanced in perfection of organization by means of the struggle for existence and the consequent 'survival of the fittest'; therefore men in society, men as ethical beings, must look to the same process to help them towards perfection.' [6]

Huxley here calls the continuity of survival of the fittest to ethics a fallacy, but he continued to maintain that mankind, and his intellectual and ethical characteristics, were all derived from the cosmic process of evolution, insisting on the doctrine that '... man, physical, intellectual, and moral, is as much a part of nature, as purely a product of the cosmic process, [of evolution] as the humblest weed.' [7] But Huxley maintained that the intelligent, energetic work of mankind is in antagonistic conflict with the cosmic process of evolution. As an analogy, Huxley compares the ethical human characteristic, which works against the natural, to the way in which human beings tend a garden, often for purely aesthetic reasons.

> 'Thus, it is not only true that the cosmic energy, working through man upon a portion of the plant world, opposes the same energy as it works through the state of nature, but a similar antagonism is everywhere manifest between the artificial and the natural...
>
> Not only is the state of nature hostile to the state of art of the garden; but the principle of the horticultural process, by which the latter is created and maintained, is antithetic to that of the cosmic process. The characteristic feature of the latter is the intense and unceasing competition of the struggle for existence. The characteristic of the former is the elimination of that struggle, by the removal of the conditions which give rise to it. The tendency of the cosmic process is to bring about the adjustment of the forms of plant life to the current

189

conditions; the tendency of the horticultural process is the adjustment of the conditions to the needs of the forms of plant life which the gardener desires to raise.' [8]

As noted, Huxley maintains that mankind's development as an ethical being has come about by the cosmic process, but that mankind's actions are now in conflict with the same natural cosmic process. Huxley recognises the logical flaw in this antagonism and even says he is sorry for logic. Huxley comments. 'I can only reply, that if the conclusion that the two are antagonistic is logically absurd, I am sorry for logic, because, as we have seen, the fact is so.' [9] Huxley's best attempt at seeking to give a logical reason why there should be a discontinuity between biological evolution and sociological evolution, is to suggest that 'fittest' should really be 'best', and that somehow 'survival of the best' has some sort of moral aspect. He comments:

'I suspect that this fallacy has arisen out of the unfortunate ambiguity of the phrase 'survival of the fittest'. 'Fittest' has a connotation of 'best'; and about 'best' there hangs a moral flavour. In cosmic nature, however, what is 'fittest' depends upon the conditions.' [10]

For Huxley, a change in circumstances may mean that smaller animals are better adapted to survive instead of the fittest, and so he changes the concept of fittest to best. Although he then plays with words and implies that best has some sort of ethical or civilising mechanism as well, without presenting any obvious logical link. It may be noted instead, in this slight modification of survival instincts, that the best may still survive as the fittest in each circumstance, and it does not provide an answer to wider ethics at all. Huxley here again failed to provide a logical reason why there should be a discontinuity between sociological and biological evolution, and his argument does not stand up to scrutiny.

Ethically speaking, Darwinism in reality is divided into two at this point, with Huxley and to a lesser extent Darwin on one side seeking to promote a modified non-conformist Comtist religion of science, with a claimed discontinuity between biological and sociological evolution, and Spencer promoting a sociological

Darwinism where unrestrained survival may apply to sociological development, to the pursuit of science and to business as a whole. Francis Galton also developed the idea that Darwinian evolution, within the human community, could be improved through the conscious effort of artificial selection, in the same way that dog breeders had produced many different kinds of dog.

To a large extent today, the views of Spencer and Galton have declined, with fascism largely rejected. With Spencer's and Galton's legacy apparently gone, the interests of big business today are supported by a belief in the inevitability of technological progress, supported in part by Huxley's positivist religion of science. However, social Darwinism remains alive in parts of the business community where greed is often still seen as being good.

In the latter nineteenth century, Spencer persisted with his idea that survival of the fittest should continue within human affairs and it was this more logical view that prevailed over the coming decades. 'How could man reverse the law of life?' was Spencer's question.[11] Spencer's ideas later became entrenched in the conduct of business, social provision and political thought. Attfield comments on Spencer's view of evolution:

'But if life-forms survive by adaptation, then there is a superficial cogency to his belief that evils, being manifestations of maladaptedness, will wither away as better adapted forms emerge and thrive.' 'Spencer's derivation of an ethic from the theory of evolution becomes all the more suspect...' 'To follow Bury's expression of the implications, 'Beings thus constituted cannot multiply in a world tenanted by inferior creatures; these, therefore, must be dispossessed to make room; and to dispossess them aboriginal man must have an inferior constitution to begin with; he must be predatory, he must have the desire to kill."

'Moreover even in future ages, to which more altruistic codes will, on his views, be appropriate, the idea of preserving or protecting vulnerable species, habitats or human cultures would be futile and misguided.'

'Spencer's conflation of the notions of evolution by natural selection and of progress was widely accepted, so that evolution in society came to be regarded as desirable, and progress as a natural necessity.' [12]

Over the years, many deists and atheistic humanists tried to overthrow faith in God, believing that mankind could on his own improve his morality, but here was the logical conclusion, that if mankind has arisen by surviving at the expense of others, then there is nothing to stop people living today by the same standard. Death and extinction of weaker people, and whole races of aboriginal people, were the natural consequences if the fittest were to survive. Hitler understood this all to well. In a time of rapid technological and social expansion, Spencer's view of survival of the fittest became popular with businessmen and industrialists alike. Lone voices calling for moral standards were disregarded, and a belief in the superiority of scientific progress became paramount, even to the extent that Nietzsche could later claim that 'God is dead'.

The more simple, but logical concept of progressive evolution, as outlined by Herbert Spencer and Francis Galton, led to the rise of the ideology of fascism, which gained strength in Europe in the 1930s. Both Hitler's national socialism, with its belief in a master race, and also Marx's brand of utopian, but tyrannical socialism, found ample food in the evolutionary idea of survival of the fittest. Richard Weikart, with his book, *From Darwin to Hitler: Evolutionary Ethics, Eugenics and Racism in Germany*,[13] has elaborated on the partial influence that Darwin himself had on the rise of fascism, and notes that Darwin discussed the benefits of eugenics in his later book *The Descent of Man.* Darwin also appeared to express some social Darwinian views in private correspondence relating to the pay of workmen.[14] Julian Huxley and H.B.D. Kittlewell also show how the rise of Darwinism led to the glorification of *laissez faire* economics and free enterprise, warfare, and to programmes of eugenics and racism, and eventually to Hitler and Nazi ideology.[15] Jerry Bergman too comments that such attitudes in business practices ruined around a million lives each year in America in the early twentieth century, with death and loss of limbs common due to unprotected machines and drivebelts.[16]

Herbert Spencer travelled to the United States on occasions where he promoted his ideas among the robber baron business leaders, and was considered for a time a greater scientist than Darwin. Among business followers were Andrew Carnegie and

John D. Rockefeller, and Spencer's reputation at the time was so great that even a journal was published, the *Popular Science Monthly*, to discuss Spencer's survival ideas. Sir Isaac Asimov has also commented that in 1884, Spencer argued that the unemployable or those who were burdensome to society should be allowed to die off, rather than be given charity and help. By doing this, the human race would be strengthened, with the weak weeded out. Asimov rightly comments that this could be used to justify some terrible impulses in human beings and society, and was a horrible philosophy.[17]

Carnegie had apparently been brought up a Christian, but appeared quick to abandon his faithful position to accept Spencer's view of pure survival of the fittest, and Spencer called him one of his closest American friends.[18] Carnegie was for a time the biggest steel producer and richest man in the world, and in his autobiography he commented that he had got rid of theology and the supernatural and found the truth in evolution instead.[19] A later biographer of Carnegie notes:

'Progress through evolution, both biological and technological, bringing nature and man, "the machine and the garden", toward perfect harmony - this was to be the essence of Carnegie's faith in the ultimate perfectibility of the universe, and he would hold that faith for the next thirty-five years.' [20]

'[Carnegie] loudly trumpeted to the world - in public speeches, books, and articles, and in private conversations, and personal letters - his intellectual and spiritual indebtedness to Herbert Spencer.' [21]

'Phrases like "survival of the fittest", "race improvement", and "struggle for existence" came easily from his pen and presumably from his lips.' [22]

Although J.D. Rockefeller and his family maintained an outward Christian front, in business he also considered survival of the fittest to be acceptable in business practices along with Carnegie. This was supported by a number of notable professors in America. Bergman identifies Professor William Graham Sumner, of Princeton

University, as concluding that millionaires were the fittest individuals in society, having been naturally selected by fierce business competition. Accordingly, they therefore deserved their status and privileges in society, and social Darwinism gave industry a 'scientific' justification for these brutal practices.[23] Steven J. Rosenthal also identifies a number of sociologists who accepted social Darwinism, therefore giving credence to racism and eugenics in social policy.[24]

However, not everyone in America agreed with such rampant survival-based capitalism. William Jennings Bryan, for instance, was the most prominent person in political life in America to oppose this move towards Darwinian extremism. Bergman comments that Bryan built his career in politics on denouncing excessive militarism and capitalism. Bryan saw Darwinism as a merciless law whereby the weak are crowded out and killed by the strong.[25]

Carnegie and Rockefeller were by no means the only robber baron businessmen committed to survival of the fittest in the United States, and others were found in car manufacturing, the oil industry and coal mining. Although Carnegie gave away a vast amount of money, it did not go to help the weak and unfit, as he would rather have thrown money directly into the sea, which he considered preferable.[26] Survival of the fittest therefore leads to the brutal conclusion that it is acceptable to have a callous disregard for the poor, the working classes, and dispose of one's enemies on the basis of death to the weakest.

Unrestrained capitalism continued to push ahead in the latter twentieth century, with sometimes the only morality appearing to be 'don't get caught'. It was Gordon Gecko in the Hollywood film, *Wall Street* who coined the phrase 'greed is good', and a number of books have highlighted this point, for instance Robert Blake et al. with *Corporate Darwinism*, published in 1966.[27] A number of big financial scandals in the later 1990s in America, such as the collapse of Worldcom and Enron, have caused one historian, Niall Ferguson to comment on the accumulation of wealth into the hands of a very small clique of top executives that he termed a *CEOcracy*.

Francis Galton, for his part, was Charles Darwin's cousin and also the grandson of Erasmus Darwin. Galton was wealthy enough to devote his life to adventure and study, spending time in Africa where he mapped out part of Namibia. He seems quite orthodox in his belief in early life, and his wife Louisa, like Charles Darwin's wife Emma, appears to have been a devout Anglican, and not impressed with evolution. However, on attending the famous annual meeting of the British Association in the summer of 1860, and reading *The Origin of Species*, Galton converted to atheism and rejected the traditions and teachings of Christianity. He wrote to Darwin that he felt '... initiated into an entirely new province of knowledge...' [28] Galton also commented on Darwin's book that:

> 'Its effect was to demolish a multitude of dogmatic barriers by a single stroke, and arouse a spirit of rebellion against all ancient authorities whose positive and unauthenticated statements were contradicted by modern science.' [29]

Ironically, while Galton considered the religious mind to be second rate, it was an Austrian Priest, Abbot Gregor Mendel who made the breakthrough in genetic research with the study of peas in 1865 and 1869.[30] However, Mendel's work remained unnoticed until 1900. Galton's mind was restless and he seemed unable to settle on single ideas for long, but instead became consumed by numerous areas of research at once and as a result had two mental breakdowns in his life. However, one area that he did settle on and promote through his later life was *eugenics*. Just as nature had often been improved through artificial selection, his vision was to develop a race of supermen through the artificial selection of the best and fittest humans. Those who were not of the fittest may live a life of celibacy and hard work. Galton's initial work was written up in two parts in *MacMillan's Magazine* as *Heredity Talent and Character* in November 1864 and April 1865. He suffered several years of mental illness before writing up his work more fully in *Heredity Genius* in 1869. It is interesting to note that Charles Darwin was also deeply troubled, as if sick with worry, before the publication of his book in 1859. In both works, Galton set out to prove that characteristics were inherited and had little to do with a person's social environment, although Galton's scientific judgement instead appears clouded, with his works ignoring obvious facts. Martin Brookes comments that:

> '...for all the practical innovation contained within *Heredity Genius* the book's critics were spot-on in their assessments. Galton's central thesis, implicit in the book's title, was deeply flawed. ... His reluctance to acknowledge the limitations of his research suggested that, consciously or otherwise, he was working to some kind of alternative agenda. Time and again he presented his argument as straightforward biological reasoning, whereas the only thing straightforward about it was its lack of objectivity ... in taking such an extreme position he gave birth to an argument that has been tainted with bias and scandal ever since.' [31]

Galton was trying to prove what he already considered true, that inheritance was the cause of genius, and he did not seem able to consider alternatives to his theory. Brookes here suggests he may have been following another agenda, although he does not elaborate on what that agenda may have been. Galton's apparent concern was that Victorian society in Britain was failing to keep up with the possible greatness of man observed in ancient Greece, even though he considered Anglo-Saxons to be two notches above the Africans. As well as racist ideas, a lack of respect for human rights and democracy were also a hallmark of *Heredity Genius*, and the poorer classes were denied the right to procreate. Brookes again quotes Galton:

> 'It is the obvious course of intelligent men - and I venture to say it should be their religious duty - to advance in the direction whither Nature is determined they shall go, that is towards the improvement of the race.' [32]

Despite the apparent confidence in evolutionary progress, the Darwinists were constantly concerned that evolution needed human intervention to prevent a regression. When challenged on the undemocratic nature of his work, he commented that the individual should count for nothing as a result of evolutionary thinking.

> 'But it [Democracy] goes farther than this, for it asserts than men are of equal value as social units, equally capable of voting, and the rest. This feeling is undeniably wrong and cannot last'. [33]

'If, however, we look around at the course of nature, one authoritative fact becomes distinctly prominent, let us make of it what we may. It is, that the life of the individual is treated as of absolutely no importance, while the race is treated as everything, Nature being wholly careless of the former except as a contributor to the maintenance and evolution of the latter.' [34]

His idea was to create a utopian state where the rights of the individual are ignored in favour of the well-being of the state programme. This lack of respect for individual human rights later became a feature of both fascism and Marxism. While Galton had many critics, his ideas slowly gained favour from those on the right and left of politics. Towards the end of the nineteenth century and beginning of the twentieth, the social problems of London were becoming extreme, with 30 percent living in poverty, and there was a great desire to do something to alleviate these problems. Galton took the opportunity, in October 1901, to promote his own ideas as a solution, at the Huxley Lecture at the Royal Anthropological Institute. [35]

Among prominent followers of Galton was Karl Pearson, a mathematics professor at University College London who established a School of Biometry at his London College. Pearson also mixed with some of the more radical sections of London society, including George Bernard Shaw and Eleanor Marx, the daughter of Karl Marx. As a result of his love for Germany, Pearson in fact changed his name from Carl to Karl, and he also presented the same rather cold emotional detachment towards people as Galton's own personality displayed. By 1904, Galton had begun to modify his eugenic views to tie in with the emerging sociological movement, and presented a lecture at the newly formed Sociological Society entitled *Eugenics: Its Definitions, Scope and Aims*. At this time he recognised that a utopian society required manual labourers as well as professional classes to function properly, although he continued to maintain that charity should only be given to the poor if they agreed to a life of celibacy. Like many others of his time, Galton was looking for a utopian state of supermen and superwomen. The Sociological Society itself offered a platform from which to promote his message across the country. Galton commented that:

> 'What nature does blindly, slowly, and ruthlessly, man may do
> providently, quickly and kindly. As it lies within his power, so it
> becomes his duty to work in that direction. The improvement of our
> stock seems to me one of the highest objects that we can reasonably
> attempt ... I see no impossibility in eugenics becoming a religious
> dogma among mankind ... The first and main point is to secure the
> general intellectual acceptance of eugenics as a hopeful and most
> important study. Then let its principles work into the heart of the
> nation, which will gradually give practical effect to them in ways that
> we may not wholly foresee.' [36]

At the Sociological Society meeting his ideas received a rather cool,
but largely favourable reception. H.G. Wells noted that often the
common criminals showed a greater degree of inventiveness than the
judges who sent them to prison, and that it would be better to select
against the bad, instead of selecting for the good, which he
considered more difficult. Wells commented that selection against
those considered a failure was the best possibility for an
improvement of the human stock.[37] Wells was a prolific writer of
science fiction, including *The Time Machine* and *The War of the
Worlds* and promoted the utopian ideals of Galton's eugenics
programme and Darwinism. He studied biology under Thomas
Huxley and came to reject his Christian upbringing. In some sense
Wells's early eugenic views were even more radical than Galton's,
wanting for instance to kill off those who were deemed to be unfit.
Wells's comments in *Anticipations*, that society should allow those
with the strongest bodies and minds and with beautiful physiques to
live, while others who are ugly and base should be checked in their
stride and even put to death.[38] Bergman shows how Wells considered
that people should have little pity for those who would be put to
death in such a way, giving the fit a more complete sense of what it
is to live. According to Wells, this ideal would make killing all the
more worthwhile.[39] One of the most enthusiastic supporters who
responded at the Sociological Society meeting was George Bernard
Shaw, who commented that they needed to face the fact that a
eugenic religion was needed to save Western civilisation from the
fate that had overtaken previous civilisations.[40]

On the other side of the ethical debate at the Sociological Society meeting, Dr. Robert Hutchinson suggested that great improvement to society would come through an improved nutrition for the poor instead. Eugenics also began to take off in Germany, and in 1904 Galton received a letter from Alfred Ploetz, who founded a journal of eugenics in Germany entitled *Archiv fur Rassen - und Gesellschaftesbiologie*. Ploetz said that he took the highest interest in Galton's eminent and important eugenics, and a year later Ploetz founded the *German Society for Race Hygiene in Berlin*.[41]

Galton also established a research fellowship in eugenics at University College London in the autumn of 1904, providing £1500 for the first three years, and Edgar Schuster was appointed from Oxford University as a young zoologist. Several years later in 1907, the *Eugenics Education Society* was established to bring together interested groups. At the time, liberals and moralists alike supported eugenics because they saw the need for improvements in society, perhaps overlooking the abuse of human rights that lay at the foundation of Galton's ideas.

However, it was in the United States where eugenics was first practiced, with Indiana beginning a programme of sterilisations in 1907 for criminals, the mentally ill, and others considered socially degenerate. This spread to another thirty states, and by 1940 a total of 35,000 people had been sterilised as a result of Galton's social agenda. In Germany, Heinrich Himmler also publicly embraced the eugenics of Alfred Ploetz, Galton's German admirer.[42] Today, while eugenics is no longer taught or widely accepted, the area of genetics that fascinated Galton continues to throw up ethical challenges, with genetic engineering being pursued by business and secular science with little regard for the ethical consequences.

On the other side of the social and political divide to fascism and unfettered capitalism, were those like Karl Marx, promoting revolution and communism, and it is noteworthy that Galton was able to discuss eugenics at a Sociological Society meeting. As with the fascists, Darwinism had a strong appeal to revolutionary theorists. Incidentally, early evolutionary ideas had previously been promoted by those who supported revolution in America and France, men like Joseph Priestly and Erasmus Darwin. In 1873, Marx, an admirer of Charles Darwin sent a second edition of his book *Das Capital* to Darwin. Darwin replied that along with his own work, their studies to increase knowledge would add to the happiness of mankind in the long run.[43] It is rather ironic that evolutionary ideas influenced Marxism, fascism and unfettered capitalism, but all may be seen as essentially materialistic creeds, with the disagreement simply around the distribution of wealth and power. Engels also commented at Marx's funeral, that Marx discovered the law of evolution in human history, just as Darwin had discovered the laws of evolution in organic nature.[44]

Marxism is inherently a *materialistic* creed that believes that mankind will reach a utopian state when freed from the capitalist system of high finance and bankers. Accordingly, all the problems in the world are due to the unequal distribution of wealth, and as such there is no need to look for spiritual solutions to life's ills. A theology of spiritual and economic prosperity through the outworking of divine grace therefore does not remain a legitimate means of increasing human happiness, and society and the economy must be managed from a humanistic centre. Engels and Marx believed in the inevitability of technological progress, and saw mankind alone as taking control of nature through exploitation, without any reference to a divine ethical standard or for the welfare of nature itself. The subsequent ecological disasters in trying to humanise nature are all too evident with the whole communist economy planned from the centre by a privileged elite.

Marx saw religion as a sort of opium that helped keep people down in order to maintain wealth and privilege in the hands of a few. Like Huxley, Marx overlooked the good that Christianity has done in raising the welfare of the poor, with for instance the preaching of Wesley, or the abolition of the slave trade by Wilberforce, and passed the blame for all society's ills to the Christian church. If fascism was partly Galton's and Spencer's logical development, communism may be seen in part as an expression of Huxley and Darwin's belief in an inevitable cosmic process of evolution, blended with belief in the rightness of materialistic science and progress. Of course, Marx formulated his radical views before Darwin, but the ideas of Marx and Engels were based on the inevitability of historical development as taught by Hegel and Feuerbach with every attempt made to humanise nature.

In 1933, John Dewey was one of those who was instrumental in drawing up the first *Humanist Manifesto*. His aim was to set up religious humanism, as he believed that traditional monotheistic religions would soon pass away and be replaced by a philosophy based on purely human achievement. In many ways, this was an extension of Comte and Huxley's belief, whereby godless science and humanity would become icons for religious devotion to form the ethical basis of society. Comte is rarely mentioned today, but present-day humanism appears as a non-conformist copy of Comte's vision of society, ordered by a religious devotion to humanity and science. Dawkins continues to promote Comte's positivist religion of science in the late twentieth and early twenty first century. Dewey was also influenced by Huxley during his university days, and finds himself caught up in the same dilemma as Huxley, with the ethical implications of extending the cosmic biological process of evolution to human ethics and society. On the one hand, he suggests there are no doubt distinctions that exist, although as yet unknown, but he then goes on to say that he has no reason to suppose that this cosmic process has become arrested. As both a humanist and pragmatist, Dewey thought it right to progress with decision making without having a logical basis for such action. He commented that:

'There are no doubt sufficiently profound distinctions between the ethical process and the cosmic process as it existed prior to man and to the formation of human society. So far as I know, however, all of these differences are summed up in the fact that the process and the forces bound up with the cosmic have come to consciousness in man ... We have, however, no reason to suppose that the cosmic process has become arrested or that some new force has supervened to struggle against the cosmic.' [45]

But Dewey was more than a philosophical humanist. Just as Huxley had encouraged others to organise and bring order to the developing sciences, Dewey also worked to promote humanism within the education system in the United States, even becoming honorary president of the National Education Association in America in 1933, after publication of the first *Humanist Manifesto*. Through his schools of education in Columbia and Chicago, his ideas gained favour among educationalists and are still prevalent in schools today, not only in America, but in Europe as well.[46] Another contributor to the *Humanist Manifesto* was Charles Francis Potter, who claimed that education could be used as a powerful tool of humanism, with the consequence that a five-day programme of humanist education could overcome the one hour per week teaching in church Sunday schools.[47] It is ironic, but Loeffler notes that in the 1930s, humanists were happy to identify humanism as a new religion, that is, until it became more advantageous to use Hegelian dialectics to separate science and faith for the purpose of undermining the latter.[48] As a result, humanists began to claim humanism as a purely objective and scientific reality, denying it ever had any inherent metaphysical reality, simply ignoring the logical flaws in such a position.

This is reminiscent of Huxley, who worked tirelessly to organise the sciences in the late nineteenth century along secular lines, again ignoring logical flaws in his materialistic philosophy. Sadly though, things did not get better as the humanists believed, and the world fell into another global conflict in 1939, with the evils of Hitler's fascism and Stalin's brand of communism. More recently in 1973, the *Humanist Manifesto* was revised, and the mistakes that were made in the pursuit of technological progress have been noted, but it still has blind confidence in scientific and technological progress without reference to any divine power.

Hitler though, hardly ever mentioned his debt to Darwinian evolution in his writings, but on closer inspection the link becomes clear. Ernst Haeckel helped popularise evolutionary theory in Germany, after encouragement to organise science along secular lines by Thomas Huxley, and as has been shown, Ploetz also promoted eugenics in Germany. Haeckel also founded the *Monistenbund* or Monistic Alliance in 1906. This league promoted a brand of Pantheism, with ideas of scientific materialism and racism, as well as the social engineering of eugenics and euthanasia. Haeckel was a biologist who became convinced of the 'fact' of evolution after reading Darwin's book *The Origin of Species*, and did a great deal to promote Darwin's work. He trained as a medical doctor and developed a number of evolutionary ideas that have since been discredited. This includes the famous 'ontogeny recapitulates phylogeny', or embryonic recapitulation, which is the idea that evolutionary change is modelled by the developing foetus. He later admitted to massaging his drawings to give a more favourable gloss to his theory.

The Nazi party under Hitler took up many of Haeckel's ideas, but in 1933 when Hitler became Chancellor of Germany, the Monistic Alliance was disbanded, as it didn't fit in with Hitler's new religion of paganism. Hitler though, had found a new philosophy to do away with traditional Christian ethics, and was able to put his new, more brutal ideas into practice once he had gained power. A few quotes from Hitler's book *Mein Kampf* (My struggle) will show just how warped his philosophy had become, and the influence that Darwinian 'survival of the fittest' played in his thinking.

> 'No more than Nature desires the mating of weaker with stronger individuals, even less does she desire the blending of a higher with a lower race, since, if she did, her whole work of higher breeding, over perhaps hundreds of thousands of years, might be ruined with one blow... When man attempts to rebel against the iron logic of Nature, he comes into struggle with the principles to which he himself owes his existence as a man.' [49]

> No, there is only one holiest human right, and this right is at the same time the holiest obligation, to wit: to see to it that the blood is preserved pure and, by preserving the best humanity, to create the possibility of a nobler development of these beings. A folkish state must therefore begin by raising marriage from the level of a continuous defilement of the race, and give it the consecration of an institution which is called upon to produce images of the Lord and not monstrosities halfway between man and ape. [50]

Hitler's aim was:

> ... finally to put an end to the constant and continuous original sin of racial poisoning, and to give to the Almighty Creator beings such as He Himself created.' [51]

The above quotes from Hitler's book are profoundly disturbing, as he craftily blends religious language with bitterness and intolerance. But the god of Haeckel and Hitler is a long way from the God of the Bible. Even though Hitler was baptised as a Catholic, he really despised Christianity in all its shades, and commented that when he had absolute power he would overcome the German church, even suggesting that Luther would be with him.[52]

Hitler's god is in fact no more than the outworking of natural science or 'survival of the fittest' according to the theory of evolution. Incidentally, all the while that Hitler was trying to build his white master race, another Austrian, Viktor Schauberger, was studying the natural world of forests, mountain streams, and jumping fish, and then copying it through the development of extremely efficient turbines. Schauberger, who was forced to work for the Nazi party under threat of death to his family, developed machines that used cyclones to generate energy, probably from the differential spin of the earth in much the same way that tornadoes continually gain their ferocious power. During a meeting with Hitler in 1934, Schauberger is reported to have told the Fuhrer that his third Reich would be lucky to last ten years, let alone one thousand, because it abused nature. Max Planck, also attending the meeting, disagreed, claiming that science had nothing to do with nature.[53]

It must also be acknowledged that at least in a small part, the rise of fascism and the Nazi Party in Germany lies in the teachings of Martin Luther, and the influence that Luther had on later German philosophers and German society. There was much that was good about the Reformation and necessary too, but there was also a lot of bitterness as well, within the German theologian's camp. Luther also preached a very nationalistic brand of Christianity, where Germans came to see their faith and patriotism as one and the same, and peasants and other groups were forced into a position of unquestioning servitude to the state and church. This helps to explain how Hitler managed to so easily gain control of the German population.

One of the most popular critiques of Luther, that is used by atheists to try and discredit Christianity, shows the influence Luther had on German nationalism during the rise of fascism. *Martin*

Luther: Hitler's Spiritual Ancestor, by Peter F. Wiener, was written as a 'Win the Peace Pamphlet' during the Second World War, when it shocked Britain and America. It was republished in 1985.[54] It is perhaps understandable that atheists should seize on this work, but even an embittered Luther does not make for an evil Christianity or Reformation as a whole. Indeed, Wiener goes to great length to show that Lutherism departed from the general Protestant Reformation, and that Luther appeared to suffer from some sort of delusion, perhaps verging on madness. Wiener appears most respectful to Christianity as a whole, and although his comments may be coloured by wartime propaganda, there appears to be some real substance to the allegations. Luther's language was often offensive and angry, and even at times appearing blasphemous,[55] but if Luther had so little respect for Christ, he had a much more elevated view of himself.

> "Not for a thousand years has God bestowed such great gifts on any bishop as He as on me" (E61, 422). "God has appointed me for the whole German land, and I boldly vouch and declare that when you obey me you are without a doubt obeying not me but Christ" (W15, 27).[56]

As far as the Jews were concerned, Luther at first embraced them to help in the power struggle against Rome, but later abandoned them when his position was secure.[57] However, the Jews were not alone in suffering persecution at the hands of Luther. The Anabaptists also suffered greatly, even though Luther had initially been an inspiration to them. Wiener quotes Luther:

> 'The principal thing ... required to protect the people against the devils who were teaching through the mouths of the Anabaptist prophets was in the case of the common people compulsion by the sword and by the law ... the law with its penalties rules over them in the same way that wild beasts are held in check by chains and bars, in order that outward peace may prevail amongst the people; for this purpose the temporal authorities are ordained and it is God's will that they be honoured and feared.' [58]

In many ways, the subject of Luther moves away from the main argument, but it does show that when looking at the Reformation,

Christians need to be very careful to sort the wheat from the chaff. Once again, we are faced with an apparent orthodoxy that is anything but orthodox, and Luther's conduct was a long way from the teachings of Christ, to love one's enemies, let alone one's friends. There is also very little comfort in Luther's conduct for atheists as well. It may indeed be true that Luther was deluded, but what does that say about Christianity as a whole, or even the rest of the Reformation? It remains true that godless evolution was the other great influence on Hitler's life, and Hitler himself was an avowed enemy of organised Christianity. The historian Andrew Walker comments further on the influence that 'Neo-Darwinism' has had on various groups, with a debasement of ethics across Europe. Walker here uses the term 'Neo-Darwinism' to refer to the ethical and social aspects of Darwinism.

> 'Neo-Darwinism also found its way into Italian fascism - directly in the writings of Mussolini, but also in the theories of two of his most enthusiastic supporters, the sociologists Pareto and Mosca. And if this was not enough, it wandered into the Nazi ideology of miscegenation and eugenic policy which ran its course in the ovens of Auschwitz.
>
> And I'm afraid we can't let feminist Mary Stokes off scot-free either, for although she championed contraception for women, she also wanted to tinker with the genes of the proletariat in order to weed out the weak and the wanton, the deformed and the depraved.
>
> Neo-Darwinism is still out of its cage today: in its benign guise it continues to underpin Fabian socialism and has informed the thinking of Peter Wilson in his magnificent study of the 20th century, A Terrible Beauty. In a more strident, seemingly scientific form we can find it in Edward O. Wilson's sociobiology.' [59]

Another main contributor to the promotion of evolution in the twentieth century was the unorthodox Jesuit Priest Pierre Teilhard de Chardin. He became a Jesuit in 1899, and gained acceptance as a Roman Catholic Priest in 1911. A couple of years later in 1913 he was involved in the discovery of Piltdown Man, which helped develop his reputation as a leading palaeontologist. However, 40 years later in 1953, Piltdown Man was exposed as a fraud, after many years of useful service for evolution. A number of people, including Malcolm Bowden, have concluded that Teilhard de

Chardin was responsible, and even the evolutionist Steven J. Gould agrees, although he considers him to have been just a joker. Although there is as yet no conclusive proof that Teilhard de Chardin was responsible, and there are indeed other suspects, he remains a contender. He gained enormously from this, and also found other very dubious fossils while in China in later years, such as remains of so-called Peking Man. The acknowledgement that Piltdown Man was a fraud came after the death of another man responsible for its discovery, and also after the discovery of Peking Man. Other alleged humanoid fossil findings made Piltdown Man anomalous to the wider developing theories of human evolution. Phillip Johnson claims that this carefully contrived concealment and management of evidence by the Natural History Museum is more of a scandal than the fraud itself.[60]

Teilhard de Chardin attempted to turn the process of evolution into God Himself, with the whole of nature being drawn upwards towards the Omega point, which Christians might view as equivalent to the second coming. Teilhard de Chardin expresses this in rather masonic terms, talking of evolution being a light to illuminate all facts and a trajectory that all lines of thought must follow. He believed that all systems, theories and hypotheses must bow down to the surpassing greatness of evolution to be considered even thinkable.[61]

For many years the Jesuits banned Teilhard de Chardin from publishing any books because the Catholic Church considered them heretical. However, after his death his major work *The Phenomenon of Man* was published by others, and the Catholic Church was powerless to stop it. This attempt to harmonise Christianity and science has appealed to many theologians and has also found appeal among pagans during the rise of the New Age movement. Teilhard de Chardin admitted that his thinking was essentially pantheist. In many ways, his views are almost identical to those of the Catholic born Hitler, who also appeared to be pantheist in thinking, believing the process of evolution to be one and the same as the God of the Bible. While there is no apparent direct link between the two men, Teilhard de Chardin promoted racism and fascism as a natural extension of evolution. At face value he appeared to see evolution as a plan of cosmic love, with some sort of Kantian respect for human rights, but his attraction to fascism may suggest otherwise. He had little respect for the Chinese, whom he worked among, nor for the Africans, believing that fascism opened its arms to the future, and progress called for the destruction of inferior races.[62]

While many New Age philosophers and theologians may find superficial appeal in the work of Teilhard de Chardin, there is perhaps a lack of understanding of the implications of applying survival of the fittest to Christian ethics. Of course some extreme biocentric environmentalists also have views that border on fascism, desiring for instance to reduce human population through varying unethical devices that impinge on people's intrinsic value. Teilhard de Chardin's work was promoted by one leading evolutionist, the Russian Orthodox Theodosius Dobzhansky, as a means of establishing a harmony between evolutionary science and Christian faith. However, C.S. Lewis was more critical, believing that Teilhard de Chardin's appeal comes from a reaction to his religious censorship.

Lewis commented that *The Phenomenon of Man* is really evolution run mad and criticized de Chardin's belief that prior to life, matter contained 'pre-life'. Lewis compared this concept to 'pre-light', which he argued is the same as darkness, and also noted that de Chardin's ideas were in fact a form of pantheism and therefore rightly banned by the Catholic authorities.[63]

An examination of the evolutionary philosophies of the past 150 years helps to explain the overriding ethical assumptions that our society utilises at the beginning of the twenty first century. Fascism has declined, but 'survival of the fittest' is still alive in the conduct of some business enterprises, especially with the pursuit of unethical practices in the field of genetic engineering, and the exploitation of nature for profit. This is wedded to an almost religious devotion to science as an answer to all life's problems, with denial that there is any objective basis for ethics. Communism has declined as well, but parts of the politically correct left continue to undermine Christianity and promote secular ethics, not considering or questioning whether there is any basis for such ethics outside of a strong and coherent faith system.

There is a growing rejection of progressive modernism today, but instead of turning to Christ, people instead turn to paganism, and a sort of pantheist *new age* faith system that is close to the thinking of Teilhard de Chardin, and ironically Hitler. The Gaia philosophy is a case in point, which in its pantheist form sees the whole earth as a living being. Within this evolutionary pantheism lurk some extreme biocentric environmentalists who care little for the intrinsic value of human beings, and in fact place animal rights above the interests of people. It would seem that although technological progress is rejected, the basis for a belief in progress, the universal cosmic process of 'survival of the fittest', is upheld. While Darwin's biological evolution is widely believed and taught in society today, it may be noted that those who did most to promote it, from Thomas Huxley, to John Dewey, to Teilhard de Chardin, to Julian Huxley, spoke in philosophical terms of a universal cosmic process at work. Even those Darwinists who have rejected pure survival instincts in sociological affairs fail to provide a convincing logical answer as to why there should be a discontinuity between sociological and biological evolution.

It is also an open question as to how much influence freemasonry and other secret societies have had on the rise of progressive deistic thought in Europe and America through the Enlightenment. These secretive societies seem to have blended ancient pagan views to the Judeo-Christian tradition, and its members are often accused of gaining positions of influence within society to mould it for their financial benefit. A number of popular secular books have been written recently, for instance *Talisman* by Robert Bauval and Graham Hancock,[64] which adopt this view, although there is also much in their work that a Christian would disagree with. Christians need to guard against getting too caught up in conspiracy theories that can lead up many blind alleys and to paranoia, but a general principle may be noted that those committed to a particular religion may seek to mould society to their own way of thinking, and if that religion is a secretive form of gnosticism, then who knows what motives have driven people to undermine other faiths. Erasmus Darwin was a known freemason, and this may have guided the work of Charles Darwin, Francis Galton and

Thomas Huxley as well. This perhaps explains their love of the great 'cosmic principle' of evolution that even Teilhard de Chardin appeals to.

Phillip Johnson also shows another negative outcome of evolutionary philosophy, evident in modern society. It is the effect that a belief in the death of God has on society, and the subsequent search for meaning, in terms of purpose, rights and ethics. Humanist education has indoctrinated the masses to a point where clarity of faith is lacking, and a sort of post-modern fatalistic nihilism has taken over. This can be seen, for instance, with the growth of violent crimes and a callous disregard for the welfare of others, especially in major cities throughout the West. Johnson summarises the problem that society faces when it rejects the ultimate divine evaluator of good and evil, and uses Leff's speech as an example. According to Johnson, Leff saw intellectual history as a losing war against nihilism. The modernists, in rejecting the unevaluated evaluator, find themselves with no basis for ultimate premises. Leff tried to reject such fatalistic nihilism, but also rejected the supernatural basis that he saw as the only logical escape route from such nihilism.[65]

The Darwinists too were faced with the logic of social Darwinism, if godless survival of the fittest were the only basis on which to build ethics. Although they tried to stem the tide of Spencer's rhetoric, they failed to provide logical reasons why Spencer was wrong if their own worldview was the only reality. The world has paid a heavy price in terms of unrestrained capitalism, materialistic progress and the rise of fascism and communism. We are basically left with two unpleasant choices in a godless evolutionary system. On the one hand, we have the subjective ethics of sympathy and sentiment, as outlined by Hume and later Darwin and Huxley. This leads ultimately to an illogical and confused basis for ethics, to loss of purpose and nihilistic fatalism, or alternatively we are left with the brutal logic of Herbert Spencer and Francis Galton, where selfish survival at the expense of others is all that matters.

A line of thought can be traced where humanity and materialistic science have been turned into icons of religious devotion, from Auguste Comte, to Thomas Huxley, to John Dewey and today to

Richard Dawkins. It would not be fair to suggest that these people accepted the ethics of social Darwinism, but all have failed to provide a logical basis for ethics, and failed to give a logical reason for a discontinuity between biological and social evolution. Huxley even said he was sorry for logic, and Dawkins too claims that science has no method of deciding ethical standards, all the while maintaining that science is the only objective reality.[66] And yet these same people have organised science, developed education, and even today Dawkins is a Professor for the Public Understanding of Science at Oxford and he continues to promote science and humanism with the same religious devotion as Comte. But the failure of this religion of humanity and materialistic science, that has evolution as a foundation, to provide an objective basis for ethics in over 150 years can be seen as the major cause of loss of ethics and purpose in the West today. It is also the cause of the growth of post-modernism and a sense of nihilistic fatalism. Western civilisation would do well to totally reject this religion of humanity that has been developed by flawed human beings, and return to the faith of Jesus Christ as revealed by God. It is also ironic that those who claim that Christianity is a man-made religion are also the ones who promote a religion that has truly been made by man.

Notes and References

[1] Lewis, C.S., The Cambridge Review 79 (November 30, 1957): 227; In: Lewis, C.S., (ed. Hooper, W.), *Poems*, Geoffrey Bles, London, pp. 55-56, 1964.

[2] Attfield, R., *The Ethics of Environmental Concern*, University of Georgia Press, p. 76, 1991. (Second Edition © 1991 by the University of Georgia Press, Athens, Georgia 30602)

[3] Open University, Wye College, University of London, *Darwin and Moral Philosophy*, Environmental Ethics, Block A, Part 3.2, p. 15, 1997.

[4] Himmelfarb, G., *Darwin and the Darwinian Revolution*, W.W. Norton, New York, p. 418, 1962. In: Bergman, J., *Darwin's Critical Influence on*

the Ruthless Extremes of Capitalism, Answers in Genesis, TJ, 16(2), pp. 105-109, 2002.

[5] Malthus, T.R., *An Essay on the Principle of Population as it Affects the Future Improvement of Society*, Reeves and Turner, London, p. 412, reprint 1887.

[6] Huxley, T.H., *Collected Essays*, Vol. 9, *Evolution & Ethics, and Other Essays*, London, p. 80, 1894, (*Evolution and Ethics*, The Romanes Lecture, 1893), <http://aleph0.clarku.edu/huxley/CE9/E-E.html>, Accessed March 2006.

[7] Ibid., p. 11, (*Evolution and Ethics: Prolegomena*, 1894), <http://aleph0.clarku.edu/huxley/CE9/E-EProl.html>, Accessed March 2006.

[8] Ibid., pp. 12-13.

[9] Ibid., p. 12.

[10] Ibid., p. 80, (*Evolution and Ethics*, The Romanes Lecture, 1893).

[11] Attfield, op. cit., p. 76.

[12] Ibid., pp. 76-77. Attfield considered Bury's view of Spencer's writing.

[13] Weikart, R., *From Darwin to Hitler: Evolutionary Ethics, Eugenics and Racism in Germany*, Palgrave Macmillan, 2004.

[14] Weikart, R., *A Recently Discovered Darwin Letter on Social Darwinism*, Isis, 86, pp. 609-611, 1995.

[15] Huxley, J., Kittlewell, H.B.D., *Charles Darwin and His World*, Viking Press, New York, p. 81, 1965. In: Bergman, J., *Darwin's Critical Influence on the Ruthless Extremes of Capitalism*, Answers in Genesis, TJ, 16(2), pp. 105-109, 2002.

[16] Bergman, J., *Darwin's Critical Influence on the Ruthless Extremes of Capitalism*, Answers in Genesis, TJ, 16(2), pp. 105-109, 2002.

[17] Asimov, I., *The Golden Door: The United States from 1865 to 1918*, Houghton Mifflin Company, Boston, p. 94, 1977. In: Ibid.

[18] Hofstadter, R., *Social Darwinism in American Thought*, Beacon Press, Boston, p. 49, 1955.

[19] Carnegie, A., (ed. Van Dyke, J.C.), *Autobiography of Andrew Carnegie*, 1920; Reprint: Northeastern University Press, Boston, p. 327, 1986.

[20] Wall, J.F., *Andrew Carnegie*, Oxford University Press, New York, p. 364, 1970.

[21] Ibid., p. 381.

[22] Ibid., p. 389.

[23] Comments by Bergman, op. cit., p. 107. Bergman quotes from Milner, R. *The Encyclopaedia of Evolution*, Facts on File, New York, p. 412, 1990.

[24] Rosenthal, S.J., *Sociobiology: New Synthesis or Old Ideology?* Paper presented at the 1977 American Sociological Association Convention, 1977.

[25] Larsen, E.J., *Summer for the Gods: The Scopes Trial and America's Continuing Debate Over Science and Religion*, Basic Books, New York, p. 183, 1997. In: Bergman, op. cit., pp. 108-109.

[26] Wyllie, I., *The Self-Made Man in America*, Rutgers University Press, New Brunswick, p. 92, 1954.

[27] Blake, R., Avis, W., Moulton, J., *Corporate Darwinism*, Gulf Publishing, Houston, 1966.

[28] Brookes, M., *Extreme Measures: The Dark Visions and Bright Ideas of Francis Galton*, Bloomsbury Publishing Plc., London, p. 142, 2004. Private letter from Galton to Darwin around 1860.

[29] Galton, F., *Memories of my Life*, Chapter 20, *Heredity*, p.287, Methuen, London, 1908. <http://galton.org>, Accessed March 2006. See also: Ibid., p. 142.

[30] Forster, R., Marston, P., *Reason, Science and Faith*, Monarch Books, Lion Hudson Plc., Crowborough, East Sussex, UK, pp. 305-306, 1999.

[31] Brookes., op. cit., p. 169.

[32] Galton, F., *Hereditary Improvement*, Frazer's Magazine, Vol. 7, p. 119, January 1873, <http://galton.org>, Accessed March 2006. See also Brookes, op. cit., p. 203.

[33] Ibid., p. 127. See also Brookes, op. cit., p.203.

[34] Ibid., p. 119. See also Brookes, op. cit., p.203.

[35] Brookes, op. cit., p. 265.

[36] Galton, F., *Eugenics: Its Definitions, Scope and Aims*. Sociological Society meeting, 1904. In: Brookes, op. cit., p. 269.

[37] Wells, H.G., response to Galton's speech, *Eugenics: Its Definitions, Scope, and Aims*. Sociological Society meeting. In: Brookes, op. cit., p. 271.

[38] Wells, H.G., *Anticipations of the Reaction of Mechanical and Scientific Progress upon Human Life and Thought*, Bernard Tauchnitz, Leipzig, 1902; Reprint: Dover, Mineola, NY, pp. 167-168, 1999. In: Bergman, J., *H.G. Wells, Darwin's Disciple and Eugenics Extraordinaire*, Answers in Genesis, TJ, 18(3), pp. 116-120, 2004.

[39] Ibid., p. 169.

[40] George Bernard Shaw, response to Galton's speech, *Eugenics: Its Definitions, Scope, and Aims*. Sociological Society meeting. In: Brookes, op. cit., p. 273.

[41] Brookes, op. cit., p. 275.

[42] Ibid., p. 289.

[43] Feuer, L.S., *Is the Darwin-Marx Correspondence Authentic?* Annals of Science, 32, pp. 11-12, 1975. In: Bowden, M., *The Rise of the Evolutionary Fraud*, Sovereign Books, Bromley, Kent, UK, p. 104, 1982.

[44] Ruhle, O., *Karl Marx: His Life and Works*, New Home Library, New York, p. 366, 1943. In: Whitcomb, J.C., Morris, H.M., *The Genesis Flood*, Baker Book House, p. 444, 1961.

[45] Dewey, J., *Evolution and Ethics*, The Monist, Vol. VIII (1897-1901); Reprint: Scientific Monthly, Vol. 78, p. 66, February 1954.

[46] Whitcomb, J.C., Morris, H.M., *The Genesis Flood*, Baker Book House, pp. 445-446,1961.

[47] Loeffler, J., *Worldview Wars*, <www.khouse.org/articles/2001/365>, September 2001. Accessed March 2006. Reference to: Potter., C.F., *Humanism, A new Religion*, 1933. Sourced by Cuddy, D., *A Chronology of Education in Quotable Quotes*.

[48] Ibid.

[49] Hitler, A., *Mein Kampf*, 1933, (trans. Manheim, R.), p. 260, Hutchinson, UK, 1969. [USA copyright © 1943, renewed 1971 by Houghton Mifflin Company, all rights reserved.] Reprinted by permission of the Random

House Group Ltd. and Houghton Mifflin Company.
See also: Nevard, A., *Hitler's Debt to Darwin*, Daylight no. 29, Autumn / Winter, 1999; Reprint: Creation Science Movement, Pamphlet 329.

[50] Ibid., pp. 365-366

[51] Ibid., p. 369

[52] Baynes, N.H., *The Speeches of Adolf Hitler*, Oxford University Press, p. 369, 1942.

[53] Cook, N., *The Hunt for Zero Point*, Arrow, p. 305, 2000.

[54] Wiener, P.F., *Martin Luther: Hitler's Spiritual Ancestor*, Gustav Broukal Press, 1985.

[55] Wiener, P.F., *Martin Luther: Hitler's Spiritual Ancestor*, Win the Peace Pamphlet, No 3, Chapter II, *Luther - The Man, Luther's Character*, Hutchinson and Co., London, (nd).

[56] Ibid. (E refers to the Erlington edition of Luther's work. W to the Weimar edition).

[57] Ibid.

[58] Ibid., Chapter III, *Luther's Political Doctrines, Martin Luther and the State*.

[59] Walker, A., *Epistles of Straw - The True Tragedy of Creationism*, Ship of Fools website, December 2001, <www.shipoffools.com/Columns/Walker/Walker1201.html>, Accessed March 2006.

[60] Johnson, P.E., *Darwin on Trial*, Monarch Books, Lion Hudson Plc., Crowborough, East Sussex, UK, p. 187, 1994.

[61] Ibid., p. 130. Quotes by Teilhard de Chardin, P., *The Phenomenon of Man* (1959).

[62] Teilhard de Chardin, P., Quoted on Christians Australia website, *Devil-ution!* (nd), <www.accsoft.com.au/~xians/teach/science-philosophy/devilution.html>, Accessed March 2006.

[63] Ferngren, G.B., Numbers, R.L., *C.S. Lewis on Creation and Evolution: The Acworth Letters, 1944-1960*, Perspective on Science and Christian Faith, 48 (1), March 1996. Personal letter from C.S. Lewis to Bernard Acworth dated 5th March 1960.

[64] Bauval, R., Hancock, G., *Talisman: Sacred Cities, Secret Faith*, Michael Joseph, 2004.

[65] Johnson, P.E., *Nihilism and the End of Law*, First Things, 31, pp. 19-25, March 1993, <www.firstthings.com/ftissues/ft9303/articles/pjohnson.html>, Accessed March 2006. See also: C.S. Lewis Society, <www.apologetics.org/articles/nihilism.html>, Accessed March 2006.

[66] Dawkins, R., *A Devil's Chaplain*, Weidenfeld and Nicolson, London, p. 34, 2003.

Chapter 10

Restoring Theistic Christianity

'Thy people shall be willing in the day of thy power'
(Psalm 110:3 KJV)

It is apparent that Enlightenment philosophy and deistic thinking in general eventually gave rise to the evolutionary theories of Charles Darwin and Herbert Spencer. This subsequently led to a rejection of traditional Christian values in the West, with the rise of atheistic humanism and belief in godless progress. As has been shown in previous chapters, this move away from Christian faith also undermined Judeo-Christian standards based on the ethic of love. Such evolutionary thinking is itself a throwback to the ancient Greek philosophers, and many of the evolutionary ideas that we are familiar with today were considered centuries before Darwin.

However, it is necessary to go back to the beginning of the Enlightenment and ask an important question. How did deism get a foothold in Europe in the first place and do such damage to a once powerful Church? When looking a little deeper, some uncomfortable conclusions become evident, that the root of deism lies in the Church's division and discord as a result of the Reformation, with fault lying on both the Protestant and Catholic sides. Luther's own character also failed to show the love of Christ to the population as a whole. This raises difficulties for Christians of both traditions.

The later reformers in effect introduced a form of Biblical deism, by stating that miracles ceased with the death of the last apostle, and the more extreme reformers introduced an over-deterministic and fatalistic teaching of limited atonement. The idea is that God elects some for salvation and some for eternal damnation. The hopeless state for those who are not of the elect is then a blank cheque to eat, drink and be merry on the high road to hell. If you are damned anyway then better have a jolly good time on the way down. Of course one way out of this hopeless fate is to try and prove that God doesn't really exist at all. This ultra-reformed theology of limited atonement also moved away from the idea of a God of justice, of passion and love, and left a fatalistic mindset for those searching for reason, love, truth and justice. The passion that Paul showed in preaching the Gospel undermines those who teach fatalistic Calvinism and a rejection of freewill. There wasn't a lot of love shown between Christians either, following the Reformation, with bitter discord and war all too real across much of Europe.

A theology of divine election misrepresents the teachings of St. Paul, who saw free will and predestination as two sides of the same coin. To Paul's mind, there appears to be a divine duality that cannot easily be bridged with human understanding, but the Bible clearly teaches about a God of love and justice, whose desire it is that no one should perish. Of course some claim that Paul never preached predestination, and appeal to everything being determined by free will, with election to do with anointing for service not salvation. Such views, for instance, see God's role in determining the future as that of a master chess player who is able to see far into the future through foreknowledge. Predestination, as taught by Paul, is also seen as God's promise of later transformation into Christ's image to those who are being saved. However, a more complete exploration of predestination is really beyond the scope of this book.

However, the Gospel of Jesus Christ should in no way be seen as cold fatalism, because the suffering and passion of Christ was very real. He suffered because of His love for all humanity. In fact, passion is a very real stumbling block for those who believe in pure determinism, whether it was Christ's death on the cross or the suffering of the saints through history. Paul himself claimed that his earnest prayers were akin to the pain a woman suffers in giving birth, *(Galatians 4:19)*, but why would Paul have prayed so earnestly if he thought it was already predetermined who would be saved and who would be eternally damned?

On the Catholic side, the clergy claimed that only they had the right to interpret Scripture. Scripture, they taught, was full of apparent contradictions and was written in several languages, and so only a trained scholar and priest could read it and interpret it correctly. Of course the Protestants pointed out that the clergy gained their authority from Scripture, and so the Catholics were undermining their own position by criticising the Bible.

Sadly though, the division of the church weakened both faith in God's ability to work miracles, and the integrity of Scripture in the minds of many. Ordinary people felt caught in the cross fire through decades of bitter and sometimes bloody division, and with both sides claiming to be absolutely right, confusion reigned. A seemingly unloving and corrupt clergy also misrepresented God in the minds of ordinary people. Enlightenment philosophers sought to bridge this confusion and darkness by looking to a progressive improvement through one's own endeavour. However, denying the need for God and His loving grace, as the philosophers increasingly did, introduced its own ethical confusion because mankind then became master of his own destiny, without an external sovereign to determine what is right or wrong. Johnson comments that as we remove God from the picture, then each human being becomes his or her own godlet with as much authority to set rules and regulations as anyone else.[1]

The main purpose of this chapter is to address the philosophical and theological question of whether miracles ceased as the Protestant reformers asserted. Ironically, those who did most to uphold the Bible at the beginning of the twentieth century, the Fundamentalists, also taught that the miracles of Jesus ceased with the death of the last Apostle, and eventually came to reject the literal creation account in favour of a belief in the process of evolution. This group, including Benjamin B. Warfield, believed that most miracles, and the creation account, should be described scientifically, and yet this is the precise movement that gave rise to Christian Fundamentalism. Modern historians such as Walker wrongly ascribe the growth of young earth creationism to the Fundamentalists, and indeed literal creationists often wearily accept the fundamentalist tag. While this word may be a fairly accurate description of those who believe that creation is foundational for Christian faith, the word in itself carries so many negative connotations that it is not really useful to use it at all. Scientific creationism, or young earth creationism, is perhaps a better description of the literalist creation view.

219

At face value, the scientific creationist Christian and the charismatic Christian should have a common cause. One believes that God worked powerfully in the past, the other that God can and still does work powerfully in the present. God after all doesn't change, and both agree that God will work powerfully in the future when Christ returns. Both also agree that by demonstrating God's power, either through logical scientific argument, or charismatic gifts, people will be won for Jesus Christ.[2] There are indeed some who would describe themselves as being both charismatic and literal creationist in theology, although often this is not the case. Many charismatic Christians adopt a progressive creationist, or gradual, theistic evolutionary approach, and believe that a too literal view of Genesis damages a modern witness to Jesus Christ.[3] It is ironic that such charismatic Christians wouldn't dream of denying Jesus's miracles in the New Testament, but both the apostle John *(John 1:3)*, and Paul *(Colossians 1:6)* also place Jesus Christ right at the centre of creation. But it is an interesting question to compare the miracles of Jesus with creation. Was it any harder, for instance, for Jesus to turn water into wine than create the vine in the first place?

On the other hand, many literal creationists believe that God no longer works miracles today, adopting a cessationist view with regard to the gifts, or *charismata*, of the Holy Spirit, which has been influenced by the followers of Calvin and Warfield. Both of these views may in fact be described as partial forms of Christian deism. As has been shown in previous chapters, the rise of deism led to a denial of God's grace in shaping society in favour of a belief in human progress, and it is uncomfortable to acknowledge that the cessationist teaching, which denies the *charismata*, is also a denial of grace in favour of human effort. The progressive creationist view of an old earth is heavily influence by deism, even if they are unaware of this, while Calvinistic cessationist teaching enabled the conditions for natural deism to rise during the Enlightenment in the first place. This process then sowed the seeds for modern cessationist thought exemplified by Benjamin B. Warfield's book *Counterfeit miracles*.[4] As already shown, Warfield believed that modern miracles violate God-given natural laws and the Protestant interpretation of New Testament Scripture, but Warfield also came to reject a recent creation in favour of a process of evolution. This view has striking similarities with the beliefs of Descartes and other deistic philosophers.

It is necessary therefore to look at the root of the cessationist and progressive creationist beliefs, and to respectfully appeal to Christians of both persuasions to consider the evidence afresh. This evidence may be uncomfortable for some, and the ground has been covered many times in the past with Christians more or less agreeing to disagree, to keep the peace, but it is important to address this issue. Christians today increasingly recognise that in order for revival to come, there is a need for unity between those who have a commitment to the Word of God, and those who have an emphasis on the Holy Spirit. After all, the Holy Spirit as God is clearly not divided between Himself, His creative power, or His inspired Word. One Pentecostal pioneer, Smith Wigglesworth, reportedly stated that 'When the [people of the] Word and the [people of the] Spirit come together, there will be the biggest movement of the Holy Spirit that the nation (i.e. Britain), and indeed the world, has ever seen'.[5] Dr. R.T. Kendall, recent minister of the reformed Westminster Chapel in London, also co-authored a book arguing for unity between those Christians who focus on the Word and those of the Spirit.[6]

Another reformed theologian, Jack Deere, has written a couple of books on the subject of charismatic gifts.[7, 8] A number of reformed teachers now recognise the reality of the grace gifts of the Holy Spirit in the present day. Arthur Wallis, one time Plymouth Brethren preacher, also longed to see revival, with God's people rising up in power. His classic book *In the Day of Thy Power*[9] took its name from *Psalm 110:3 (KJV)*, 'Thy people shall be willing in the day of thy power'.

The root of cessationist theology can be traced back to the Reformation. The reformers were unhappy with the excesses of the Roman Catholic Church at the time, which included payment for forgiveness of sins in the form of indulgences, and spurious claims of miracles. The Calvinists therefore adopted the belief that Scripture alone was sufficient for godliness, and rejected Christian miracles. Jack Deere notes that *Sola Scriptura* ('only the Scripture') was a great battle cry of the Reformation period.[10] In return, the Roman Catholic Church questioned the legitimacy of the reformers' doctrine because of a lack of miracles. The Roman Church on the other hand could point to a long history of miracles, which they believed made their faith and doctrine legitimate. Deere highlights the response to this claim by the reformers. He shows that without hard Scriptural evidence, the reformers had to rely on deduction to teach that miracles were meant to cease with the death of the Apostles. He notes that this is still the main line of reasoning of cessationists today, because clearly Scripture has not changed. Deere believes that the reason the reformers tried to deduce cessationist teaching from Scripture was really born out of a lack of *experience* of miracles.[11]

The Calvinists denied miracles in the post-apostolic Christian age, believing that God had given the Church a miraculous start during the first century, and then allowed it to coast through history with Scripture alone. This is in fact similar to the argument of natural deists who believe in a distant creation and a purely natural, clockwork universe with God at best reduced to the role of absentee landlord. In a later book, Jack Deere goes on to claim that cessationist teaching is really Biblical deism, commenting that this position has a lot in common with natural deism.[12]

There were, of course, very good reasons for the Reformation, but the reformers rebelled against the authority of the Roman Church and denied that it had power to work miracles in the past and present, claiming that Church age miracles were counterfeit.[13] But if the Christian reformers could rebel against the Roman Church and deny its power, then others could rebel against Protestant Christianity and deny all miracles. This was in fact what happened when the deists began to teach that God was both distant and powerless to act. Enlightenment thinkers included men like Spinoza (1632-1677), Hume (1711-1776), Voltaire (1694-1778), Rousseau (1712-1778) and Fichte (1762-1814).[14]

It is also likely that there was a general reaction against the ultra-Calvinistic teaching of limited atonement and double predestination[15] within society, which then led to an acceptance of other more deistic doctrines. With such a fatalistic view of life, and an apparently cruel and unjust God, is it any wonder that men like Hume and Spinoza rebelled against organised Judaism and Christianity, and gained such strong followings in later centuries? Spinoza was to some extent a pantheist, believing God to be an integral part of the universe, but both Spinoza and Hume were totally opposed to all miracles because they believed miracles violated the laws of nature. Jon Ruthven described this process as follows:

> 'John Calvin turned the cessationist polemic against Roman Catholicism and the radical reformation, undercutting their claims to religious authority they based on miracles and revelations. Calvin popularized the restriction of miracles to the accreditation of the apostles and specifically to their gospel, though he was less rigid about cessationism than most of his followers. Nevertheless from Aquinas through the Enlightenment, the concept of miracle assumed an increasingly rationalistic cast, until it became a cornerstone of the Enlightenment apologetic of Locke, Newton, Glanville and Boyle, but a millstone in Hume.
>
> Hume's skepticism about the possibility of miracles, the ultimate cessationist polemic (which exemplified Warfield's historical critical method in his examination of post-biblical miracle claims), precipitated the response of Scottish Common Sense Philosophy (SCSP), a somewhat rationalistic apologetic made widely popular by William Paley's *Christian Evidences*. Paley argued from the divine design of nature, predictive (Messianic) prophecy and from (biblical) miracles.
>
> … Warfield's concept of miracle required an essentially deistic view of nature…' [16]

Colin Brown comments that deism initially started out as an attempt by Edward, Lord Herbert of Cherbury (1583-1648) to show that faith in God was rational without recourse to special revelation.[17] John Locke, in *The reasonableness of Christianity*, published in 1695, also appealed to reason and Scripture to try and prove the reality of Christian faith. Later deists turned increasingly hostile to Christian faith.

> 'The deists also attacked the arguments based on fulfilled prophecy and miracles. Anthony Collins claimed that the Old Testament prophecies did not really fit Jesus, and Thomas Woolston wrote a series of bitter discourses on the miracles of Jesus, leading up to an attack on the resurrection.' [18]

It is apparent therefore that the reformers claimed that the God who works miracles was restricted to the New Testament age and before, with Scripture alone sufficient for building faith in the present. Subsequently, Christians attempted to prove the existence of God and the reasonableness of Christianity, through reason and Scripture alone. Later, natural deists, if they considered the miraculous at all, pushed divine intervention back to a very distant past with a denial of all subsequent miracles. The natural deism of the Enlightenment was therefore, at least in part, born out of the division, rebellion, and denial by the reformers of God's power to work miracles.

However, not all reformers were cessationist in theology. Jack Deere highlights the fact that many of the Scottish reformers used *charismata* of prophecy, words of knowledge and healing. This included George Wishart (1513-46), John Knox (1514-1572), John Welsh (1570-1622), Robert Bruce (1554-1631) and Alexander Peden (1626-1686).[19] Knox, one time student of Calvin, '... emphasised the evangelical doctrines of grace and forgiveness, the Word and Scripture, and the Holy Spirit and the Church.'[20] As an example of Knox's prophetic gift, he is reported to have predicted the impending death of his friend William Kirkaldy for supporting the Catholic Mary Queen of Scots against the Protestant English armies. It happened as John Knox said, with Kirkaldy lowered from the castle in shame on the 3rd of May 1573 and hung before the sun on the 3rd of August 1573.[21] Wishart was also stated by John Howie to have 'possessed the spirit of prophecy in an extraordinary degree'.[22] Jack Deere later shows how this evidence was air brushed out of history by reformed Christians who rejected the possibility of charismatic gifts. The statement above, regarding Wishart, was changed by William McGavin in a revised 1846 edition of Howie's book to 'He possessed an extraordinary degree of sagacious foresight.'[23] It would seem that the cessationist Calvinists, who denied the possibility of present day miracles and prophecies, were revising history, perhaps a result of the growing influence of deism. This change in attitude towards modern miracles mirrored the increasing rationalism of the time.

The two main Scottish Church historians of the period were Robert Fleming (1630-1694) and Samuel Rutherford (1600-1661).

Both were leading Scottish reformed ministers and theologians. Fleming wrote a book entitled *The Fulfilling of the Scripture* in 1669, in which he noted that God poured out a prophetic and apostolic spirit on his servants in Scotland during this time, which was close to the outpouring of the New Testament period.[24] During the ministry of Robert Bruce, there was also evidence of healing of epilepsy and insanity, angelic visitations, and many other gifts of the Holy Spirit.[25] Fleming believed that all of this occurred to fulfil Scripture. Rutherford, for his part, commented that 'There is a revelation of some particular men, who have foretold things to come, even since the ceasing of the Canon of the Word...'[26] Rutherford mentioned John Hus, John Wycliffe, Martin Luther and George Wishart as having 'foretold things to come'.[27]

Manifestations of the Holy Spirit have also been documented throughout Church history. Dr Patrick Dixon, in *Signs of Revival*,[28] refers to a lengthy study of some 650,000 words by John Gillies,[29] a friend of George Whitfield. Dixon comments that owing to the magnitude of accounts of manifestations and different kinds of enthusiasm, it is difficult to know what to leave in and what to leave out.[30]

The history of miracles and spiritual manifestations can be traced right through the history of the church, and there is insufficient space to go into great detail. Eusebius, for his part, in his *Ecclesiastical History*, highlights two works by Irenaeus entitled *Refutation and Overthrow of False Doctrine*. The second book of the same work shows that the miracles that were carried out by Jesus and the apostles continued in the churches after the death of the apostles, until at least the time of Irenaeus. Eusebius highlights the following passages from Irenaeus:

'... from the raising of the dead, as the Lord raised, and as the apostles by means of prayer, for even among the brethren frequently in a case of necessity when a whole church united in much fasting and prayer, the spirit has returned to the ex-animated body, ...'. 'But if they say that our Lord also did these things only in appearance, we shall refer them back to the prophetic declarations, and shall show from them that all those things were strictly foretold, and were done by him, and that he alone is the Son of God. Wherefore, also, those that were truly his disciples, receiving grace from him, in his name performed these things for the benefit of the best of men, as every one received the free gift from him.' [31]

Spiritual gifts mentioned later in this passage include the casting out of demons, the gift of knowledge of things to come, visions and prophetic communications, and the healing of the sick. Irenaeus, like Fleming, comments that all of this was done according to the promise of Scripture. What Scripture might they have been referring to? The text that Peter referred to on the day of Pentecost was *from Joel 2:28-32.* This passage, also recorded in *Acts 2:17-21* says, your '... sons and daughters will prophecy ... young men will see visions ... old men will dream dreams. ... I will show wonders in the heavens above and signs on the earth below ... before the great and glorious day of the Lord. ... And everyone who calls on the name of the Lord will be saved.' A plain reading of this text shows that God's gifts will be available before the glorious return of Christ, and during the period in which people may be saved. Another passage is from Mark's Gospel, *(Mark 16:9-20)* where Jesus says that '... signs will accompany those who believe: In my name they will drive out demons ... they will place their hands on sick people, and they will get well.' [32]

While Scripture is rightly asserted to be divinely inspired by most evangelical Christians, we need to understand how and why it was written, to understand the culture and the background. It is too easy for a Christian to simply quote from Scripture without understanding the historical context. There in fact arises a serious problem of logic for those who believe the Spiritual gifts died out with the death of the last apostle. The complete canon of the New Testament, that we believe to be divinely inspired, was not finally agreed until AD 400 at the Council of Carthage,[33] although use was made prior to this of the recognised four Gospels, Acts and Paul's letters. If we are to maintain the integrity of Scripture, then we must accept that the Roman Catholic Church of the fourth and fifth century AD had the authority and the *charismata* of wisdom and knowledge to take this decision. If we say they had no such grace gifts then we invalidate Scripture, and the canon of the New Testament becomes a matter of human debate.

There is evidence that ultimately progressive creationism had its roots in the Calvinist cessationist teaching of the Reformation, which gave rise to deism. Promoters of both cessationism and progressive creation may be uncomfortable to discover that their beliefs have a common foundation, as often they are diametrically opposed, but both have deistic characteristics. One believes that God can work miracles in the present, but not in creation, the other that God worked powerfully in the past, but not today. Both views may be seen as forms of deism and not true to the supernatural theistic characteristic of the Judeo-Christian faith. The God of the Bible is clearly revealed as one who is able to work miracles, during creation, during the Old and New Testament period, in the present day and in the future, without our permission or approval.

The reformed cessationist teaching of Calvin unwittingly gave birth to the Enlightenment, with the rise of deism and later atheistic humanism. Calvin's cessationism grew into the denial of all miracles, and this subsequently influenced the beliefs of geologists and biologists, with the growth of a full blown, purely materialistic science. Deism then fed back into Christian thought and weakened faith during the nineteenth and twentieth centuries with the rise of progressive creationist teaching among educated people in the West.

Written evidence from Church history shows that indeed miracles have occurred at various times in this period, with *charismata* given to various Christians to build the Church. What is more is that a plain reading of the Bible shows that the continuation of the *charismata* is in fact a fulfilment of Scripture, and not its denial. This does not mean we should accept everything uncritically, but we should test everything. 'Do not put out the Spirit's fire; do not treat prophecies with contempt. Test everything. Hold on to the good.' *(1 Thessalonians 5:19-21)*. Many Christians, including reformed theologians, increasingly recognise the need for a commitment to God's Word and the need to be filled with the Holy Spirit, if we are to see a restoration of the authority of the Church and revival in the West. It also needs to be recognised that acceptance of the reality of present day *charismata*, does not mean acceptance of what is often called *charismania*, or imply that the charismatic movement is above criticism. Paul, while upholding the *charismata*, had a great deal to say about the abuse of such gifts in the first letter to the Corinthian Church, and we must bear this in mind. There is often found a lack of discipline, immature leadership, an over-emphasis on wealth, and a willingness to even dare to command God to act. All of these abuses actually undermine the acceptance of the continuation of the grace gifts among Christians, and this hinders the Gospel.

On the other side of the fence, the continued promotion of progressive creation by leading charismatic evangelical Christians may be seen as a form of deism, and may in fact undermine the authority and power of Jesus Christ and His Church in the world today. The assertion that scientific young earth creationism in itself damages a modern Christian witness to Christ is without foundation, and negates one's own responsibility. As has been shown, looking for scientific evidence for a recent creation is a valid pursuit for Christians committed to upholding the integrity of God's Word. Progressive creationists should reconsider this in all seriousness, and also give greater respect to those seeking to defend the Bible against attacks from materialistic voices.

Forster and Marston, for instance, assert wrongly that young earth creationism is a major break from traditional evangelicalism, favouring instead progressive creation or theistic evolution.[34] It is rather ironic that Forster and Marston should favour the deistic position of the fundamentalist Warfield and his rejection of miracles, instead of the theistic creation theology of Henry Morris who upholds the creational miracles and the continuation of miracles even in the present time.[35] It is my assertion that both theistic evolution and progressive creationism are forms of deism or semi-deism, and that a deistic spirit, endemic in Western Christianity, is a major stumbling block to the health and growth of the Christian church in the West. Young earth creationists are seeking to restore faith in a God of love and power.

Notes and References

[1] Johnson, P.E., *Nihilism and the End of Law*, First Things, 31, pp. 19-25, March 1993, <www.firstthings.com/ftissues/ft9303/articles/ pjohnson.html>, Accessed March 2006. See also: C.S. Lewis Society, <www.apologetics.org/articles/nihilism.html>, Accessed March 2006.

[2] As an aside, St Paul (1 Corn. 1and 2, and Romans 1:16) shows how Christian faith comes by powerful revelation of who Jesus Christ is, by the Holy Spirit, and not through signs, or human wisdom. (Power = *dunamis*: Greek - from which we get the English word dynamite.)

[3] See for instance: Forster R., Marston P., *Reason, Science and Faith*, Monarch Books, Lion Hudson Plc., Crowborough, East Sussex, UK, 1999. [Roger Forster is a well respected charismatic Christian leader, and pastor of the large Icthus Fellowship in London. He believes a literal reading of Genesis is unnecessary for effective Christian faith]. Hugh Ross, a Canadian scientist, charismatic Christian and promoter of progressive creation has also recently spoken critically of young earth creationists along these lines. See the interview with Hugh Ross in Charisma magazine, June 2003, by Andy Butcher - Senior writer and news director of the magazine. [Review: Sarfati, J., *Shame on Charisma!*, Answers in Genesis, 29th May 2003. <www.answersingenesis.org/docs2003/0529charisma.asp>, Accessed March 2006].

[4] Warfield, B.B., *Counterfeit Miracles*, The Banner of Truth Trust, Edinburgh, UK, 1918.

[5] Wigglesworth, S., Reportedly spoken in 1947, shortly before his death. Researched and paraphrased: Price, C., *Revival Prophesied*, Renewal magazine, 284, p. 50, January 2000. Monarch Magazines Ltd., Lion Hudson Plc, Crowborough, East Sussex, UK. See also: <www.thewayofthespirit.com/about/wigglesworth.aspx>, Accessed March 2006.

[6] Kendall, R.T., Cain, P., *The Word and the Spirit*, Creation House, June 1999.

[7] Deere, J., *Surprised by the Power of the Spirit*, Kingsway Publications, Eastbourne, England, 1994. [Jack Deere spent many years as professor in the Old Testament department at Dallas Theological Seminary].

[8] Deere, J., *Surprised by the Voice of God*, Kingsway Publications, Eastbourne, England, 1996.

[9] Wallis, A., *In the Day of Thy Power*, Christian Literature Crusade, England, 1956.

[10] Deere, op. cit., *Surprised by the Power of the Spirit*, p. 100.

[11] Ibid., pp. 99-103.

[12] Deere, op. cit., *Surprised by the Voice of God*, p. 251.

[13] Deere, op. cit., *Surprised by the Power of the Spirit*, p. 100.

[14] See for instance: Attfield, R., *The Ethics of Environmental Concern*, University of Georgia Press, Ch.5, pp. 67-87, 1991. (Second Edition © 1991 by the University of Georgia Press, Athens, Georgia 30602)

[15] This teaching asserts that God has pre-ordained or elected some for eternal salvation, and some to eternal damnation.

[16] Ruthven, J., Adaptation from Chapter 4 of his book, which is based on his PhD dissertation. <http://www.logosword.co.uk/articles/cessationCharismata.htm>, Accessed March 2006. Complete title: Ruthven, J., *On the Cessation of the Charismata: The Protestant Polemic on Post Biblical Miracles*, Sheffield University Academic Press, UK, 1993. [Jon Ruthven is Professor of Systematic and Practical Theology, School of Divinity, Regent University, Virginia Beach].

[17] Brown, C., *Reason and Unreason*; Dowley, T., (ed.), *The History of Christianity: A Lion Handbook*, Lion Hudson Plc., Revised ed., p. 492, 1990.

[18] Ibid., p. 492.

[19] Deere, op. cit., *Surprised by the Voice of God*, pp. 64-78.

[20] Atkinson, J., *Reform*; Dowley, T. (ed.), *The History of Christianity: A Lion Handbook*, Lion Hudson Plc., Revised ed., p. 390, 1990. [From Knox's confession of Faith and Doctrine, 1560].

[21] Howie, J., (ed. McGavin, W.), *Scots Worthies*, W.R. McPhun, Glasgow, p. 63, 1846. (Orig. 1775). And: Ridley, J., *John Knox*, Clarendon Press, Oxford, pp. 517, 519, 1968. In: Deere, op. cit., *Surprised by the Voice of God*, pp. 72-73.

[22] Ibid., *Scots Worthies*, p. 27. Based on John Knox's writing. In: Deere, op. cit., *Surprised by the Voice of God*, pp. 78-79 and endnotes.

[23] Ibid., *Scots Worthies*, p. 27. In: Deere, op. cit., *Surprised by the Voice of God*, p. 79 and endnotes.

[24] Fleming, R., *The Fulfilling of the Scripture*, Rotterdam, (no pub.), pp. 422-423, 1671, (Orig. 1669). In: Deere, op. cit., *Surprised by the Voice of God*, Note 11, p. 83.

[25] Ibid., pp. 416-440. In: Deere, op. cit., *Surprised by the Voice of God*, pp. 75-76.

[26] Rutherford, S., *A Survey of the Spirituall Antichrist. Opening the Secrets of Familisme and Antinonmianisme in the Antichristian Doctrine of John Saltmarsh...* , Printed by J.D. & R.I. for Andrew Crooke, London, p. 42, 1648. In: Deere, op. cit., *Surprised by the Voice of God*.

[27] Ibid., p. 42.

[28] Dixon, P., *Signs of Revival*, Kingsway, East Sussex, England, 1994.

[29] Gillies, J., *Historical Collections of the Accounts of Revival*, 1754; Reprint: Banner of Truth, 1981. In: Ibid., p. 116.

[30] Dixon, op. cit., p. 116.

[31] Cruse, C.F. (trans.), *Eusebius' Ecclesiastical History*, Book V, Chapter VII, pp. 186-187, Baker Book House, 1995.

[32] Although some have tried to claim that this passage is not part of Scripture, one leading Bible scholar, Carsten Peter Thiede, believed this longer ending to Mark's Gospel was from a second draft prepared by Mark himself, with Peter's oversight, and therefore it naturally belongs to Scripture. It is indeed acknowledged very early. See: Thiede, C.P., *Jesus: Life or Legend?*, Lion Publishing, Oxford, England, 2nd ed., p. 59, 1997. Eusebius states that Mark was Peter's 'interpreter'. See: Ibid., p. 188.

[33] Hurtado, L.W., *How the New Testament Has Come Down to Us*; Dowley, T. (ed.), *The History of Christianity: A Lion Handbook*, Lion Hudson Plc, Revised ed., pp. 134-135, 1990.

[34] Forster, R., Marston, P., *Reason, Science and Faith*, Monarch Books, Lion Hudson Plc., Crowborough, East Sussex, UK, p. 241, 1999.

[35] Morris, H.M., *Miracles*, Master Books, 2004.

Chapter 11

Suffering and the Evolutionary Theodicy Problem

'The creation waits in eager expectation for the sons of God to be revealed. For the creation was subjected to frustration, not by its own choice, but by the will of the one who subjected it, in hope that the creation itself will be liberated from its bondage to decay and brought into the glorious freedom of the children of God.'
(Romans 8:19-21)

The issue of suffering is problematic for Christians, and a complete understanding has eluded mankind throughout history. This is a complex question, but atheists and secularists often use suffering and the presence of evil, to make rather simplistic attacks on Christianity and deny the existence of God. One of the most popular is to accuse religious people of causing wars and strife, but as the following evidence suggests, a rejection of Christian faith does not lead to a better world, but to greater suffering. One atheist who is willing to acknowledge the weakness of such arguments is Andrew Kenny. Writing in the Spectator he comments that crimes committed by Christians such as Richelieu, Torquemada, and Richard the First are hardly comparable with the much greater crimes of more recent atheists, Lenin, Stalin and Mao Tse-Tung. He notes that only the pagan Hitler matches them, and he ranks these leaders in order of people killed. Mao comes in at number one, followed by Stalin, Hitler and then Lenin at number four.[1]

It is a common accusation levelled at Christians that religious people are responsible for all wars and violence. However, this doesn't stand up to critical scrutiny, especially in comparison to wars and violent acts committed by those who claim to be atheist or pagan. In fact a clear understanding of evil is impossible for the atheist. David Hume, for instance, placed evil in the mind of the observer, not in the object of suffering. Evil then becomes a matter of human debate and opinion, which perhaps explains why godless political systems have such a brutal legacy.

Not only do religious people get the blame for war and political violence, but another question that Christians are often asked is; if there is a God of love, then why does he allow suffering? This question is asked by those who are seeking a genuine answer, and by more militant atheists seeking to undermine Christian faith. Recently, in a BBC TV documentary David Attenborough asked a similar question. How, he asked, could a God of love create the guinea worm that burrows into the eye of a young boy? [2] Attenborough's question is really based on the concept of *natural evil* and perhaps recognises that *moral evil* comes from the human will. Moral evil includes such things as war, murder and acts of violence, for instance, and these are caused by mankind's wickedness and should not therefore be blamed on God. However, philosophers struggle to come to terms with what is termed natural evil, for instance accounting for earthquakes, volcanoes, hurricanes, disease and general accidents etc. These are often called 'acts of God'. John Stuart Mill for instance comments:

> 'Not even on the most distorted and contracted theory of good which ever was framed by religious or philosophical fanaticism, can the government of Nature be made to resemble the work of a being at once good and omnipotent.' [3]

Trying to harmonise this 'government of Nature' with the character of a loving God as revealed in the Bible appears problematic. David Hume further expounds this point by appealing to the questions set out by the ancient Greek atheist Epicurus. Hume claims that Epicurus's questions have not been answered. Hume asks whether God is willing to prevent evil, but not able; then such a God would be impotent. He then asks whether God is able, but not willing; such a God would then be malevolent. Hume finishes by asking if God is both willing and able, then he asks why does evil continue? [4]

This is a challenging question and appears to suggest that God cannot be both loving and omnipotent in allowing evil to run unchecked. Accordingly, the conclusion set out by such philosophers is that the Judeo-Christian God cannot exist. But before we answer this challenging question more fully, we need to assess the logical consequence of the question. The question of natural evil that Epicurus, Mill, Hume and Attenborough point to, in fact has an assumption that suffering and natural evil are wrong, but we might ask another question. If the God of love does not exist, then why does suffering matter? In saying natural evil is bad, we make a value judgement, but value judgements are meaningless in a godless universe where meaning and purpose are denied. How can we evaluate evil in a world where ultimate value has no meaning? If ethical values do have meaning, then where does it come from? In a universe without meaning and purpose, why should anyone care about anything? If there is no God of love, then where is the basis for any sort of moral code at all? Who is to judge what is right and wrong if we deny the ultimate evaluator? Phillip Johnson[5] has shown that a rejection of the God of the Bible, who wants to be approached as Father, does not produce a more loving ethical society, but a more brutal, nihilistic one, where the ultimate evaluator of good and evil is rejected. We have already covered much of this debate, but we can only make sense of suffering and evil in the context that there is a God, and that He is a God of love.

Of course one possibility is that instead, God is a malevolent and brutal tyrant, but if so, then he may still be omnipotent, in which case you will be assimilated, and resistance is futile, to pinch a phrase from the fictional Borg of Star Trek fame. But we can see in the suffering and sacrifice of Jesus Christ, how God demonstrated his love towards mankind in an effort to bring an end to humanity's suffering, and indeed the suffering of nature also. For this He is worthy of our praise. The issue of suffering is far more profound than simplistic attempts to discredit God by Epicurus, Hume or Attenborough.

The other alternative, as the deists would have us believe, is that God is both weak and very distant. It is understandable how people might consider this possibility when they see the suffering in the world, and do not perceive any direct divine intervention. However, according to Judeo-Christian theology, God has bound himself to work through mankind in the form of prayer and faithful service. God deals with mankind through covenants that he puts in place, and under these he respects our moral decisions. Today we live under a New Covenant. It is not that he is powerless to intervene. It is that mankind is disobedient and rebellious. In fact, if God did intervene every time that we sin, we would soon all be destroyed. However, the God of the Bible is one who offers mercy and desires mankind to approach him with faith. God has made all power available to us, but we simply do not take hold of it by faith. The Bible also teaches that it is mankind's duty to serve Him in the earth. This is found in the original great commission 'to go forth and multiply, to fill the earth and subdue it', and also in the second great commission of Jesus to make 'disciples of all nations'. *(Matthew 28:19)*. The truth is that God has intervened and He has done so through Jesus Christ, who as God came down to Earth to bring the world under his authority. Christ means *Anointed One*, and Jesus the *One who Saves*. Therefore his very name, Jesus Christ, means that he has absolute authority to save mankind from sin and rebellion. Later the Holy Spirit was poured out on the day of Pentecost to enable mankind to live by God's grace and to establish the church, whose job it is to preach righteousness across the world. A lot of suffering is caused today because people reject His power and authority. So in answer to the deist's claim, God is both very near and very powerful, but we must take hold of that power through faith.

In the Christianised West, it seems obvious to all of us that it is wrong for children to suffer in pain, but Hitler's logic, based on the 'iron logic of nature', allowed him to send children from the wrong race to the gas chamber. Hitler's ideal was based on the logic of survival of the fittest and the brutal eugenics programme of the utopian Social Darwinists. As an evolutionist, Darwin was perhaps far more concerned with the suffering of children than Hitler, seeing his own beloved child die. I am sure Attenborough has similar sympathies, but where does Darwin's and Attenborough's parental and filial affection come from? As we have seen, Darwin tried to make out that such parental concern was the product of nature, and that nature as a whole has filial affection for its different members.

However, quite clearly this filial affection does not extend from the parasitic guinea worm to humanity. The only conclusion is that nature often is *red in tooth and claw*, and the development of some sort of ethical standard from evolution cannot answer the question of suffering. Parental and filial affection is not how nature operates overall at all. In a godless universe, the only logic is one where the fit survive, and there is no reason to care for those who suffer as a consequence. Evolutionists have failed to provide an answer to the discontinuity question between biological and sociological evolution. The question of suffering cannot be answered in a godless universe, and in fact the question becomes meaningless, or worse, the application of survival of the fittest is seen as good. It is more likely that the moral conscience of Darwin and Attenborough derives from their own nature as created human beings. These men have gained their parental and filial affection from their essential creation, being made in the image of a God of love who wants to be known as a Father.

As an aside, we might consider how the parasitic guinea worm problem is being tackled today. In 2002 the incidence of this disease has dropped to 65,000 from 3.5 million cases in 1986. This is mainly a result of the work of the Carter Centre, set up by the Christian and ex-president of the United States, Jimmy Carter, Carter's aim being to eradicate this disease as a result of a Christian conscience.[6] In doing this, Carter is fulfilling the original great commission to be a faithful steward, and to rule over nature and subdue it, to work with God and restore nature to its original perfect state.

The book of Genesis teaches very clearly about a God who made everything, and then created mankind in His own image. God saw that it was good, and God wanted to have fellowship with Adam and Eve. Mankind was commanded to obey God, by not eating of the fruit of the knowledge of good and evil, or else death would ensue. Perhaps predictably Adam and Eve failed, with a resultant fall from grace. Death, suffering, brambles and the parasitic worm were the consequence. The physical mechanism of this fall is not entirely clear. Was it a sudden destructive act, or was it the result of entropy, or micro-evolution? Perhaps this will always remain an open question and there have been a number of theories put forward by theologians.

Another aspect will remain somewhat of a mystery as well. This is the question why God allowed this test in the first place, or why God gave mankind free will. The classic response is that God wanted people to choose to love and serve him from a position of freedom, but giving free will risks allowing evil to gain a foothold instead. God is not like the fictional Borg Queen, in wanting to assimilate people against their will, but it would seem that God's desire is that we choose to love and serve Him freely. The Bible does teach about the negative consequences of rejecting Christ's offer of eternal life, but still God wants us to approach him from a position of love and freedom, not compulsion. This leads to the free will defence of moral evil, as it would seem that the benefit of free will outweighs the consequences of rebellion. Later we find God repenting of his creation of mankind, because of mankind's brutality, greed and wickedness.

We begin to see as well that God Himself is subject to suffering and has shared in the suffering of mankind. But in the suffering of God we see a divine dilemma. The choice appears to be between living for eternity on one's own, or creating beings in your own image that will be able to freely worship and have fellowship with you. But what if they choose not to be obedient, not to live in harmony with creation, but seek power over others? Then one has allowed evil and suffering to arise. If mankind chooses to disobey, then it will require an act of redemption and sacrifice on God's part to redeem mankind.

From this we begin to see that it was a rebellious act against God that is the cause of all suffering in the world. Rebellion caused the perfect creation to fall into a state of decay. This rebellion against God is basically what the Bible calls sin. In fact ultimately all of the suffering in the world is the result of mankind's greed, wickedness and brutality. It is people who fight wars, and enjoy plenty while others starve or become innocent victims. War and social upheaval are the main cause of poverty and starvation. Famines occur in one country, but other nations enjoy plentiful harvests. First world banking systems and global companies exploit the poor, and corrupt third world governments fill their personal foreign bank accounts while their people go hungry, and food aid is distributed according to political affiliation, or held back through corruption.

But how are we to answer the charge that is made against God, that He is not a God of love, but a brutal but omnipotent tyrant? Antony Flew, one time leading atheist, has recently come to see the design evidence in nature, but at present, he continues to view organised Christianity as being despotic,[7] with God seemingly forcing people to believe under threat of hell. Flew seems to struggle to come to terms with the presence of evil, although he does have greater respect for Jesus, who he sees as an attractive charismatic figure.[8]

The thought that anyone will end up in hell for eternity causes many people to struggle with their faith, and perhaps grieve for the lost. But the will and pride in mankind to seek power over others is part of the rebellion seen in the Garden of Eden, which if left unchecked, would cause the destruction of the world and possibly even the universe itself. This will to power is aided and abetted by dark spiritual forces seeking to overthrow God himself, and the strongest sanctions are necessary to bring order to creation.

Most of us may be tempted from time to time to feel sorry for those locked in jail, but if there were no sanctions in human society to stop criminals running unchecked, then our society would be degraded by anarchy. In the same way, it would seem that God has to set up sanctions to stop rebellious forces from over-running his creation. If evil were left to continue unchecked, then we would soon be all living in an anarchic hell, or worse, one where unjust laws are enforced by truly despotic and demonic powers. As shown earlier in the chapter, it is godless powers of atheism and paganism that have caused more suffering in the world than the Judeo-Christian faith tradition. When we look at the depth of depravity endemic in the world because of the will to seek power over others, then hell appears the only option as the ultimate sanction. It is almost as if some people are unable to escape the grip of pride which clouds rational thought, with mortal man seeking immortality without God, forgetting it is God who sustains our very being. It is such rebellion that causes so much suffering. People will not end up in hell because

God is a despotic tyrant, but because God has to maintain order in his creation. God's desire has always been that all people should respond to him with love, but sanctions exist to stop those whose will it is to seek power over others. When we submit to God, we also submit to our fellow humanity as good team players, and also to our purpose in restoring creation. Otherwise, all humanity and creation would descend into hell. Pascal, in his *Pensees* expresses some of these issues well. These show how each of us should seek truth, which is findable, but the motives of those who refuse to seek truth are clouded and not loving. In Pensee 174, Pascal quotes St. Augustine, who suggests that reason judges that there are occasions when we should submit to God. In Pensee 176, Pascal argues that those who refuse to submit to God love neither truth nor charity.[9]

The answer to the question of evil, and the accusation that God is despotic, is also seen in Christ, who came down to earth and allowed himself as God to suffer on the cross. It is this act of love and humility that shows that God himself has the capacity to share in the suffering of mankind. In fact the basic thrust of the Bible since the fall is one of rebuilding society and setting up civilised systems of government under Christ's authority around the world, to ensure social and environmental standards. God appeared to Abraham and promised to bless all nations through his seed. Later, Christ as a descendant of Abraham made this a reality. He commanded his followers to go into the whole world and make disciples of all nations, teaching people to obey His commands of love, even to love one's enemies and forgive those who sin against us. This is the action of a God of love, who came down to earth, suffered and died for mankind, and taught mankind how to live in love. All suffering ultimately is caused by mankind's rebellion against God, but God's desire is to bring this rebellion to an end.

God calls mankind to work to 'subdue' the world, to reduce the level of suffering around us, and maintain biodiversity, to ensure that rare species of animals are not wiped out, but remain for the glory of God on earth.[10] Much of the Mosaic Law can also be seen as health and safety legislation, with a social and environmental dimension as well, with for instance instructions about sowing and reaping, and about allowing ground to lie fallow in a jubilee year. Provision was made to ensure that the poor could gather crops around the edge of a field and pick up sheaves that had fallen to the ground. Every house built also had to have a wall around the roof to prevent people from falling off.

In fact, in this Mosaic Law we begin to see God's answer to natural evil, which perhaps attempts to formalise the original instruction given to Adam to 'subdue' the world. Mankind, it would seem, is called to develop mitigation strategies against natural disasters, and to provide food and clothing for the poor. It is claimed that 98 percent of people affected by natural disasters come from developing nations.[11] Often the developed nations have put in place mitigation strategies and few die from natural disasters. In Florida, evacuation procedures allow people to escape from well-forecasted storms. In developed nations, houses and office blocks are built to withstand earthquakes and remain largely undamaged, whereas mud brick houses collapse quickly in poorer nations and thousands die. Death from natural disasters may therefore be seen as sins of omission and are really moral evil.

It may also be seen, with the fall of Adam in the Garden of Eden, that God cursed the ground because of man's sin. The Noahic Flood was also a result of moral wickedness, and once again natural disasters may be stated as moral evil, as opposed to natural evil. In these senses the concept of good and evil become defined as obedience and disobedience to God's given commands, and this idea itself is a very useful definition of good and evil. However, while these concepts may be asserted as being true, they do not fully answer the question of suffering, and good and evil.

One of the oldest stories in the Bible is that of Job, who it is claimed lived a good life before God, and yet suffered greatly. His friends claimed that he must have sinned to have fallen into such great suffering, but he protested his innocence. At the end, God shows his love to Job by restoring his blessing, but the ultimate question of why people suffer, even without personal moral evil, remains unanswered. There is still much in this story that remains a mystery, and questions of suffering remain mysterious for many. The devil often gets the blame for a lot of our ills. He certainly gets the blame in the story of Job, and in the Garden of Eden as the lying serpent, but this raises other questions. It is though perhaps too easy for mankind to pass the buck to the devil, with the issue of suffering, although the connection between suffering and evil is recognised.

In one sense, our suffering brings forth a better humanity, although this is not to denigrate the suffering of children. Jesus spoke a proverb, '... unless a grain of wheat falls to the ground and dies, it remains only a single seed. But if it dies, it produces many seeds' *(John 12:24)*. In Romans *(8:17)* Paul states that we are to share in Christ's suffering in building God's church, and indeed the Christian's role is to lead the whole of creation from its suffering *(Romans 8:18-22)*. Suffering is a mystery, but we cannot really know what the depth of love is until we experience suffering for ourselves. How would we know what joy was, unless we knew sadness too? As Queen Elizabeth II said at the memorial service to the 9/11 events in New York, 'grief is the price we pay for love'. The message is that if you don't want to suffer, then don't bother loving anyone. We find therefore that we often suffer because we love, and we can only make moral judgements about suffering in the context that there is a God, and that he is a God of love. Anything else is meaningless.

The problem of suffering, for the atheist, where survival of the fittest is all there is to work with, is a difficult one indeed. This issue has been discussed at length, but it is an issue that is widely ignored and denied by those who want to discredit Christianity. No coherent or strong basis for a loving morality has ever been presented by the Darwinists, despite various weak attempts by Hume, Darwin and others. Loving ethics are simply assumed as an *a priori* fact, with little if any consideration for the foundational teaching of Christ and the Church. Failure to recognise this problem by atheists has been part of the underlying problems of suffering encountered within the twentieth century. We also find a loss of purpose within the West as well, as a result of Darwinism. While the scientific elite may be able to live with this, the ordinary person in the street fails to come to terms with it. As a result, suicides are increasingly common among the young. As Paul said, *faith, hope and love* remain, but with evolution all three are denied, and people cannot cope with a distrustful, hopeless, and emotionally cold existence.

However, for the Christian who believes in progressive creation or theistic evolution, the issue of suffering is a far more serious problem, whether Christians are aware of the problem or not. This may be expressed as the evolutionary theodicy problem and it asks how a theistic God of love and power can be harmonised with millions of years of evolution by survival of the fittest.[12] Theodicy is concerned with the justice of God, or the justification of God in the light of evil and suffering, and dealing with this in evolutionary terms is extremely difficult when we consider the struggle and suffering of nature that evolution asserts happened over millions of years. If, as Christians, we believe in a God of love, then how can we accept a God who created according to survival of the fittest? This implies hundreds of millions of years of suffering, waste and death of weaker strains, with human social conduct also seemingly reliant on survival instincts alone. This problem gap has not yet been closed. David Hull expressed the problem with reference to the Galapagos Islands, asking what type of God can be inferred from the species found there.

> 'What kind of God can one infer from the sort of phenomena epitomised by the species on Darwin's Galapagos Islands? The evolutionary process is rife with happenstance, contingency, incredible waste, death, pain and horror. ... Whatever the God implied by evolutionary theory and the data of natural selection may be like, he is not the Protestant God of waste not, want not. He is also not the loving God who cares about his productions. ... The God of the Galapagos is careless, wasteful, indifferent, almost diabolical. He is certainly not the sort of God to whom anyone would be inclined to pray.'[13]
> *(Reprinted by permission from Nature, copyright 1992 Macmillan Publishers Ltd.)*

The Creator God is not seen as being perfect, but aspects of the fall from grace are used as evidence against God. Christians come up against this problem in part because of a rejection of Augustine's doctrine of original sin, a process that started with Locke. The concept of original sin is closely tied in with the fall from grace in the Garden of Eden, and belief in evolution has superficial appeal because it completely does away with the fall, and original sin, and allows mankind room for self-improvement. Incidentally the term *original sin* is not helpful, because the fall occurred sometime after creation and God made man originally perfect, so it might better be described as *Adamic* or *Edenic sin*. However, in trying to escape Augustine's doctrine altogether, the Christian runs straight into the evolutionary theodicy problem. How, for instance, can we worship and accept a God of love and justice if he created by survival of the fittest, over hundreds of millions of years? How can we ever say that God is good, or that he created everything good? How can we treat others with love if we are not created in the image of a good God of love, but evolved through a blind, careless process?

Many commentators have criticised Augustine because of his over-emphasis on mankind's fallen nature, and total inadequacy for self-improvement being wholly dependent on grace for every area of our lives. This was certainly John Locke's criticism, and he believed moral improvement could come through secular education. Attfield comments that:

'The Theology of Augustine, indeed, allows so low a place of human self-determination that numerous Christians down through the ages have had to qualify it to acknowledge the role of human effort in any consistent scheme of Christian ethics. Thus even if Locke's positive views misconstrue human instincts and inherited capacities, his claim that there is for each generation of new-born humans the possibility of moral development, and that it can be fostered by entirely secular means, was both an influential and a salutary one. It was, indeed, a modification of the Judeo-Christian tradition vital for all branches of ethics, environmental ethics included.' [14]

It is indeed recognised that mankind has a capacity for self-improvement through education, as Locke suggests, but we do not need to totally reject Augustine in order to deal with the excesses of his doctrine. Although Attfield claims that this rejection of original sin led to improvement in ethics of all kinds, the total rejection of Augustine's position has had exactly the opposite effect, with the subsequent total denial of grace by later humanists. Locke too appears to be rejecting all grace by suggesting that moral improvement is attainable through secular education alone. This has meant that ethics have become entirely man-centred, with God's authority rejected.

Trying to determine where grace begins and human self-help ends is perhaps intangible and indeterminate. Do we for instance need grace to get out of the bed in the morning? If we wake up bright eyed and bushy tailed, is that grace or is it self? If we wake up depressed and tired, is that self or lack of grace? God's power at work in us is so closely interwoven in the life of the Christian that these questions defy tangible answers, but grace is often working quietly and out of our sight.

It must also be recognised that many Christians who reject original sin, while accepting theistic evolution, do not necessarily deny the need for grace as secularists do. However, those who dismissed Augustine's original sin did so to reduce the need for God's grace, and finally, as noted, deists and atheists denied the need for grace altogether, blending this rejection with a completely materialistic theory of origins. The Christian who then accepts progressive creation or theistic evolution, and denies original sin from the Edenic fall from grace, while upholding God's grace in the present and man's need for grace, struggles to maintain a credible theological and logical position, because the naturalistic theory of evolution denies grace. Where did grace begin, and where did sin enter? Some theistic evolutionists do accept a limited fall, but only in terms of its effect on human affairs. However, mankind has responsibility towards nature, and if macro-evolution were true, then death and suffering would have existed before the fall, and God would be responsible for causing natural evil.

It may be asked how the theistic evolutionist is to deal with the problem of evolutionary theodicy if God did not create everything good, but created according to the brutal and amoral process of evolution. Steve Chalke appears to run into this problem. In his book, *The Lost Message of Jesus*,[15] he questions Augustine's theology of original sin, and also the work of atonement by Jesus.[16] He also rejects a recent creation in favour of some form of theistic evolution or progressive creation, but at the same time asserts there is a good God behind creation,[17] and also suggests that Jesus emphasised mankind's original goodness.[18] But how can such a God be good, or his creation be good, if he used hundreds of millions of years of death and suffering to create the natural world?

Christopher Southgate highlights three responses that have been proposed to this problem.[19] Firstly, some dismiss the problem altogether and suggest that the suffering of animals is of no moral concern; it is just a fact of nature, and morality only affects humanity. Others, such as Descartes, suggest that animals do not really suffer, as they are without souls, but this is really beyond common sense as it is a simple observation of nature that animals flee from danger and cry out in distress. Some have tried to claim that the process of survival of the fittest, which uses suffering in order to create, is in itself good, but this has huge moral implications for the environment and society. People who enjoy causing suffering to animals often have psychopathic tendencies towards people as well. This is no way can be seen as being good. While it is recognised that suffering and death in nature are real, and perhaps even necessary to maintain life today, our only humane response to this is to view it as somehow ultimately wrong and part of a broken perfection. Those who object to fox hunting do so because they see it as intrinsically wrong to kill animals for human pleasure. Those who enjoy watching the song birds feed on the bird table are saddened when a sparrow hawk takes one for its food, or to feed its young. It is perhaps a natural human response to grieve over the loss of a life, even if only a robin or swallow. Trying to pretend that survival instincts are good does not accord with human nature, and leads to a rejection of our very humanity. This problem only becomes worse when we try and apply survival instincts to human social affairs, as Herbert Spencer proposed.

Secondly, the theodicy problem is disregarded, with no account of the cost given in creating through the process of evolution. John Polkinghorne suggests that suffering and death of animals, disease and cancer are allowed to happen by God as necessary side effects of creation through the process of survival of the fittest. By rejecting the notion of a fall from grace, he places these entities as part of God's gradual evolutionary change process of creation, through various laws of probability from for instance chaos theory and stochastic quantum mechanics.[20] The idea of God as a skilled watchmaker, as Paley described Him, is rejected in favour of God as a sort of juggler, where many balls are held in the air at once, and occasionally some fall to the ground. Southgate comments that in doing this, the free will defence of the existence of moral evil is extended to a defence of physical or natural evil.[21] This is known as the *free process defence*, and claims that death and suffering are necessary even if regrettable side effects to the process of gradual evolution, in order to create life. Death and suffering of animals therefore has beneficial consequences in terms of the life of others. Not only does this utilitarian approach, as a sort of cost-benefit analysis, reject the creation account and fall from grace, it undermines the whole thrust of Scripture, which is one of restoration and intervention through grace, prayer and faithful service.

The main objection to the free process defence is that it does not have the same weight as the free will defence. While God is seen as omnipotent in physical terms, he must always be true to his own character whereby he must respect mankind's right to make bad choices. It would appear impossible to give human beings genuine free will without allowing the moral choice of obedience or rebellion. Either people have moral choices or they do not, and God, who gave genuine free will respects people's right to choose. However, in creation God is simply not limited physically as to how he chooses to create. There is no physical dilemma in creation over a short period, as there is in respecting people's moral choices. God could simply get around the wasteful nature of an evolutionary process by creating everything perfectly in a short period of time, as the Genesis account asserts he did.

Instead it has been shown that according to Scripture, natural evil is really a function of mankind's moral evil, following the fall from grace. This is seen in *Genesis 3:17*, where God says to Adam, 'Cursed is the *ground* because of you...', and Paul asserts that, 'sin entered the world through one man, and death through sin.' *(Romans 5:12)*. If natural evil as well as moral evil came about through the free will choice of mankind to rebel, then the free will defence should be applied to natural evil as well. But having created everything perfect, we may assert that God simply did not use, nor needed to use natural selection over hundreds of millions of years to bring about a wide and diverse creation. However, we can observe that there is suffering in nature, and that it does rely on survival instincts, following the fall from grace. The free process defence to natural evil leaves God guilty of creating through a brutal process, when he had all the power in the cosmos to create perfectly in a short period of time, if we maintain that he is physically omnipotent, but only limited by the need to remain true to his own character.

Applying the free will defence of moral evil to natural evil still leaves open the question of why God created mankind with free will, perhaps knowing Adam and Eve would fall. Not only would this fall lead to moral evil, we now can see that it leads to the death and suffering of animals, to a cursed ground and therefore to natural evil. Suffering and death of animals is a constant reminder of mankind's rebellion against God, but it is man and not God who is responsible for both moral and natural evil.

Many writers have demonstrated that the Bible speaks of God's plan of restoration for humanity and nature. Robert Gurney,[22] for instance, shows how a couple of passages in Isaiah *(11:6-9 and 65:17-25)* refer to the restoration of nature towards the original created order where vegetarianism was the order of the day for both mankind and people. *Isaiah 11* is a Messianic prophecy, wherein God is said to raise up a 'root of Jesse', that is Jesus, in verse one, although it really speaks of the return of Christ when perfection will be fully restored.

'The wolf will live with the lamb,
the leopard will lie down with the goat,
the calf and the lion and the yearling together;
and a little child will lead them.
The cow will feed with the bear,
their young will lie down together,
and the lion will eat straw like the ox.
The infant will play near the hole of the cobra,
and the young child put his hand into the viper's nest.
They will neither harm nor destroy
on all my holy mountain,
for the earth will be full of the knowledge of the LORD
as the waters cover the sea.' *(Isaiah 11:6-9)*

Abraham too was called to live by faith, and the desert he settled in blossomed and allowed him to prosper, and this is offered as a promise to the faithful Christian children of Abraham who are called to live by faith to bring God's message of salvation to the world *(Galatians 3:14)*. This is again reflected in Isaiah where the cursed ground becomes well watered and restored once more.

> 'The desert and the parched land will be glad; the wilderness will rejoice and blossom. Like the crocus, it will burst into bloom; it will rejoice greatly and shout for joy ... Water will gush forth in the wilderness and streams in the desert. The burning sand will become a pool, the thirsty ground bubbling springs.' *(Isaiah 35:1-2,6-7)*

God's desire is to intervene through Christ to redeem and heal both moral and natural evil, through human cooperation of repentance, prayer and faithful service. It may also be seen that viewing death and suffering as necessary side effects to survival of the fittest absolves mankind of responsibility towards human society and nature. An indifferent fatalism would appear to be the logical consequence of Polkinghorne's free process defence, and Hull's theodicy challenge against God is not answered. God has instead called mankind to work with God to bring about restoration.

The final solution to the theodicy problem is to reject entirely the God of the Bible, although Southgate comments correctly that this is a form of deism.[23] In this idea, God no longer has any active part in the process of evolution and again simply allows it to happen. Southgate himself proposed that God's desire is to heal and redeem the suffering of humanity and nature, within and through the process of evolution. God is seen as being alongside nature in the evolutionary process of suffering and wants to heal and redeem it.[24]

However, healing implies that nature is sick, and redemption implies that it is in debt or in a state of rebellion. These terms only have meaning in the context of a fall from grace, which the process of evolution denies. Trying to apply these terms to evolution, outside of a fall from grace, leaves God responsible for creating through a sick process of evolution, and the theodicy problem is not adequately solved as Southgate recognises. It may be considered in response that the evolutionary theodicy problem is unbridgeable, in theistic evolutionary terms, leaving us with the requirement for a paradigm shift back towards the traditional perfect creation followed by a fall.

It needs to be recognised as well that Scripture speaks fully of mankind's need for *sustaining* grace as well as appealing to a powerful creation and fall, and grace itself is given according to faith. 'Abram believed the Lord, and he credited it to him as righteousness.' *(Genesis 15:6)*. This concept lies at the heart of the Christian Gospel, and Paul alludes to it in *Romans 1:16-17*. The well-being of nature is therefore intrinsically linked in Scripture to human faithfulness and God's sustaining power. Although this may not be measurable scientifically, it is a matter of faith and taught in Scripture as being part of the Judeo-Christian faith system. This concept of fruitful prosperity and restoration, for obedient, loving service and faithful lifestyle offers a compelling solution to environmental and social ethics, but it can only be accepted fully in terms of faith and not science. On the flip side, the land is often seen in Scripture as being cursed as a result of mankind's rebellion, with the world of Noah for instance receiving a watery curse because of disobedience and wickedness. However, as has been quoted previously, Scripture asserts that:

> 'The creation waits in eager expectation for the sons of God to be revealed. For the creation was subjected to frustration, not by its own choice, but by the will of the one who subjected it, in hope that the creation itself will be liberated from its bondage to decay and brought into the glorious freedom of the children of God.' *(Romans 8:19-21)*.

Southgate has also appealed to this concept as expressed in *Romans 8*. [25] However, it may be noted that this passage talks about restoration and salvation from bondage and decay. The passage seems to leave open the question of who subjected nature, but Gurney suggests that it was God as a reminder of mankind's fallen nature. [26] The whole plan of Scripture and salvation is one of restoration following a fall from grace. Trying to marry up Darwinian survival of the fittest with an originally good creation as recorded in Genesis is problematic in the extreme, as to appear an impossible gap to bridge. For the Judeo-Christian, God made everything perfect, but brutal survival instincts only developed after an act of rebellion by mankind. In this sense, the death and suffering of people and animals can be seen as in need of healing and redemption, but it only makes sense if we see natural survival processes as being evidence of a broken perfection.

God appeared to Abraham and promised to make him a nation, and that all nations on earth will be blessed through his seed. The family became a clan, and then went through a period of slavery, followed by escape and nationhood. With various periods of success and exile, and with words from fearsome prophets, the nation eventually gave birth to the promised Messianic Son. This Son grew up, had a short but powerful ministry, and then died. His followers claimed to have seen him risen from the dead, and were so convinced and filled with the Holy Spirit that they turned the Roman Empire upside down. Two thousand years later, this Christian church has indeed fulfilled the words spoken to Abraham, and all nations have followers of the faith of Abraham among their population.

This chapter has attempted to show that understanding suffering and death is extremely problematic for a purely materialistic faith, where purpose and meaning are denied. Suffering and meaning only make sense in the context that there is a God, and that he is a good God of love. How are we to account therefore with the fact that the world appears broken, with suffering, death and struggle for survival all too evident?

This is most effectively dealt with through the fall from grace of mankind, and any attempt to construct theistic evolutionary theodicy without this is extremely problematic, as to be unbridgeable. Materialism also fails to recognise the whole thrust of Scripture which is one of restoration, and fruitful prosperity for faithfulness working with God's grace. God has not only created everything good, but he wants to be actively involved with mankind in restoring nature from its fall and bondage to decay. The outworking of this is in terms of both direct human action, and also through a work of divine grace. Human self-help and grace are often so closely linked that it is virtually impossible to say where one ends and the other begins. An analogy often given in the Bible, and found in Genesis 1-3, is that of the cooperation between the gardener and God.

Mankind uses God's good creation and blends it into a human creation. God sends rain and sunshine, and provides the plants and nutrients. In this sense, mankind is beginning to subdue nature and work in harmony with God and creation. On the broader scale, a game reserve or national park must also be considered land set aside for this same purpose of cooperation with God's creation. It is though recognised that Augustine overstated the case for grace, making mankind totally dependent on grace to a point of powerlessness, but some modification to Augustine's idea of original sin should not lead to a total rejection of grace altogether, as later humanists have done.

Christians, who accept some form of theistic evolution or progressive creation, without a real Adam and a real Eve and a real fall from grace, struggle to maintain a credible theological position. At what point does sin enter into the equation and need for grace begin? Progressive creationists, or theistic evolutionists who believe in the original goodness of creation, need to ask how God could have created everything good, through a process that does not look at all good, but instead broken. Survival of the fittest, with nature *red in tooth and claw*, has all the hallmarks of brokenness from perfection. Death and suffering entered into the world through mankind's sin, and we need to work with God's grace to restore society and nature towards perfection. Restoration towards an original perfect state provides a Christian basis for a coherent and loving ethic for society and the environment. That does not mean that we will be able yet to return to a perfect vegetarian state, because the death and suffering seen in nature is a sign of mankind's rebellion.

It has been shown that according to Scripture, natural evil is really a function of moral evil, and that the free will defence argument may therefore apply to both natural and moral evil, even though it is recognised that the free will defence does not fully answer the presence of suffering and evil, which remains a mystery. But if we adopt the alternatives and say that the process of survival and struggle is good, then we end up falling into the errors of Herbert Spencer and we are back with eugenics and the Nazi death camps. If we say that nature is driven by blind chance where God is rejected, then we also lose all ability to evaluate suffering and evil.

251

While the issue of suffering has not been fully answered and perhaps never will be, the traditional reading of Scripture forms a basis on which to build a coherent and loving morality and society. The alternatives are brutal or at best meaningless. These alternatives have serious implications for mankind's attitude to nature and those who desire to gain power over others. Mankind then becomes master of his own destiny, and evaluator of his own ethical conduct.

Notes and References

[1] Kenny, A., *Down with Superstition*, Spectator, pp. 14-15, 20th March, 2004.

[2] Attenborough, D., *Life on Air*, BBC1 TV, 5th December 2002.

[3] Mill, J.S., *Three Essays on Religion*, Henry Holt & Co., New York, p. 38, 1874; In: Miller, E.L., *Questions that Matter: An Invitation to Philosophy*, 3rd edition, McGraw-Hill Inc., New York, p. 350, 1992.

[4] Hume, D., (ed. Aiken H.D.), *Dialogues Concerning Natural Religion*, Hafner, New York, p. 64, 1948.

[5] Johnson, P.E., *Nihilism and the End of Law*, First Things, 31, pp. 19-25, March 1993, <www.firstthings.com/ftissues/ft9303/articles/pjohnson.html>, Accessed March 2006. See also: C.S. Lewis Society, <www.apologetics.org/articles/nihilism.html>, Accessed March 2006.

[6] Walley, C., Letter in Christian Herald, Worthing, Sussex, 21/28 December 2002.

[7] Wavell, S., Iredale, W., *Sorry, says atheist-in-chief, I do believe in God after all*, The Sunday Times, 12th December 2004.

[8] Flew, A., Habermas, G.R., *Atheist Becomes Theist: Exclusive Interview with Former Atheist Antony Flew*, Philosophia Christi, Evangelical Philosophical Society, Winter, 2004.

[9] Pascal, B., (trans. Krailsheimer, A.J.), *Pensees*, Penguin Classics, London, pp. 51-54, 1995.

[10] However, if diseases and parasites such as HIV and the Guinea worm are products of micro-evolution, then eradication may be considered morally

acceptable. They are then products of the fall, not of God's designed creation. This argument is worthy of a much more detailed consideration.

[11] Tear Fund report. *Before Disaster Strikes*, p. 4, February 2004.

[12] Southgate, C., *God and Evolutionary Evil: Theodicy in the Light of Darwinism*, Zygon, Vol. 37, no. 4, pp. 803-824, Dec. 2002.

[13] Hull, D.L., *God of the Galapagos*, Nature, 352, pp. 485-486, 1992.

[14] Attfield, R., *The Ethics of Environmental Concern*, University of Georgia Press, p. 70, 1991. (Second Edition © 1991 by the University of Georgia Press, Athens, Georgia 30602)

[15] Chalke, S., Mann, A., *The Lost Message of Jesus*, Zondervan Publishing, 2004.

[16] Publishers Weekly, Book review of Chalke, & Mann, (ibid.), Reed Elsevier Inc. 2004. As placed on amazon.com website. <www.amazon.com/exec/obidos/tg/detail/-/0310248825/>, Accessed March 2006.

[17] Curtis, P., *Christian Charity to Open London Academy*, Guardian news report, 13th July 2004.

[18] Publishers Weekly, op. cit.

[19] Southgate, op. cit., pp. 809-811.

[20] Polkinghorne, J., *Science and Providence*, SPCK, London, pp. 66-67, 1989.

[21] Southgate, op. cit., p. 809.

[22] Gurney, R.J.M., *The Carnivorous Nature and Suffering of Animals*, Answers in Genesis, TJ, 18(3), pp. 70-75, 2004.

[23] Southgate, op. cit., p. 810.

[24] Ibid., p. 816-821.

[25] Ibid., p. 818.

[26] Gurney, op. cit., p. 73.

Chapter 12

Bearing Fruit

Jesus replied, "I tell you the truth, if you have faith and do not doubt ... you can say to this mountain, 'Go, throw yourself into the sea,' and it will be done. If you believe, you will receive whatever you ask for in prayer."
(Matthew 21:21-22)

The above statement in Matthew's gospel comes after an incident where Jesus cursed a fig tree because it was not bearing fruit. However, the passage records that it was not the season for figs, but instead the tree was full of glorious new green leaves. Jesus must have been aware of this fact, but the fig tree still received a verbal cursing and shrivelled up at his words. There is an important message here. On the outside we may be like the fig tree, full of glory, but lacking fruit in our lives. The desire of Jesus is that we bear fruit in terms of acts of love to our fellow human beings and be concerned for the world in which we live, both in season and out of season. Of course environmentalists may throw their hands up in horror at the thought of a cursed fig tree, but that is to miss the point. Jesus was at the time remonstrating with legalistic Pharisees, the ruling classes in the Sanhedrin and corrupt businessmen who were defrauding the poor, all in the name of organised religion. They, as rulers of Israel, were like the fig tree, full of outward glory but lacking real fruit in their lives.

And this is really the message of this book, that there is a need for us to maintain a faith that bears fruit in terms of caring for the poor and weak in society, to maintain justice, righteousness and mercy, and to care for the environment. However, it may be noted that the traditions of Darwinism have damaged ethical concern within the Western world, and this has crept into the church. At worst, ethical standards derived from Darwinian beliefs have led to fascism, eugenics, racism, greed is good capitalism, a rejection of social provision for the poor, and even influenced materialistic Marxism. At best, the implication of the so called 'death of God' has led, and continues to lead to a sort of nihilistic fatalism, where people live for selfish pleasure with little regard for others. We have gained Epicurean pleasures, but lost a sense of duty towards others. Others find despondency in the loss of purpose that atheism brings. While academics may be happy with this state of affairs, Phillip Johnson states that such confidence in godlessness is misplaced. Johnson comments that in replacing God with a mindless process of evolution, any objective notion of responsibility for good ethical conduct is lost, with the whimsical nature of human reason and feeling providing a very poor subjective substitute. As a result, the subjective nature of ethics, that modernist rationalism gives to society, is giving way to post-modernist nihilism as a sort of natural offspring.[1]

People in the West have so much materially, and the church manages to maintain a degree of light in Western values of justice and mercy, but in many nations corruption and war are running out of control. There is increasing pressure in the West, as well as from big business and materialistic science, to allow ethically questionable practices. Martin Jacques, writing in the Guardian, also asserts that we live in an increasingly disjointed world driven by selfishness and market forces. This he calls the ego-market, and it is eroding our basic humanity and our ability to communicate at an emotional level with one another.[2] Although he suggests that this state of affairs arose in the 1960s, he fails to address the deeper root causes and offers a fatalistic response, suggesting that nothing much can be done. The best hope, he states, is that we first identify the problem.[3]

What really happened in the 1960s was a loss of faith by a post-war generation that did not know the horrors of war first hand. However, people were concerned about environmental damage and the threat of nuclear weapons through the Cold War. As we have seen, many blamed Christianity for the pursuit of progress and environmental damage caused, and then sought answers in alternative eastern mysticism, or pagan faiths, together with a sexual revolution and the easy availability of drugs. Teilhard de Chardin's vision of a pantheist faith, derived from evolution, also informs the underlying faith position today.

Perhaps as well, with war in Vietnam, American military domination of the world and Christian values were seen as being aligned together with right wing politics. Christians too easily swallow the lie that extreme right wing politics is Christian, forgetting that Jesus called us to be humble and to love our enemies. That is not to say that there is not sometimes a self-defence justification for war, but Christians are often oblivious to darker forces at work in politics on both the left and right. Of course secularised people in the West did not know first hand about the human rights abuse of communist states, but instead rejected Christianity on the basis of anti-right wing sentiment. On the other hand, that which looks like good wholesome Christianity is no more than a cover for powerful groups to maintain power and wealth over others, with little regard for loving Christ-like ethics, but Christianity is maligned none the less. Christianity is often used as a cover by godless forces to gain wealth and power.

This rejection of Christianity spread to the wider population, where short term pleasure was seen as being preferable to the long term benefit of Christian values. It is really the rejection of Christianity in the West that is the root cause of the loss of intimacy, and we have accepted post-modern nihilism as our basis for faith. All of this has echoes in Darwinian theory, where ethical values are based on sentiment, and the self is placed above society, together with a dominant market economy.

Previous chapters have provided a partial critique of Darwinian thought in the past 150 years, with its belief in technological and scientific progress as a sort of inevitable cosmic process, and subsequent implications for ethical conduct. Darwinism grew out of general deistic enlightenment philosophy, which moved away from the traditional Judeo-Christian concepts based on natural law and natural theology. Deism perhaps started out as an attempt to defend and explain Christian faith in a rational manner from the natural world, with a progressive movement towards a millennial and eternal perfection working within God's grace. However, it slowly turned into a positivist religion of science, sometimes called scientism or scientific naturalism, with God's grace completely denied.

With the advent of Darwinism, leading evolutionists found their theory of survival of the fittest facing a major challenge over the ethical implications. As a result, Darwin and Huxley tried to claim some sort of discontinuity between biological and sociological evolution based on the whim of human sentiment. This appealed back to Epicurus and Hume. However, the more logical argument of Herbert Spencer prevailed, that there would be a continuity of survival instincts from biological to human sociological affairs, with a subsequent debasement and rejection of compassionate Christian ethics. This ethic informed social and business conduct.

Darwinism has also undermined the traditions of natural law and natural theology. The twin books of Scripture and nature provided evidence for the existence of God, and also to His good and loving character. Francis Bacon, at the beginning of the enlightenment, appealed for the scientific quest to be tamed by 'sound reason and true religion'. These natural traditions gave mankind rights and duties towards one another, as outlined by St. Paul and later Thomas Aquinas. Many Christians through the ages found that their faith produced a deep love for nature as well as humanity, including the Celtic saints, St. Francis of Assisi and the German Albert Schweitzer, who desired a reverence to be given towards nature. Natural theology also gave mankind a purpose to live, which Darwinism destroyed. With a rejection of a higher divine purpose for humanity, people find reason to live in purely personal gain and selfish pleasure instead.

However, the advent of Darwinism has swept aside the natural law tradition, and philosophers have searched for other ethical bases on which to defend their deistic or atheistic beliefs. One is utilitarianism, which proposes the sentimental value of sympathy, or parental and filial affection, as a means of understanding ethics. This accordingly may even apply to the level of the tribe through a sort of herd mentality. However, as has been shown, these are partial and weak, and continue to be defined in survival terms. Rights theory in the West is also increasingly defined in Darwinian survival terms, where competing pressure groups seek to defend their rights, with little regard for the rights of others, or the rights of those with no voice. Rights are no longer linked to duties, but are given to the most vocal pressure groups according to who can command the most sympathy. The cunning fox, for instance, has now won his first victory against the hunters in the UK, through use of sentiment and sympathy alone.

And where is the church in all of this? In many ways, faults with the Reformation led to a weakening of Christianity's voice in society. With different factions fighting war across Europe, and with rivals put to death with little regard for their divinely created humanity, is it any wonder that people turned away from organised religion? The Calvinists, for their part, denied that miracles should continue through the church age, and also seemed to turn away from the natural theology tradition, proclaiming that Scripture alone was sufficient for faith. One leading theologian, Jack Deere, has suggested this to be a form of Biblical deism. The Catholics, on the other hand, attacked the reformers by claiming that only priests had the right to interpret Scripture, due to apparent contradictions. This helped to weaken faith in the Bible and drive people away from the authority of the church.

However, after the cosmic process of Darwinism became the overriding paradigm in Western society, most Christian leaders simply fell into line and accepted it with little thought for the ethical consequences. The design argument, that natural theology gave us to inform our conduct, was rejected in favour of atheistic philosophy and evolution as originally proposed by Epicurus, Empedocles, Thales and Anaximander. Whereas St. Paul demolished the Epicurean argument in Athens by appealing to natural theology *(Acts 17:16-34)*, many nineteenth century theologians simply capitulated. A belief in a literal Genesis account was widely discarded as a form of allegory or high mythology, even sweeping aside previous compromises such as the gap theory or pre-Adamic races. Today, many leading evangelicals continue to accept some sort of old earth progressive creation or theistic evolution position, although it may be noted that deistic evolution may be a more accurate description of this latter position. Division continues within the Christian church, with modern thinking evangelicals showing little respect for the remaining Christians who maintain a literal reading of Genesis 1-3. Literalists are considered naïve and simplistic. This minority position has become known as scientific creationism or young earth creationism, with a commitment to look for scientific answers to the Genesis account, but this does not mean that creationists are looking for answers to all natural science in the Bible, as often wrongly claimed.

Of course in one sense, looking for scientific answers to miracles that are once-only events is a waste of time, but a desire to falsify macro-evolution and gradualism forms the main thrust of creationists' work. This is a legitimate exercise for young or old earth creationists alike, but modern thinking Christians seem to accept evidence presented by secular scientists without even questioning the underlying assumptions. This approach by old earth creationists or theistic evolutionists may instead be considered naïve and simplistic. In fact modern evangelical or charismatic Christians may pride themselves on their radical methods of evangelism and social action, but in many ways the young earth creationist position may be considered equally necessary, and in many ways as effective and radical. As shown, when Paul preached in Athens, he started by proclaiming God as the Creator of mankind and the world, and explained God's purpose in all this before moving onto the resurrection of Jesus.

However, the purpose of this book is not to prolong Christian division by passing insults backwards and forwards, but to seek to bridge the gap and look for greater respect between evangelical Christians of different persuasions. In the current godless climate, division is a luxury the Church cannot afford. Recent pioneers of scientific methodology, such as Karl Popper, have called on scientists to look for the weaknesses in their theory instead of only looking for confirmation. Young earth creationists have a right and duty therefore to undertake this falsification task, which is not being done by evolutionary scientists themselves.

The main problem for Christians of all persuasions, in seeking to uphold a belief in a young earth is the speed of light and the distant starlight problem. However, a number of solutions have been proposed to solve this problem, for instance a variable speed of light, or the effects of general relativity on the dimension of time in an expanding universe, and some secular scientists are now considering these as serious possibilities as well. Progressive creationists should consider these as imaginative ways of harmonising science with Scripture.

One of the problems for progressive creationists or theistic evolutionists is that in the New Testament, Jesus also talks about the reality of the Genesis account. Both Paul and John also ascribe Jesus as being at the heart of creation, even speaking everything into being as the Genesis record suggests. Indeed, in the passage quoted at the start of this chapter *(Matthew 21:21-22)*, Jesus gives ordinary Christians the power to speak things into motion as well. 'I tell you the truth ... say to this mountain, 'Go, throw yourself into the sea,' and it will be done.' This passage is a major challenge to all of us as Christians, but especially to Christians who reject present day miracles and to those who believe that God needed millions of years to create the world and everything in it. In fact the spoken Word of God, and information seen in DNA, appear to form a more fundamental reality in the cosmos than the material itself.

In more recent times, the denial of the miraculous may be in part attributable to the teachings of Benjamin B. Warfield and other Fundamentalists, who presented a form of Biblical deism as fundamental Christianity. Another prominent theologian, who saw the creation account as a high form of mythology, was C.S. Lewis, but it would seem that in later life through private correspondence with Bernard Acworth, a co-founder of the Evolution Protest Movement, he began to soften his view, seeing evolution as a 'central and radical lie' because of subsequent debasement of ethics.

It is also necessary for Christians to defend their faith against the growth of post-modernism. This stems partly from the paper by Lynn White, which blamed Christianity for environmental destruction. This paper has faced many criticisms since, and a lot of White's attacks are unwarranted. However, partly as a result of White's paper, people have not returned to Christianity, despite a widespread rejection of the scientific modernism of the evolutionists. Instead, they have moved to a sort of pantheistic view of evolution, similar to that outlined by Teilhard de Chardin, perhaps not really being aware of the full implications. Teilhard de Chardin promoted an agenda that was once again similar to Darwin, Huxley and Dewey, but expressing the cosmic process of evolution in apparent Christianised terms. Philip Johnson has also shown that post-modernism and nihilism are natural offspring of the humanist religion where any objective reality to ethics and purpose is denied.

Within the modern deep or romantic biocentric environmental movement, there continues to be the promotion of views that are almost fascist in nature, seeking for instance to reduce human population by disregarding people's basic human rights and intrinsic value, or even justifying the murder of people in the name of upholding animal rights. Although people increasingly reject a belief in scientific progress, they do not seem as yet to reject the main evolutionary base that degrades environmental and social ethics.

One area where Christians are beginning to seriously look again at origins is with the growth of the Intelligent Design Movement. Evidence from design may well lead to a return to the natural law and natural theology position of Aquinas, and to a greater respect for the twin books of Scripture and nature argument of Francis Bacon. Other theologians, such as Alister McGrath and Albert Schweitzer, have also called for a return to a sense of reverence and wonder for natural life, as a means of informing a Christian attitude to the natural environment. In fact, a return to the natural theology of Aquinas may form the basis for Christian-centred environmental and social ethics, with greater respect and reverence for humanity and nature. This would also restore a sense of purpose in an increasingly nihilistic age. Restoration and the concept of blessing or fruitful prosperity for obedience is also a profound environmental principle found in Scripture. Obedience to the will of God leads to the land in which we dwell being blessed, which then runs with milk and honey. *(Exodus 3:8)* On the flip side, natural evil can be seen as a result of moral evil and rebellion in theological terms.

On the wider issue, there really is a need for Christians to stand up for humanity and the environment, as God's creation, and once again be salt and light in the world, ensuring it is managed properly. Perhaps there may even be some truth in White's assertions that Christians have failed in their duty to protect the ecosystem from destruction in the past. This care for the world is part of God's initial great commission to subdue the earth and rule over it, not in a tyrannical fashion, but as God's stewards and managers of the land, working against the worst excesses of survival of the fittest, to protect the weak and poor and maintain biodiversity. Sadly, Christianity is often seen as being entrenched with the scientific establishment, which allows big business in the name of science and technology to exploit the environment and society for profit.

So this is the field that Christians find themselves in. Not only has the Darwinian theory of evolution led to a degradation of the sanctity of human life and abuse of nature, it has also removed a sense of reverence and wonder towards nature and the environment, which the Bible states as being part of God's good creation. No longer is man seen as steward of the planet, but he has the right to exploit nature for profit and progress. This is a social and political conspiracy, which has crossed the political divide from left to right and has infected the church as well. The blame must surely rest with the acceptance of the theory of evolution, which denies God's role in, and ownership of His creation.

I would urge genuine Christians who accept theistic evolution, or progressive creation, to look again at the implications of this compromise. The theory of evolution is not morally neutral, but has arisen through people who have tried to build a godless and atheistic system of science and ethics with a determination to undermine traditional Christian faith for whatever reason. Whether the reason for this is a general disappointment with Christian conduct since the Reformation, or an underlying commitment to a different theology or philosophy from various societies who seek power and wealth over others and nature, in a sort of Faustian pact, is an open question. Despite the best efforts of evolutionists, the only logical ethic that can be derived from evolution is that given by Spencer, the ethic of survival of the fittest, even extending to human social affairs.

If we want to restore our Christian society and regain the faith of people, then Christians must consider teaching once again the power and wisdom of God in creation within the school system. Much of the Western education system has been established on purely humanistic lines as a result of John Dewey's efforts, but Christians have a right and duty to work against this and restore a theistic Christian education system for their own children. While secular parents may reject a change of this nature, Christian parents may conclude that their children have a right to understand the scientific and ethical arguments in favour of special creation and against evolution. This is an area that Christians must engage in, especially with the increasing development of faith-based schools by Christian groups.

The reason for this is the need to understand the debauched ethical implications of Darwinian evolution, and that the only consistent system of loving ethics is one derived from a loving God, whose character is evident in nature. The Christian message is one of restoration and stewardship over the earth. The present civilisation that we enjoy in the West has not come about through advances in godless science, as humanists would have us believe, but through the faithfulness of Christian people, striving to restore God's creation to its previous perfect state throughout the Christian age.

It is Christian civilisation itself that is at stake if we don't grasp the nettle and tackle the arguments in favour of faith. For too long, Christians have allowed atheistic humanists to make the running, but defending Christian teaching on origins, and more generally Christianity as a whole is most important. This is for the sake of civilisation, for the sake of law and order in the West, for the sake of human rights and environmental concern, for the sake of the weak, and for those who are not even Christian. There are many forces at work who would, and do deny human rights whenever they have the chance. Obviously it is not right, nor productive to force people to have Christian faith, and there is a need for respect for those who have different faiths or lifestyles, but Christianity provides the best foundation for protecting the environment, and a strong and stable human civilisation and loving ethical standards.

Today, fascism has gone underground, although it still exists in clandestine groups in Europe and America, and Marxism has declined dramatically in the former Soviet Union as well since communism collapsed, although once again there may possibly be a latent brand of Marxism in many union offices and socialist political parties throughout the West. Indeed, in many Western countries, socialism has been re-branded as political correctness, both in liberal and socialist traditions. However, political correctness appears to have become impaled on its own contradictions, wanting to support, for instance, militant gay groups and fundamentalist Islamic groups at the same time, overlooking the fact that these groups are opposed to one another and therefore mutually exclusive. Interestingly, both the gay rights groups and Islamic ones are opposed to traditional Biblical Christianity, which makes them attractive to those politicians who are fundamentally opposed to Christianity and all it stands for.

Political correctness is hard to define, and not all of it is bad, as treating other races, for instance, with dignity and respect has always been part of Christian tradition. However, there is a darker side to political correctness, or the liberal consensus, whatever we might call it, that is constantly undermining society, although whether this is deliberate or by accident is not entirely clear. But we can see evidence of parental rights and authority over children being undermined. Children's innocence is being stolen through teenage magazines promoting adult issues, these aimed at ever-younger kids. These pre-teenage children then dress like adults in response. Pop videos are increasingly suggestive and revealing with poor singing talent compensated for by lack of clothing. Children in schools in Britain have been offered contraceptives even as young as eleven, and fourteen year olds given abortions without parental consent. Laws passed in Parliament take away a parent's right to discipline a child according to traditional methods of chastisement, and yet children are increasingly running riot, even stabbing and beating each other up in schools and outside. Teachers fail to gain control of school kids in the classroom, with teachers facing bullying from school children, and yet possible court action for the most minor incidents if they respond. All of this affects the education of those who want to learn. Chaotic children, causing tyranny for other children and public servants, seems to be one outcome of political correctness.

The gay issue is being used to undermine people's own dignity and well-being, and to undermine society and the church, and this is said without wishing at all to insult, harass or stigmatise individuals.

The gay lobby teaches young people that if they have gay feelings, then it means it is part of their genetic make-up. As such they should just give in to it. All the while, young people are manipulated to have gay feelings through media imagery, popular music and pressure from the gay lobby in schools and colleges. But if you dare to ask how a gay gene might reproduce itself, you are accused of being prejudiced or committing a hate crime. Instead, I believe that the rise of gay sentiment has more to do with the concept of a gay meme than a gay gene. Richard Dawkins[4] developed the idea of the meme from F.T. Cloak,[5] to describe the way religious beliefs spread through society, but it may also be used to describe the spread of any system of ideas or belief. Although far from perfect, the concept of the meme is a useful tool to describe how ideas spread through society from mind to mind. As noted already, the thoughts we choose to meditate upon determine the people we become, and enact mental and physiological changes within us. 'For as he thinketh in his heart, so is he'. *(Proverbs 23:7 KJV)*

As with the issue of abortion, an increase in gay activity reduces reproduction rates and stops people finding intimacy, happiness and fulfilment in traditional family units. Today, an ever increasing number of young men and women are confused about their sexual identity, and misled to believe that they were born one way or the other. By asserting that a gay gene exists when there is no evidence that it does, in effect enslaves some people to a particular lifestyle that is not in their best interest. Gay feelings have much more to do with possible sexual abuse or mental or emotional manipulation as young adults and as children, but very few if any are born with a gay gene. It is not possible to make a logical case for a gay gene being passed through generations, whether you look at the issue from an evolutionary or special creation perspective. A gay gene by definition cannot reproduce itself, so it represents an evolutionary dead end. If it could be passed on, then it would not truly be gay. Christians believe that God created everyone male and female, although it is noted that as a result of the fall from grace, genetic mutations have made some eunuchs. However, there is no reason to suppose that our genes determine the thoughts we choose to think, and the rapid growth of gay feelings in modern society clearly shows that it is cultural and not genetic. It is almost as if the politically correct liberal left is deliberately promoting the gay agenda and abortion to decrease or reduce human population growth rates.

Following on the heels of the issue of women priests, the issue of gay clergy is being used to drive a wedge between Christians, and undermine the church. The gay lobby is not satisfied with rights for itself, but is directly attacking Christianity and marriage. But if there is no evidence that gay feelings are passed on by genes, then one's sexuality is a matter of human choice, and cannot be considered an issue of human rights as the gay lobby claims. Whether we accept a gay meme into our minds and hearts is a matter of choice, although the false assertion that a gay gene exists in effect takes away that choice for many people. Christianity has always set certain standards for its members, and although people do not always live up to them, we must agree that those standards are good for all on an equal basis, whether we are tempted in certain ways or not. Whether we live by those standards is a matter of choice, and not part of our genetic make-up. The issue of the church not accepting gay clergy cannot therefore be considered a matter of human rights, because all are called to live by the same standards whatever temptations we struggle with.

All of these politically correct liberal issues are being driven by Hegelian dialectics, which is perhaps one of the best weapons against the church that the devil has. Don't Christians just love a consensus? This secular concept seeks to build a synthesis between a thesis and an antithesis. By exerting pressure it is possible to progress towards the utopian thesis that you want. Marxists used this idea to establish communism in many countries, but since Marxism has declined, it has become the tool of politically correct forces instead. Often these are ex-socialists trained in political activism, but now looking for a trendy cause to fight for. Christians also love a synthesis, and are often willing to make small compromises to maintain consensus and respectability, but before long the church and society is driven away from Christian values, with debasement of ethical standards. But Hegelian dialectics should be fairly easy to counteract if Christians will simply make a firm stand for traditional values and accept short term unpopularity. Hegelian dialectics is a two-way street.

Both fascism and Marxism are in part the products of a belief in the grand cosmic process of materialistic evolution, courtesy of Darwin, Galton, Huxley, Spencer and others. Today, the more obvious tyrannical regimes have collapsed, but the fruits of evolution are still in evidence. There is an ongoing quest, for instance, to develop genetically engineered crops, and the cloning of human embryo's by large bioscience corporations for the sake of profit. At a superficial level, scientists indoctrinated in evolution make this scientifically respectable, but there is little concern for the ethical problems implicit in using human entities as a means to an end. This is commerce and godless science working together outside of basic Christian-centred ethics. It is surely time for Christians, and society in general, to begin to look at the false foundations that a belief in evolution through natural selection gives to society, and expose it to fresh critical analysis. In over one hundred years of searching, evolutionary scientists have failed to find a credible ethical basis that does not allow power over others and nature. It is belief in evolution, and survival of the fittest, that makes society selfish. It is surely time for Christians to make a stand for sound ethical standards to be re-established within commerce, society and science. There is a need for the message of God's love to all humanity and nature, the message of redemption by a Creator God who sacrificed himself on a cross, to be heard among the nations once again.

There has been an increase in lawlessness in our time as well. Not all of this is the direct fault of evolution, but the basic atheistic humanism that underpins much of education today in the West, although such attitudes are indirectly supported by the belief in evolution. Wherever Epicurean philosophy is tried, it always ends up in short term hedonism. The education system and the broadcast media teach evolution as an assumed fact, with no absolute moral authority, and so people begin to rebel against traditional morality and do as they please. But animals have no knowledge, understanding or wisdom. A cow chewing the cud in the fields has never pondered for a moment, and asked the question why? So whereas animals are driven by basic survival instincts, to fight for food and drink and to mate, mankind, as a sapient being, has much greater capacity for good and evil, sometimes devising cruel and wicked ways to hurt one another for selfish gain, or on the opposite side occasionally sacrificing him, or herself for the sake of others.

It is therefore rather ironic that many blame God for the suffering that exists in the world, but much of this suffering is caused by mankind's selfishness and wickedness. It may be acknowledged that religious people are far from perfect, and have been responsible for wars and some brutality in the past, as shown by Luther's failings, but how many people died in the twentieth century from atheistic dogma, from the likes of Lenin, Stalin, Mao or Pol Pot? Or consider the pagan Hitler, who tried to exterminate an entire race with his extreme commitment to social Darwinism? Today, the greed of unrestrained capitalism, the corruption of third world regimes, and unnecessary wars, and the poor distribution of resources, which can't be blamed on God, but mankind, cause much of the starvation and suffering in the world.

Still though, some try and pin the blame on organised religion for the many wars that occur, and it must be admitted that many wars have been fought over theological issues, but as shown previously, the tyranny of those who have no faith has been greater. Ruling classes, who are only nominally Christian for the sake of respectability, are usually responsible for starting wars, but they seek to gain power over others and hoard wealth for their own selfish interest. And to be fair to Christianity, we must also look at the achievements that have occurred in the last two thousand years of Christian civilisation, from Augustus to Charlemagne to the present Pope. The Christian Church overcame the horrors and decadence of the Roman Empire, through the faithful lifestyle of people who led peaceful lives despite tremendous suffering. Many Christians since, such as Wilberforce with the abolition of slavery, and Martin Luther King with civil rights, have overcome wrongs through peaceful protest. All through the Dark Ages, Christians established religious communities and organised agriculture, education and health care. Christians continued to be at the forefront of building hospitals and schools through the middle ages, right up to the present day. Christians have produced great works of art, from Gregorian chant and the Lindesfarne Gospels, to renaissance art, and choral pieces such as Handel's Messiah and Bach's St. John's Passion. And at the same time that Darwin was writing his book, a Prussian minister, George Muller, was feeding thousands of children in Bristol, simply through a life of prayer and faith. Christians and Jews have led in science as well, with many great discoveries attributable to people like Galileo, Faraday, Maxwell and Einstein. Einstein claimed that in order to understand the universe, he tried to think God's thoughts after Him.

Of course the theories of Einstein and other physicists have led to weapons of mass destruction as well, and the chemical industry has polluted the environment for profit, but that really highlights part of man's fallen nature, which is to desire knowledge and power without wanting a moral or ethical conscience which should go with it. This Faustian pact shows the pride and arrogance of mankind, which overthrows faith in God, and ends up causing environmental and sociological damage because we haven't the sense to use the knowledge wisely. Today, scientists are pursuing many different fields, for instance finding new medicines to treat incurable diseases, but others are toying with genetic engineering, and taking human parts such as stem cells from human embryos, for the same purpose of finding new medicines and treatments. This shows that we need to differentiate between ethically good and ethically bad science. Is it too much to ask that Christians take a stand and insist that the pursuit of science has an ethical dimension? Is it too much to demand a moral dimension to science, and to claim that Christianity provides the basis for that morality? The widespread belief in the Darwinian theory of evolution promotes godless progress and allows unethical practices such as the genetic engineering of plants, animals and human beings, including such practices as human embryonic stem cell research, all carried out in the name of scientific research. As a result the reputation of scientific research itself is damaged by Darwinism and a belief in godless progress.

It appears that the discipline of biology produces more atheistic and godless students than other disciplines such as physics and chemistry, and it seems that the blame for this should be placed at the feet of the theory of evolution, which is so widespread. With the ethos of social Darwinism still alive in some commercial enterprises, together with continued belief in Comte and Huxley's religion of science among many scientists, conditions are ripe for the ongoing abuse of nature and humanity. There may perhaps be little difference today between the practices of some genetic research programmes in biotechnology corporations and the biological eugenics of the 1930s. Sadly in Britain in 2004, such embryonic stem cell research is considered acceptable by a government where many cabinet ministers claim to be both socialist, and Christian. Is it too much to ask that stem cell research be carried out without the conception and destruction of human embryos?

This book has not tried to look in detail at individual ethical issues, but to take a close look at the broader context and seek to rebuild the traditional Christian framework on which to judge all social and environmental issues. This is found in the twin book approach, which sees the Word of God and the Works of God as telling the same story of God's power, wisdom and goodness. The appearance of design, clearly evident in nature for any who will open their eyes, points to the existence of God, and also informs us of His wisdom, power and goodness. As we spend time enjoying God's good creation, it then informs our conduct towards nature and humanity. But we can also see brokenness in nature that should also cause us to work with God in His long term plan of redemption and restoration.

But as a result of the abuse of society and the environment, which is often wrongly ascribed to Christianity, today many people have lost faith in Christianity and also true science, and become environmentally aware, preferring various brands of new age paganism. They have not returned to Christian faith, but have found eastern mysticism and paganism much more to their taste. But why have they not returned to the Christian fold? Is it because Christianity is seen as too close to the very establishment that has caused the damage, swimming with the evolutionary tide? There are some serious issues here that need to be addressed.

Notes and References

[1] Johnson, P.E., *Nihilism and the End of Law*, First Things, 31, pp. 19-25, March 1993, <www.firstthings.com/ftissues/ft9303/articles/ pjohnson.html>, Accessed March 2006. See also: C.S. Lewis Society, <www.apologetics.org/articles/nihilism.html>, Accessed March 2006.

[2] Jacques, M., *The Death of Intimacy: A Selfish, Market-Driven Society is Eroding Our Very Humanity*, The Guardian, UK, 18th September 2004. (Martin Jacques is a visiting fellow at the London School of Economics Asia Research Centre).

[3] Ibid.

[4] Dawkins, R., *The Selfish Gene*, 2nd ed., Oxford University Press, Oxford, 1989.

[5] Cloak, F.T., *Is a Cultural Ethology Possible?*, Human Ecology, 3, pp. 161-181, 1975.

Bibliography

Adams, D., *The Cry of The Deer*, Triangle/SPCK, London, 1987.

Ager, D. V., *The Nature of the Stratigraphical Record*, Macmillan Press Ltd., London, 1981.

Albrecht, A., Magueijo, J., *A Time Varying Speed of Light as a Solution to Cosmological Puzzles*, Phys. Rev. D 59, 043516, 1999.

Asimov, I., *The Golden Door: The United States from 1865 to 1918*, Houghton Mifflin Company, Boston, 1977.

Attenborough, D., *Life on Air*, BBC1 TV, 5th December 2002.

Attfield, R., *The Ethics of Environmental Concern*, University of Georgia Press, 1991.

Bacon, F., *Advancement of Learning*, 1605; Oxford ed., 1906.

Bacon, F., *The Works of Francis Bacon*, 10 vols., London, 1819.

Baillie, J., *The Belief in Progress*, Oxford University Press, London, Glasgow, Toronto, 1950.

Barker, K.L., et. al., (eds.), NIV Study Bible, Hodder & Stoughton, 1987. (Hodder Headline since 1993).

Barrow, J.D., *Cosmologies With Varying Light Speed*, Phys. Rev. D, 59, 043515, 1999.

Bartholomew, M., *Lyell and Evolution*, British Journal for the History of Science, Vol. 6:23, 1973.

Bauval, R., Hancock, G., *Talisman: Sacred Cities, Secret Faith*, Michael Joseph, 2004.

Baynes, N.H., *The Speeches of Adolf Hitler*, Oxford University Press, 1942.

Behe, M.J., *Darwin's Black Box: The Biochemical Challenge to Evolution*, The Free Press, New York, 1996.

272

Bentham, J., *An Introduction to the Principles of Morals and Legislation*, first published 1789.

Berggren, W.A., Van Couvering, J. A., (eds.), *Catastrophes and Earth History: The New Uniformitarianism*, Princeton University Press, Princeton, New Jersey, 1984.

Bergman, J., *Darwin's Critical Influence on the Ruthless Extremes of Capitalism*, Answers in Genesis, TJ, 16(2), pp. 105-109, 2002.

Bergman, J., *H.G. Wells, Darwin's Disciple and Eugenics Extraordinaire*, Answers in Genesis, TJ, 18(3), pp. 116-120, 2004.

Blake, R., Avis, W., Moulton, J., *Corporate Darwinism*, Gulf Publishing, Houston,1966.

Bowden, M., *Ape-Men: Fact or Fallacy?*, Sovereign Books, Bromley, Kent, UK, 1981.

Bowden, M., *The Rise of the Evolutionary Fraud*, Sovereign Books, Bromley, Kent, UK, 1982.

Brookes, M., *Extreme Measures: The Dark Visions and Bright Ideas of Francis Galton*, Bloomsbury Publishing Plc., London, 2004.

Buckland, W., *The Bridgewater Treatises On the Power, Wisdom and Goodness of God as Manifested in the Creation*, Treatise VI, 2 vols., *Geology and Mineralogy Considered with Reference to Natural Theology*, William Pickering, London, 1837. There were eight published Treatises and a partially completed ninth, written by different authors. See also Kirby, W.

Burgess, S., *Hallmarks of Design*, 2nd ed., Day One Publications, Leominster, England, 2004.

Bury, J.B., *The Idea of Progress*, Macmillan Press, London, 1920.

Butcher, A., Interview with Hugh Ross, Charisma magazine, June 2003.

Cadbury, D., *The Dinosaur Hunters*, Fourth Estate, London, 2001.

Callicott, J.B., *In Defense of the Land Ethic*, State University of New York Press, Albany, 1989.

Calvin, J., *Genesis*, 1554; Banner of Truth, Edinburgh, UK, 1984.

Carnegie, A., (ed. Van Dyke, J.C.), *Autobiography of Andrew Carnegie*, 1920; Reprint: Northeastern University Press, Boston, 1986.

Chalke, S., Mann, A., *The Lost Message of Jesus*, Zondervan Publishing, 2004.

Church of Scotland, General Assembly, *Act Approving the Shorter Catechism*, (Agreed upon by the Assembly of Divines at Westminster), Session 19, Edinburgh, 28th July 1648. <www.epcew.org.uk/wsc/>, Accessed March 2006.

Cloak, F.T., *Is a Cultural Ethology Possible?*, Human Ecology, 3, pp. 161-181, 1975.

Cockburn, W., *The Bible Defended Against the British Association* (1844), 5th ed., Whittaker, 1845.

Coleridge, S.T., *The Rime of the Ancient Mariner*. First published 1798. Revised version with marginal glosses, 1817, 1828, 1829, 1834. <http://etext.lib.virginia.edu/stc/Coleridge/poems/Rime_Ancient_Mariner.html>, Accessed March 2006.

Colling, A., *Science Matters: Discovering the Deep Oceans*, Open University, 1995. See also *Open University* for other course materials.

Cook, N., *The Hunt for Zero Point*, Arrow, 2000.

Cooper, D.E., Palmer, J.A., (eds.), *The Environment in Question: Ethics and Global Issues*, Routledge, London,1992. Includes Rolston III, H., *Challenges in Environmental Ethics*.

Cruse, C.F. (trans.), *The Ecclesiastical History of Eusebius Pamphilus - Bishop of Caesarea, In Palestine*, 1850. Reprinted as *Eusebius' Ecclesiastical History*, Baker Book House, 1995.

Bibliography

Curtis, P., *Christian Charity to Open London Academy*, Guardian news report, 13th July 2004.

Dalrymple, T., *The Evil That Men Do*, The Spectator, p. 16, 20th March 2004.

Darwin, C., (ed. Darwin, F.), *Life and Letters*, John Murray, 1887.

Darwin, C., *On the Origin of Species*, Murray Publishing, London, 1859; *The Origin of Species*, 6th ed., Collier Books, New York, 1872.

Davies, P.C.W., Davis, T.M., Lineweaver, C.H., *Black Holes Constrain Varying Constants*, Nature, 418 (6898), pp. 602-603, 2002.

Dawkins, R., *A Devil's Chaplain*, Weidenfeld and Nicolson, London, 2003.

Dawkins, R., *The Selfish Gene*, 2nd ed., Oxford University Press, Oxford, 1989.

Deere, J., *Surprised by the Power of the Spirit*, Kingsway Publications, Eastbourne, England, 1994.

Deere, J., *Surprised by the Voice of God*, Kingsway Publications, Eastbourne, England, 1996.

Dembski, W.A., *The Intelligent Design Movement*, Cosmic Pursuit, Spring 1998, <www.leaderu.com/offices/dembski/docs/bd-idesign.html>, Accessed March 2006.

Denslow, W. R., *10,000 Famous Freemasons*, 4 vols., Missouri Lodge of Research, Trenton, Missouri, 1957-61.

Denton, M., *Evolution: A Theory in Crisis*, Adler and Adler, Maryland, USA, 1986.

Des Jardins, J.R., *Environmental Ethics: An Introduction to Environmental Philosophy*, 3rd ed., Wadsworth Group, Thomson Learning Inc., Belmont, USA, 2001.

Dewey, J., *Evolution and Ethics*, The Monist, Vol. VIII (1897-1901); Reprint: Scientific Monthly, Vol. 78, p. 66, February 1954.

Dixon, P., *Signs of Revival*, Kingsway, East Sussex, England, 1994.

Dorset County Council, Devon County Council, and Dorset Coasts Forum, *Nomination of the Dorset and East Devon Coast for Inclusion in the World Heritage List*, 2000. (This nomination and publication was supported by the British Geological Survey)

Dowley, T. (ed.), *The History of Christianity: A Lion Handbook*, Lion Hudson Plc, Revised ed., 1990. Includes the following articles:
Atkinson, J., *Reform*, p. 390
Barnes, S., *Time and Progress*, p. 27
Brown, C., *Reason and Unreason*, pp. 485-496
Hurtado, L.W., *How the New Testament Has Come Down to Us*, pp. 134-135.

Ferngren, G.B., Numbers, R.L., *C.S. Lewis on Creation and Evolution: The Acworth Letters, 1944-1960*, Perspective on Science and Christian Faith, 48 (1), March 1996.

Feuer, L.S., *Is the Darwin-Marx Correspondence Authentic?* Annals of Science, 32, pp. 11-12, 1975.

Fleming, A., Speech at the first public meeting of the Evolution Protest Movement, London, 12th February 1935. Reported in: The Times, *Teaching of Organic Evolution: A Protest Meeting*, 13th February 1935.

Fleming, R., *The Fulfilling of the Scripture*, Rotterdam, (no pub.), 1671, Orig. ed. 1669.

Flew, A., Habermas, G.R., *Atheist Becomes Theist: Exclusive Interview with Former Atheist Antony Flew*, Philosophia Christi, Evangelical Philosophical Society, Winter, 2004.

Forster, R., Marston, P., *Reason, Science and Faith*, Monarch Books, Lion Hudson Plc, Crowborough, East Sussex, UK, 1999.

Foster, M., Lankester, E.R. (eds.), *The Scientific Memoirs of Thomas Henry Huxley*, 4 vols. + supplement, Macmillan & Co., London, 1898-1903.

Bibliography

Galton, F., *Hereditary Improvement*, Frazer's Magazine, Vol. 7, pp. 116-130, January 1873, <http://galton.org>, Accessed March 2006.

Galton, F., *Memories of my Life*, Methuen, London, 1908. <http://galton.org>, Accessed March 2006.

Gillies, J., *Historical Collections of the Accounts of Revival*, 1754; Reprint: Banner of Truth, 1981.

Ginsburg, M., *The Idea of Progress: A Revaluation*, Greenwood Press, Westport, Connecticut, 1953.

Gurney, R.J.M., *The Carnivorous Nature and Suffering of Animals*, Answers in Genesis, TJ, 18(3), pp. 70-75, 2004.

Hamblin, T., *On Whose Authority?*, Pamphlet 298, CSM, January 1995.

Harrison, P., *The Bible and the Emergence of Modern Science*, Christians in Science, Public Lecture, Cambridge University, 24th May 2005. <www.st-edmunds.cam.ac.uk/cis/harrison/Peter%20Harrison%20-%20index.htm>, Accessed March 2006.

Herbert, S., *The Place of Man in the Development of Darwin's Theory of Transmutation*, part II, Journal of the History of Biology, Vol. 10, no. 2, p. 161, Fall, 1977.

Himmelfarb, G., *Darwin and the Darwinian Revolution*, Chatto and Windus, 1959; W.W. Norton, New York, 1962.

Hitler, A., *Mein Kampf*, 1933, (trans. Manheim, R.), Hutchinson, UK, 1969.

Hobbes, T., *Leviathan*, 1651; Reprint: Oxford University Press, 1996.

Hofstadter, R., *Social Darwinism in American Thought*, Beacon Press, Boston, 1955.

Howie, J., (ed. McGavin, W.), *Scots Worthies*, W.R. McPhun, Glasgow, 1846. (Orig. 1775).

Hull, D.L., *God of the Galapagos*, Nature, 352, pp. 485-486, 1992.

Hume, D., (ed. Aiken, H.D.), *Dialogues Concerning Natural Religion*, Hafner, New York, 1948.

Humphreys, D.R., *Starlight and Time*, Master Books, Green Forest, AR., 1994.

Huxley, J., Kittlewell, H.B.D., *Charles Darwin and His World*, Viking Press, New York, 1965. (Julian Huxley was the son of Leonard Huxley and grandson of Thomas Henry Huxley).

Huxley, L., (ed.), *The Life and Letters of Thomas Henry Huxley*, 2 vols., Macmillan, London, 1900; Reprint: Gregg International Publishers, Hants, 1969. (Leonard Huxley was the son of Thomas Henry Huxley).

Huxley, T.H., *Collected Essays*, 9 vols., London, 1893-94. <http://aleph0.clarku.edu/huxley/bib1.html>, Accessed March 2006. Also published by Macmillan and Co., London, 1894-1908.

Huxley, T.H., *Lay Sermons, Addresses and Reviews*, London, 1870; D. Appleton & Co., New York, 1871.

Huxley, T.H., *Science and Religion*, The Builder, Vol. 17, Museum of Geology, pp. 35-36, January 1859.

Irvine, W., *Apes, Angels, and Victorians*, Weidenfeld and Nicolson, 1956.

Jacques, M., *The Death Of Intimacy: A Selfish, Market-Driven Society is Eroding Our Very Humanity*, The Guardian, UK, 18th September 2004.

Jensen, J.V., *The X-Club*, British Journal for the History of Science, p. 59, pp. 63-72, p. 179, 1970.

Johnson, P.E., *Darwin on Trial*, Monarch Books, Lion Hudson Plc, Crowborough, East Sussex, UK. 1994.

Johnson, P.E., *Nihilism and the End of Law*, First Things, 31, pp. 19-25, March 1993. <www.firstthings.com/ftissues/ft9303/articles/pjohnson.html>, Accessed March 2006. See also: C.S. Lewis Society,

<www.apologetics.org/articles/nihilism.html>, Accessed March 2006.

Kant, I., (trans. Paton, H.J.), *Groundwork of the Metaphysic of Morals*, Hutchinson University Library, London, 1948.

Kendall, R.T., Cain, P., *The Word and the Spirit*, Creation House, June 1999.

Kenny, A., *Down with Superstition*, Spectator, pp. 14-15, 20th March 2004.

King-Hele, D., *Erasmus Darwin*, Charles Scribner's Sons, New York, 1963.

Kirby, W., *The Bridgewater Treatises On the Power, Wisdom and Goodness of God as Manifested in the Creation*, Treatise VII, 2 vols., *On the History Habits and Instincts of Animals*, William Pickering, London, 1835. There were eight published Treatises and a partially completed ninth, written by different authors. See also Buckland, W.

Larsen, E.J., *Summer for the Gods: The Scopes Trial and America's Continuing Debate Over Science and Religion*, Basic Books, New York, 1997.

Le Fanu, J., *Of Mouse and Man, and a New Sense of Wonder*, Review, Sunday Telegraph, UK., p. 4, 22nd December 2002.

Leopold, A., *A Sand County Almanac*, Oxford University Press, New York, 1949.

Lewis, C.S., (ed. Hooper, W.), *Poems*, Geoffrey Bles, London, 1964.

Locke, J., *Second Treatise of Civil Government*, 1690; Reprint: *Two Treatises of Civil Government*, Dent, Everyman ed., London, 1953.

Loeffler, J., *Worldview Wars*, <www.khouse.org/articles/2001/365>, September 2001. Accessed March 2006.

Lubenow, M.L., *Bones of Contention*, Baker Book House, Grand Rapids, Michigan, 1992.

Mackie, J.L., *Ethics: Inventing Right and Wrong*, Harmondsworth, Penguin Books, 1977.

Magueijo, J., *Faster than the Speed of Light*, William Heinemann, London, 2003.

Malthus, T.R., *An Essay on the Principle of Population as it Affects the Future Improvement of Society*, Reeves and Turner, London, reprint 1887.

Mantell, G., *The Geological Age of Reptiles*, New Philosophical Journal, Edinburgh, Vol. XI, pp. 181-185, Apr-Oct 1831.

McGrath, A., *Dawkins' God*, Blackwell Publishing, 2005.

McGrath, A., *The Re-enchantment of Nature*, Hodder Headline, London, 2003.

Mill, J.S., *Three Essays on Religion*, Henry Holt & Co., New York, 1874.

Mill, J.S., *Utilitarianism*, Longman, Green and Co., London, 1863.

Miller, E.L., *Questions that Matter: An Invitation to Philosophy*, 3rd edition, McGraw-Hill Inc., New York, 1992.

Milner, R., *The Encyclopaedia of Evolution*, Facts on File, New York, 1990.

Missler, C., *Cosmic Codes*, Koinonia House, 1999, <www.khouse.org>, Accessed March 2006.

Moffat, J.W., *Superluminary Universe: A Possible Solution to the Initial Value Problem in Cosmology*, Int. J. Modern Physics, D, Vol. 2, No. 3, pp. 351-365, 1993.

Moore, G.E., *Principia Ethica*, Cambridge University Press, 1903. Revised edition: Baldwin, T., (ed.), Cambridge University Press, 1993.

Moreland, J.P., Craig, W.L., *Philosophical Foundations for a Christian Worldview*, IVP, 2003.

Morris, H.M., *A History of Modern Creationism*, Master Books, 1984.

Morris, H.M., *Miracles*, Master Books, 2004.

Morris, H.M., *The Troubled Waters of Evolution*, Creation Life Publishers, San Diego, 1980.

Mortenson, T., *British Scriptural Geologists in the First Half of the Nineteenth Century - Part 1: Historical Setting*, Answers in Genesis, TJ, 11 (2), pp. 221-252, 1997. This was the introduction to a series of articles that appeared in subsequent issues, each about a specific geologist.

Mortenson, T., *The Great Turning Point*, Master Books, 2004.

Nevard, A., *Hitler's Debt to Darwin*, Daylight No. 29, Autumn / Winter 1999; Reprint: Creation Science Movement, Pamphlet 329.

Nisbet, R., *History of the Idea of Progress*, Heinemann, London, 1980.

Norman, T.G., Setterfield, B., *The Atomic Constants, Light and Time*, Invited Research Report of the Stanford Research Institute / Flinders University, 1987. (This paper was invited by physicist Lambert Dolphin of SRI in 1987. The committee of the SRI later tried to withdraw the invitation after they realised the implications, and the paper is not an official report of the SRI).

Open University, Wye College, University of London. Course in *Environmental Ethics*, 1997, including:
- *Darwin and Moral Philosophy*;
- *Religion and Environmental Values, Christian Stewardship*;
- *Utilitarianism, Ethical Theory and Environmental Values*.
See also Colling, A., for Open University course material on *Science Matters*.

Owen, Rev. R., *The Life of Richard Owen*, 2 vols., John Murray, London, 1894. (The author was the grandson of Richard Owen).

Pascal, B., (trans. Krailsheimer, A.J.), *Pensees*, Penguin Classics, London, 1995.

Passmore, J., *Man's Responsibility for Nature*, 2nd/3rd editions, Duckworth Publishing, 1980.

Passmore, J., *The Perfectibility of Man*, Duckworth, London, 1970.

Polkinghorne, J., *Science and Providence*, SPCK, London, 1989.

Popper, K., *Unended Quest*, Open Court Pub. Co., La Salle, Illinois, 1985.

Presky, M., *Mike's World History*, July 2003, Galileo Library, <www.galileolibrary.com/history/index.html>, Accessed March 2006.

Price, C., *Revival Prophesied*, Renewal magazine, 284, p. 50, January 2000. Monarch Magazines Ltd., Lion Hudson Plc, Crowborough, East Sussex, UK.

Price, G.M., *The New Geology*, Pacific Press, California, 1923.

Rawls, J., *A Theory of Justice*, Clarendon Press, Oxford, 1972.

Reddie, J., *Scientia Scientiarum*, Journal of the Transactions of the Victoria Institute, Vol.1, 1867-68. First published as a circular in May 1865.

Regan, T., *The Case for Animal Rights*, University of California Press, Berkeley, 1983; Routledge, London, 1984.

Repcheck, J., *The Man Who Found Time: James Hutton and the Discovery of the Earth's Antiquity*, Simon and Schuster, London, 2003.

Ridley, J., *John Knox*, Clarendon Press, Oxford, 1968.

Rosenthal, S.J., *Sociobiology: New Synthesis or Old Ideology?* Paper presented at the 1977 American Sociological Association Convention, 1977.

Rosevear, D., *Creation Science*, New Wine Press, Chichester England, 1991.

Rudwick, M.J.S., *The Meaning of Fossils*, Chicago University Press, 1972.

Ruhle, O., *Karl Marx: His Life and Works*, New Home Library, New York, 1943.

Rupke, N.A., *The Great Chain of History: William Buckland and the English School of Geology 1814-1849*, Clarendon Press, Oxford, 1983.

Rutherford, S., *A Survey of the Spirituall Antichrist. Opening the Secrets of Familisme and Antinonmianisme in the Antichristian Doctrine of John Saltmarsh...* , Printed by J.D. & R.I. for Andrew Crooke, London,1648.

Ruthven, J., *On the Cessation of the Charismata: The Protestant Polemic on Post Biblical Miracles*, Sheffield University Academic Press, UK, 1993.

Sarfati, J., *Shame on Charisma!*, Answers in Genesis, 29 May 2003. <www.answersingenesis.org/docs2003/0529charisma.asp>, Accessed March 2006.

Schneer, C.J., *Towards a History of Geology*, MIT Press, Boston, Mass., 1967.

Schweitzer, A., Lemke, A.B. (trans.), *Out of My Life and Thought*, Holt, New York, 1990.

Sibley, A., Brown, A., McIlwaine, T., *Bristol Channel Waterspout, 11 January 2004*, Weather, 59 (6), Royal Met Soc., pp. 158-161, 2004.

Simpson, G.G., *The World Into Which Darwin Led Us*, Science, Vol. 131, pp. 966-974, 1st April 1960.

Singer, P., *Practical Ethics*, Cambridge University Press, 1979.

Southgate, C., *God and Evolutionary Evil: Theodicy in the Light of Darwinism*, Zygon, Vol. 37, No. 4, pp. 803-824, Dec. 2002.

Spokes, S., *Gideon Algernon Mantell, LLD, FRCS, FRS, Surgeon and Geologist*, John Bale and Sons and Danielson, London, 1927.

Tax, S., (ed.), *Evolution after Darwin*, 3 vols., University of Chicago Press, 1960.

Tear Fund report, *Before Disaster Strikes*, February 2004.

Teilhard de Chardin, P., Quoted on Christians Australia website, *Devil-ution!* (nd). <www.accsoft.com.au/~xians/teach/science-philosophy/devilution.html>, Accessed March 2006.

The Eye (pseudonym), *Erasmus Darwin Centre opens in Lichfield*, Freemasonry Today, Issue 9, Summer 1999. <www.freemasonrytoday.net/public/index-09.php>. Accessed March 2006.

Thiede, C.P., *Jesus: Life or Legend?*, Lion Publishing, Oxford, England, 2nd ed., 1997.

Trollope, A., Huxley, T.H., et. al. (founders, 1865), *The Fortnightly Review*, London: Chapman and Hall (1865-1931), Horace Marshall (1931-1954).

Victoria Institute, Council Members, *Objects of the Victoria Institute*, Journal of the Transactions of the Victoria Institute, 1866-67.

Walker, A., *Epistles of Straw - The True Tragedy of Creationism*, Ship of Fools website, December 2001. <www.shipoffools.com/Columns/Walker/Walker1201.html>, Accessed March 2006.

Walker, A., *Restoring the Kingdom*, Hodder & Stoughton, London, 1985. (Hodder Headline since 1993).

Wall, J.F., *Andrew Carnegie*, Oxford University Press, New York, 1970.

Walley, C., Letter in Christian Herald, Worthing, Sussex, 21/28 December 2002. Discusses the work of the Carter Centre, to eradicate the disease caused by the parasitic guinea worm.

Wallis, A., *In the Day of Thy Power*, Christian Literature Crusade, England, 1956.

Warfield, B.B., *Counterfeit Miracles*, The Banner of Truth Trust, Edinburgh, UK, 1918.

Wavell, S., Iredale, W., *Sorry, says atheist-in-chief, I do believe in God after all*, The Sunday Times, 12th December 2004.

Weikart, R., *A Recently Discovered Darwin Letter on Social Darwinism*, Isis, 86, pp. 609-611, 1995.

Weikart, R., *From Darwin to Hitler: Evolutionary Ethics, Eugenics and Racism in Germany*, Palgrave Macmillan, 2004.

Wells, H.G., *Anticipations of the Reaction of Mechanical and Scientific Progress upon Human Life and Thought*, Bernard Tauchnitz, Leipzig, 1902; Reprint: Dover, Mineola, NY, 1999.

Whitcomb, J.C., Morris, H.M., *The Genesis Flood*, Baker Book House, 1961.

White, L., Jr., *The Historical Roots of our Ecologic Crisis*, Science, Vol. 155, No. 3767, pp. 1203-1207, 10th March 1967.

Wiener, P.F., *Martin Luther: Hitler's Spiritual Ancestor*, Gustav Broukal Press, 1985. Originally written during World War II as a Win the Peace Pamphlet, No 3, Hutchinson and Co., London, (nd).

Wiseman, P.J., (ed. Wiseman, D.J.), *Ancient Records and the Structure of Genesis*, Thomas Nelson Publishing, Nashville, 1985.

Wyllie, I., *The Self-Made Man in America*, Rutgers University Press, New Brunswick, 1954.

Wynne-Tyson, J., *The Extended Circle: An Anthology of Humane Thought*, Sphere, London, 1990.

Zacharias, R., *Jesus Among Other Gods*, Word Publishing, Nashville, Tennessee, 2000.

Index

National Academy of Education,
1
National Curriculum (UK
schools), 15
national socialism, 192, *See also*
fascism.
natural deism. *See* deism.
natural history, 140
Natural History Museum, 207
natural law. *See also* teleology.
ethical, 98, 99, 100, 102, 103,
104, 112, 120, 121, 124,
129, 149, 256, 257, 261
scientific, 39, 51, 164, 165,
220
scientific and ethical, 100
natural philosophy, 30, 31, 32,
33, 35, 37, 44
natural science, 6, 41, 62, 67, 74,
75, 76, 77, 79, 141, 146, 149,
204, 259, *See also* positivism
and scientism.
natural selection, 12, 17, 21, 40,
49, 82, 86, 139, 187, 191, 242,
246, 267, *See also* survival of
the fittest.
natural theology, 21, 31, 37, 39,
40, 53, 86, 96, 100, 103, 112,
129, 132, 136, 149, 159, 160,
161, 166, 167, 168, 256, 257,
258, 261
scientific, 39, *See also*
physical theology.
naturalism, 38, 75, 77, 257
naturalistic fallacy, 39, 41, 101,
124, 125
nature
government of, 233

law of nature, 97, 99, 102,
104, *See also* natural law
and teleology.
state of nature, 97, 105, 120,
189
nautilus, 174
Navarre, 133
Nazi, 192, 203, 204, 206, 251
Nebuchadnezzar, 154, 155
nebular theory, 45
neology, 167, 168
neurosurgery, 80
new age, 87, 207, 208, 209, 270
New Covenant, 235
New Testament, 5, 51, 168, 220,
260
age or period, 224, 225, 227
canon, 225, 226
New York, 241
Newton, Isaac, 133, 163, 223
Newtonian mechanics, 39
Nietzsche, Friedrich Wilhelm,
181, 192
nihilism, 80, 121, 210, 211, 234,
255, 256, 261
Noah, 28, 34, 137, 154, 249
Norman, Trevor G., 19, 91
nuclear weapons, 160, 255
Numbers, Ronald L., 46, 56
oil, 85, 134, 194
Old Testament, 5, 166, 168, 223
age or period, 227
omega (Greek), 59
omega point, 207
ontogeny, 203
opium of the people, 200
opossum, 176, 178
Origen of Alexandria, 27, 28
original sin. *See* sin.
orphans, 188